Please return this boo
below.

Fines will be charged on book

LANGUAGE AND STYLE
SERIES

General Editor
STEPHEN ULLMANN

III

JEAN DOMINIQUE BIARD

THE STYLE OF
LA FONTAINE'S
FABLES

OXFORD

BASIL BLACKWELL

1966

PRINTED IN GREAT BRITAIN IN THE CITY OF OXFORD AT THE ALDEN PRESS

TO MY WIFE

ACKNOWLEDGMENTS

I WISH to thank Professor L. C. Sykes of the University of Leicester for introducing me to the method of research and for his unfailing interest and guidance throughout the preparation of this thesis.

I am indebted to Professor S. Ullmann of the University of Leeds for his encouragement in the early stages of my research, to Professor P. J. Yarrow of the University of Newcastle for his very generous advice and assistance, and Dr L. W. Tancock of University College, London, for his comments and suggestions.

I also wish to thank the University of Leicester for the research award which enabled me to pursue two years' full-time research.

I wish to express my appreciation to the many librarians who have provided me with the necessary material for the preparation of this work.

This book was originally prepared as a thesis approved by the University of London for the award of the Ph.D. Degree.

J. D. BIARD

CONTENTS

INTRODUCTION

La Fontaine enjoys the reputation of being the best known writer in France; the *Fables* are traditionally learnt by heart in primary schools and thus most French people who have no other knowledge of literature have at least some acquaintance with La Fontaine. This fame has little to do with artistic appreciation, but the popularity of the *Fables* is reflected by the editions of La Fontaine's works and the critical studies devoted to him. Nevertheless, while there are many editions of the *Fables*, including innumerable inaccurate and incomplete editions for children, the rest of his work has known no such favour with the public. It seems paradoxical to say that La Fontaine has not been given the attention he deserves as a writer; yet there are far fewer critical studies on him than on any other classical writers, Molière or Corneille for example. Furthermore, among the most serious of these studies, whether books or articles, very few indeed deal solely with the style of La Fontaine's *Fables*. This is particularly striking since so many critics have praised his mastery of style; his contemporaries saw in him an imitator of classical models, whose chief merit was his inimitable style.

Baillet, in his *Jugement des Savants*, comments:

> 'Ce n'est que dans les manières qu'il a prises et dans ce tour heureux qu'il donne aux choses qu'il doit passer pour original. Car on ne peut pas nier qu'il ne doive beaucoup de ses inventions aux anciens auteurs de la Grèce et de l'Empire Romain et qu'il n'en ait pris même quelques-unes dans les faiseurs de contes qui ont écrit en notre langue avant lui et dont il a changé la prose en vers: mais il y mêle tant de choses du sien qu'on peut dire que c'est son bien propre.'[1]

La Bruyère writes of him:

> 'Homme unique en son genre d'écrire; toujours original, soit

---

[1] Baillet, *Jugement des Savants sur les principaux ouvrages des auteurs*, Paris, 1686, vol. IV, part 5, p. 353.

ix

qu'il invente, soit qu'il traduise; qui a été au delà de ses modèles, modèle lui-même difficile à imiter.'[1]

Furetière admits that France owes him gratitude for gathering fables hitherto scattered in the works of ancient poets and orators and adds:

'Encore y en a-t-il beaucoup qui languiraient s'il n'en avait relevé le sujet par la beauté de son style et ses heureuses expressions.'[2]

Madame de Sévigné urges Bussy-Rabutin to acquire the newly published *Fables*:

'Faites-vous envoyer promptement les Fables de la Fontaine: elles sont divines. On croit d'abord en distinguer quelques-unes, et à force de les relire, on les trouve toutes bonnes. C'est une manière de narrer et un style à quoi l'on ne s'accoutume point.'[3]

Many other lesser known seventeenth-century critics make similar remarks.[4] Since the seventeenth century, this view has been held by all those who have studied La Fontaine's writings closely: La Harpe writes in the *Eloge* which he entered for the *Concours de l'Académie de Marseille* in 1774:

'On nous crie: il n'a presque rien inventé. Il a inventé sa manière d'écrire, et cette invention n'est pas devenue commune. Elle lui est restée toute entière. Il en a trouvé le secret et il l'a gardé. Il n'a jamais été ni imitateur ni imité. A ce double titre, quel homme peut se vanter d'être plus original?'[5]

'Lorsqu'on a parcouru ses divers mérites, il faut ajouter que c'est encore par le style qu'il vaut le mieux', admits Sainte-Beuve in his *Portraits litté-*

---

[1] La Bruyère, *Discours prononcé dans l'Académie Française le quinzième juin 1693*, in *Œuvres*, Grands Ecrivains de la France, Paris, 1922, vol. III, part 2, p. 461.

[2] Furetière, *Fables morales et nouvelles*, Paris, 1671, Preface.

[3] Madame de Sévigné, Letter to Bussy-Rabutin and Mme de Coligny, July 20th 1679, in *Lettres*, Pléiade, Paris, 1955, vol. II, p. 436.

[4] Contemporaries praised the excellence of the style not only of the *Fables* but also of the *Contes*; it is for its style that the author of the *Dissertation sur Joconde* places La Fontaine's tale far above Bouillon's and even ahead of Arioste's:

'Je soutiens que non seulement la nouvelle de Monsieur de La Fontaine est infiniment meilleure que celle de Monsieur Bouillon, mais qu'elle est elle-même plus agréablement contée que celle d'Arioste. . . . M. de La Fontaine a pris à la vérité son sujet d'Arioste; mais en même temps il s'est rendu maître de sa matière: ce n'est point une copie qu'il ait tirée un trait après l'autre sur l'original, c'est un original qu'il a formé sur l'idée qu'Arioste lui a fournie.' In Boileau, *Œuvres complètes*, Paris, 1870–73, vol. III, pp. 144–5. Jules Brody establishes Boileau's authorship of the *Dissertation* convincingly in *Boileau and Longinus*, Geneva, 1958, pp. 24–9.

[5] La Harpe, *Eloge de La Fontaine*, in *Recueil de l'Académie de Marseille*, Paris, 1774, p. 11.

raires.[1] Remy de Gourmont, himself a specialist on style, declares: 'Ce don du style, La Fontaine le possède à un degré unique.'[2] Valéry comes to the same conclusion about *Adonis*[3] and critics with such varied standpoints and of such different importance as Paul Bourget, Brereton, Guillemin, Haraszti, Ernest Hello, Georges Lafenestre,[4] agree that 'cette puissance qui immortalise La Fontaine c'est le style'.[5]

Nevertheless, this almost unanimous acknowledgment of La Fontaine's stylistic merits has given rise to a relatively small number of serious studies of his style. There are paragraphs, sometimes chapters, on the subject in all the works which aim at giving a comprehensive survey of La Fontaine's writings but, although most of them bring out interesting characteristic features of his style, they often remain superficial and it is not uncommon to find, under the same heading, remarks which, in fact, concern prosody rather than style. Bailly, Bray, Clarac, Lafenestre, Vossler and Moreau[6] have made substantial contributions to criticism in this line but, however extensive and systematic their investigations may be, their conclusions remain very general as befits works whose aim is to give a comprehensive estimate of an author. Taine[7] occasionally deals with questions of style but it is to Gohin, Haraszti, Lugli, Wadsworth and Mesdames O. de Mourgues and M. Guitòn[8] that we must turn in order to find the most searching criticism in that field. These scholars are concerned with the analysis of the writer's technique as well as with the aesthetic effect of his writings. Valéry applies his

[1] Sainte-Beuve, *Œuvres*, Pléiade, Paris, 1949, vol. I, p. 718.
[2] Remy de Gourmont, 'La Vie des animaux et la morale dans les Fables de La Fontaine', *Mercure de France*, LVII (1905), pp. 510–23 and LVIII (1905), pp. 24–39; also in *Promenades littéraires*, Paris, 1904–13, 2ème série, pp. 182–235.
[3] P. Valéry, 'A propos d'Adonis', in *Variété I*, Paris, 1921, pp. 59–97.
[4] Paul Bourget, *Etudes et portraits*, I, *Portraits d'écrivains et notes d'esthétique*, Paris, 1905, pp. 23–38. Geoffrey Brereton, *An Introduction to the French Poets, Villon to the Present Day*, London, 1956, pp. 75–92. Henri Guillemin, *La Fontaine, Fables*, Geneva, 1945. J. Haraszti, *En glanant chez La Fontaine*, Paris, 1922. Ernest Hello, *L'Homme*, Paris, 1941, pp. 408–17. Georges Lafenestre, *La Fontaine*, Paris, 1895.
[5] Ernest Hello, op. cit., p. 408.
[6] Auguste Bailly, *La Fontaine*, Paris, 1937. René Bray, *Les Fables de La Fontaine*, Paris, 1929. Pierre Clarac, *La Fontaine, l'homme et l'œuvre*, Paris, 1947 and *La Fontaine par lui-même*, Paris, 1961. Georges Lafenestre, op. cit. Karl Vossler, *La Fontaine und sein Fabelwerk*, Heidelberg, 1919. Pierre Moreau, *Thèmes et variations dans le Premier Recueil des Fables de La Fontaine*, Cours de Sorbonne, Paris, 1960.
[7] H. Taine, *Essai sur les Fables de La Fontaine*, Paris, 1853 and *La Fontaine et ses Fables*, Paris, 1860.
[8] Ferdinand Gohin, *L'Art de La Fontaine dans ses Fables*, Paris, 1929. J. Haraszti, op. cit. Vittorio Lugli, *Il Prodigio di La Fontaine*, Milan, 1939. Philip A. Wadsworth, *Young La Fontaine, a Study of his Artistic Growth in his Early Poetry and First Fables*, Evanston, USA, 1952. Odette de Mourgues, *La Fontaine, Fables*, London, 1960; and *O Muse, fuyante proie*, Paris, 1962. Margaret Guiton, *La Fontaine: Poet and Counterpoet*, Rutgers University Press, New Jersey, USA, 1961.

subtle critical power to two of the lesser known works of La Fontaine, yet he draws conclusions about the poet's attitude towards his art which shed a new light on the whole of his work.[1] Interesting and valuable as they may be, Louis Arnould's[2] and Félix Boillot's[3] works concerning more particularly La Fontaine's language remain outside the field of this study. Boillot is more concerned with the frequency and significance of the vocabulary of sensorial impressions and the figures of speech derived from it than with the effects resulting from their use by the poet in a given context. He certainly helps us to understand the range of La Fontaine's vocabulary and imagery, but he and Arnould do little more than identify, classify and list linguistic elements. The use of these elements for artistic purposes is still to be analysed. The same remarks apply to the vocabulary and grammatical introduction compiled by Henri Régnier in volumes X and XI of the *Edition des Grands Ecrivains de la France*[4]. Boillot in his *Psychologie de la construction dans la phrase française moderne*[5] and Fischer and Hacquard in *À la découverte de la grammaire française*[6] draw many examples from La Fontaine:

> 'Nous avons souvent fait appel, dans le choix des exemples, à celui qui reste un éternel contemporain, à La Fontaine. Virtuose de la langue, il est le plus varié de nos écrivains; les autres ont tous plus ou moins des "habitudes": La Fontaine n'en a pas.'[7]

The comments which often introduce or follow these examples are most useful but inevitably limited. Brunot's *Histoire de la langue française* also contains invaluable material in the form of occasional remarks on various aspects of La Fontaine's language but these are purely linguistic and nowhere amount to a comprehensive study of our poet's style.[8] There are also several annotated editions of La Fontaine's works, of the *Fables* and even of individual fables, which, while providing the reader with valuable analytical linguistic or grammatical comments, hardly make a more comprehensive and synthetical study superfluous.[9]

[1] P. Valéry, op cit. and 'Oraison funèbre d'une fable', in *Variété II*, Paris, 1926, pp. 47–51.
[2] L. Arnould, *La Terre de France chez La Fontaine, bêtes et gens*, Tours, 1924.
[3] F. Boillot, *Les Impressions sensorielles chez La Fontaine*, Paris, 1926.
[4] *Œuvres de Jean de La Fontaine*, 11 vols & 1 'album', Paris, 1883–92.
[5] Paris, 1930.
[6] Paris, 1959.
[7] M. Fischer & G. Hacquard, op. cit., p. xvii, note.
[8] F. Brunot, *Histoire de la langue française des origines à 1900*, Paris, 1911, vol. IV, parts I & II, passim.
[9] *Fables*, ed. P. Clarac, Paris, 1946; ed. G. Couton, Paris, 1962; ed. L. Geslin, Paris, 1950; ed. H. Guillemin, Geneva, 1945; ed. H. Régnier in *Œuvres de J. de La Fontaine*, Grands

A few works have been devoted entirely to particular aspects of La
Fontaine's style but they are unfortunately out of date both in outlook
and information and do not seem to assist us to understand the aesthetic
value of the style. Leon Wespy, Clemens Siegert and Otto Kötz[1] have
listed points of linguistic interest; but they comment on them exclusively
from the linguistic standpoint. J. Gudra's study[2] is nothing but a list of
archaic and rare words used by La Fontaine, without any reference to the
history of the language or to style. W. Potthoff's work[3] contains more
interesting remarks than its unaccountable omission from the standard
bibliographies would suggest. Potthoff stresses the effects which La
Fontaine endeavours to obtain through his deliberate use of archaisms.
Although the contribution made by this dissertation to the study of the
style of La Fontaine remains rather limited, its author makes valuable
comments about the use of syntactical devices to give style more variety
or to make it more lively. Heinrich Wiemann, Joseph Mousset and
Richard Auerbach[4] use a common method which consists of reviewing
systematically the various grammatical categories used by La Fontaine in
the particular work under examination and tend to account for the features
of his style in terms of 'impressionism', by which they imply stylistic
vividness, emphasis and a subjective approach to writing which does not

[1] Leon Wespy, 'Die historische Entwickelung der Inversion des Subjekts in Französischen
und der Gebrauch derselben bei La Fontaine', in *Zeitschrift für französische Sprache und
Literatur*, Oppeln, Bd. VI, 1884, pp. 150–209. Clemens Siegert, *Die Sprache La Fontaines mit
besonderer Berücksichtigung der Archaismen*, Meissen, n.d. (1885). Otto Kötz, 'Der Sprachgebrauch La Fontaines in seinen Fabeln' in *Die neueren Sprachen*, Bd. XVII, 1909, Heft 5, 6, 7.
This article inspires little confidence. For example, we cannot agree with the assertion that 'Les
renards gardant la maison', in Fables, VI, 14, means 'se gardant de la maison du roi' and with
the comment 'sie blieben hübsch draussen' (p. 258). The phrase *garder la maison* in the modern
sense of staying at home was commonly used in the seventeenth century as can be seen, for
example, in Mme de Sévigné's letter of July 3rd 1676: 'Vous savez que je garde mon logis huit
jours après mon retour de Vichy, comme si j'étais bien malade'; in *Lettres*, vol. II, p. 137.
[2] J. Gudra, *Die Sprache La Fontaines in seinen Fabeln*, Zweiundzwanzigster Jahres-Bericht
der kaiserl-kön. Ober-Realschule im III. Bezirk (Landstrasse) in Wien, für das Schuljahr
1872–73, Vienna, 1873.
[3] W. Potthoff, *La Fontaines Stil mit besonderer Berücksichtigung der syntaktischen Archaismen*, Marburg, 1894.
[4] Heinrich Wiemann, *Impressionismus im Sprachgebrauch La Fontaines*, Münster, 1934.
Joseph Mousset, *Der Stil La Fontaines in seinen Contes*, Münster, 1936. Richard Auerbach,
Der Stil La Fontaines in seinen Briefen, Mainz, 1953, unpublished dissertation.

Écrivains de la France, Paris, 1883–92, vol. I, II, III; ed. V–L. Saulnier, Paris, 1950.
La Fable troisième du livre onze, commentée par Louis Roussel, Paris, 1951. *Discours à Madame
de La Sablière, commentaire littéraire et philosophique par H. Busson & F. Gohin*, Geneva & Lille,
1950. Mention should be made, too, of *Fables, Contes et Nouvelles, introduction par Edmond
Pilon & René Groos, notes et variantes aux Fables par E. Pilon et R. Groos, aux Contes par
Jacques Schiffrin*, Pléiade, Paris, 1932, which is unfortunately very inferior to its companion
volume of *Œuvres diverses*, edited by P. Clarac.

fit in with what is known of La Fontaine's attitude to his work. None of these critics ever refers the reader to the usage of the seventeenth century and this omission leads them to a wrong assessment of the originality and vividness of La Fontaine's style.

C. W. Rosen's thesis *Style and Morality in La Fontaine*[1] tries to relate two elements which, by their very nature, seem to preclude any possible relationship but it contains many remarks bearing exclusively on style, which are valid if not altogether original. One would expect to find the name of Royère[2] mentioned in this treatment of poetry in La Fontaine, since Rosen takes prosody and sound effects into consideration. Other studies, though sometimes brilliant and illuminating like that of Spitzer, *Die Kunst des Übergangs bei La Fontaine*[3], remain limited to a narrow field and give only a fragmentary view of our author's style. Karl Ettmayer's article *Die Rolle der Verba Vicaria im poetischen Stil La Fontaines*[4] deserves attention since both its method and its conclusions are ambitious; however, the impressive documentation gathered together in its pages is more of linguistic than of stylistic value. But however tempting the enterprise may be, it is not our aim to give here an exhaustive critical bibliography of works dealing with La Fontaine's style, and further reference to any particular critic will be found in the course of the discussion of his merits in the subsequent chapters.

At the outset of this study, the relatively small output of La Fontaine seemed to make a comprehensive, though detailed, study of his style possible; indeed, such a study is needed. However, the variety of genres attempted by the poet, the range of his inspiration, the independence of his artistic conceptions result in a variety of styles which made discrimination necessary. The style of the *Fables*, for example, whatever partial analogies it presents with that of the *Contes* and certain of the *Œuvres Diverses*, is a distinctive style. It is this style which has been chosen as the main subject of this work. This choice was guided by several considerations: neither in classical antiquity nor in seventeenth-century France was the fable considered as a genre in its own right. Quintilian mentions the fable as a rhetorical device between the historical parallel and the simile, only to liken it to the proverb,[5] but has no place for it in his

---

[1] Princeton, 1951, unpublished thesis.
[2] J. Royère, 'Le symbolisme verbal chez La Fontaine', in *La Renaissance Politique, Littéraire, Artistique*, July 9th 1921. Also *Clartés sur la poésie*, Paris, 1925; and *Le Musicisme, Boileau, La Fontaine, Baudelaire*, Paris, 1929.
[3] In *P.M.L.A.*, LIII, (1938), pp. 393–433.
[4] In *Hauptfragen der Romanistik*, Festschrift für P. A. Becker, Heidelberg, 1922, pp. 3–36.
[5] Quintilian *Institutio Oratoria*, V, XI, 19–21, Loeb Classical Library, London, 1921–22, vol. II, p. 282.

comprehensive review of Latin and Greek literary genres.[1] Had it not been for La Fontaine's *Fables*, Boileau's omission of the fable from his *Art Poétique* might never have been questioned. Thus, the fable allowed greater freedom in matters of style and tone than any other genre. Indeed, it was not even a genre, but only a lengthy rhetorical device closely related to allegory and favoured by moralists. It is La Fontaine who, by working out his own definition of the fable and choosing it as his favourite medium, turned it into a literary genre. Naigeon, in his *Eloge de La Fontaine*, one of the entries for the *Concours de l'Académie de Marseille* in 1774, was the first to stress the originality of La Fontaine in this matter:

> 'Lorsqu'il fit imprimer ses fables on connaissait, il est vrai, celles d'Esope et de Phèdre mais personne alors n'avait médité sur le caractère, la forme, et le but de l'apologue, sur le style propre à cette espèce de poème, sur la marche qu'il faut donner au dialogue, sur les ornements qui lui conviennent, sur les défauts qui peuvent en détruire l'effet, sur les moyens de porter ce nouveau genre à un plus haut degré de perfection. On n'avait même aucune idée de la variété infinie des talents qu'il exige et qu'il est rare de voir rassemblés en un seul homme.'[2]

It is easy to see the interest of examining a style in which La Fontaine set a very high standard, in the only genre which could possibly allow him complete artistic freedom. It is striking also that, while the *Fables* represent the most comprehensive, the most mature achievement of La Fontaine, they have been universally acknowledged as his masterpiece and their literary merit has never been disputed since their publication, even by those who criticized their moral implications. We know from Maucroix that La Fontaine himself 'regardait ses Fables comme le meilleur de ses ouvrages'.[3]

It remained to choose a coherent method of investigation into the components of style. The reading of several recent studies of the style of various writers led me to the conclusion that, whilst a systematic review of the different parts of speech and stylistic elements was the very basis

---

[1] Quintilian, op. cit., X, I, vol. IV, pp. 2–74. Seneca, ignoring Phaedrus, calls the fable 'haec hilariora studia' and 'intemptatum Romanis ingeniis opus'. *Ad Polybium, De consolatione*, VIII, 3, in *Moral Essays*, Loeb Classical Library, London, 1932, vol. II, p. 376. As late as 1734, the fable is still considered as a figure of speech: '. . . la fable qui n'est autre chose qu'une allégorie.' Rémond de Saint-Mard, *Réflexions sur la Fable*, in *Œuvres*, The Hague, 1734, vol. III, p. 103.
[2] Bouillon, 1775, p. 41.
[3] F. de Maucroix, *Lettre au P . . . de la C. de J.*, March 30th 1704, in *Œuvres diverses*, Paris, 1854, vol. II, p. 233.

of such a study, the final presentation of the material in that form was often monotonous and repetitive, and left the reader with a fragmentary picture of the aesthetic achievement of the writer under examination. Valéry gives a definition of literary criticism with which I shall endeavour to make the present study conform:

> 'L'objet d'un vrai critique devrait être de découvrir quel problème l'auteur (sans le savoir ou le sachant) s'est posé, et de rechercher s'il l'a résolu ou non.'[1]

This striking formula has also the merit of being in perfect harmony with the opinion of such an authority on stylistics as Marouzeau:

> 'Ce que j'imagine, c'est par exemple une série de recherches sur l'adaptation du langage à la pensée: comment l'auteur de l'énoncé utilise le matériel de la langue, soit pour réaliser un parallélisme méticuleux entre la pensée et l'expression, soit au contraire pour pratiquer des équivalences approximatives, pour rechercher même des substitutions, des détours.'[2]

It is obvious that such an examination of an author's writings requires a systematic and methodical approach; I therefore conducted my analytical investigations in the traditional manner whilst trusting that, as I progressed, patterns of stylistic significance would emerge, shedding light on the technique of the artist. I then endeavoured to relate the various techniques to the aesthetic effects they produce, in an attempt to assess the success of La Fontaine as a writer. This study is therefore presented in the form of a synthesis bringing out the psychological and aesthetic effects of La Fontaine's use of language, since this presentation of conclusions ought to be aesthetically more revealing than one closely following the original scheme of the early investigations. Marouzeau considers the possibility of such an approach to the problem of style and makes no fundamental objection against it:

> 'On peut songer à prendre pour point de départ des considérations de psychologie générale, du fait que dans le langage comme dans la vie, prédominent suivant les cas, les éléments intellectuels ou affectifs ou imaginatifs; il y aurait lieu de faire dans l'énoncé, la part des uns et des autres et d'aboutir par là à une caractérisation du style: logique, abstrait, discursif, expressif et émotif, concret, visuel.'[3]

[1] P. Valéry, *Tel Quel*, Paris, 1941, vol. I, p. 161.
[2] J. Marouzeau, 'Comment aborder l'étude du style', in *Le Français Moderne*, XI, 1943, pp. 1–6.
[3] J. Marouzeau, op. cit.

By keeping close to the text and the text only during the first stage of my
research, it seemed that it might be possible to avoid preconceived ideas
leading to a tendency to read into it what one expected to find there; and
by endeavouring to relate the language of La Fontaine to that of the seventeenth century, it was hoped to avoid irrelevant and anachronistic discussions on matters of aesthetics and psychology. There were many
difficulties to overcome in this attempt to present a survey of La Fontaine's
style from this angle: there are few other works which could be used as
models or consulted for reference. This is partly due to the fact that the
study of an individual style requires the adaptation of a given technique
to bring out effectively the characteristic features of that style. Moreover
some fields of stylistics have so far been only summarily explored; such is
the question of the relationship between humour and style which is of
some importance for a full appreciation of La Fontaine.

Finally the terminology to be adopted throughout this work also
presented a serious difficulty. Confronted with a variety of terms used
in different senses by different critics, I decided to choose reliable technical
lexicons as standards and use the terminology as defined therein. Thus,
the reader is referred to the third edition of Marouzeau's *Lexique de la
terminologie linguistique*, Paris, 1951, and to Heinrich Lausberg's *Elemente
der literarischen Rhetorik*, Munich, 1961 and *Handbuch der literarischen
Rhetorik*, Munich, 1960, 2 vols., for a definition of technical terms used
in this study; whenever necessary, the meaning attached to any term not
found in these books will be given.

The edition of the *Fables*[1] by Gohin and of the *Contes* by Clarac, in the
Collection des Textes Français, Paris, 1934, and the edition of the *Œuvres
Diverses*[2] by Clarac, *Bibliothèque de la Pléiade*, Paris, 1948, have been used
throughout the present study and all references, except where otherwise
stated, are to these texts. The spelling of titles and quotations has been
modernized throughout.

[1] All quotations from the *Fables* will be immediately followed by a reference to the book
and number of the fable.
[2] Abbreviation: *O.D.*

B

CHAPTER I

LA FONTAINE–THEORIST AND PRACTITIONER

1. The Importance of Style

LA FONTAINE's attitude towards literature and his own theory about the art of writing may easily be traced in his works, his prefaces, his correspondence. Critical remarks and discussions abound, revealing a thoughtful and very lucid artist, conscious of the requirements of the genres he attempts, of his own taste and that of his public. We cannot but agree with Coppin that 'nul peut-être, si ce n'est Corneille, n'a plus réfléchi sur son art'.[1] and wonder with Haraszti 'que l'on ait su écrire tout un livre sur l'évolution de la critique en France, voire une étude spéciale sur la critique au dix-septième siècle, et négligé La Fontaine'.[2] It is not our intention to give a detailed analysis of the evolution of the poet's literary taste and ideas: Haraszti, Adam, Gohin, Lugli, Borgerhoff, Renée Kohn and Wadsworth[3] have already done much in this field whilst Vial and Denise, and recently Clarac[4] have gathered together passages from La Fontaine's writings which may cast some light on these points. In this study, we shall only consider La Fontaine's approach to the technical problems of writing.

His remarks concerning style not only strike the reader by their frequency, they inspire also admiration by their variety and the evidence they give of his penetrating insight into the techniques of style. We are in the presence of a writer who is fully conscious of the technical means at his disposal. It is on style and form that, in his view, a writer must concentrate his efforts; the subject-matter of any literary work is only the necessary pretext, the framework of an author's exercise in language and style: the perfection of form remains the standard by which he himself wishes to be judged:

[1] *Histoire de la Littérature française*, ed. J. Calvet, Paris, 1934, vol. IV, p. 137.
[2] J. Haraszti, *En glanant chez La Fontaine*, p. 44.
[3] J. Haraszti, ibid.; A. Adam, *Histoire de la Littérature française au XVIIème siècle*, Paris, 1962, vol. II, pp. 108–113, vol. IV, pp. 7–72, vol. V, pp. 297–301; F. Gohin, *L'Art de La Fontaine*; V. Lugli, *Il Prodigio di La Fontaine*; E. B. O. Borgerhoff, *The Freedom of French Classicism*, Princeton, USA, 1950, pp. 131–49; Renée Kohn, *Le Goût de La Fontaine*, Paris, 1962; P. A. Wadsworth, *Young La Fontaine*.
[4] F. Vial and L. Denise, *Idées et doctrines littéraires du XVIIème siècle*, Paris, 1920, pp. 187–93; P. Clarac, *La Fontaine par lui-même*.

'On me peut encore objecter, que ces contes ne sont pas fondés . . .
Je réponds en peu de mots que j'ai mes garants: et puis ce n'est ni le
vrai, ni le vraisemblable, qui font la beauté et la grâce de ces choses-
ci; c'est seulement la manière des les conter.'[1]

Contons; mais contons bien; c'est le point principal;
C'est tout: à cela près, censeurs, je vous conseille
De dormir comme moi sur l'une et l'autre oreille.
Censurez tant qu'il vous plaira
Méchants vers et phrases méchantes;
Mais pour bons tours, laissez-les là.[2]

Et supposé que quant à la matière
J'eusse failli, du moins pourrais-je pas
Le réparer par la forme en tout cas?[3]

However these remarks come from the *Contes* and it might be objected
that the stylistic quality on which La Fontaine insists is characteristic of
the genre, especially as we find in the preface of the first collection of
fables a statement which may seem to advocate an entirely different
approach to the fable:

'Mais ce n'est pas tant par la forme que j'ai donnée à cet ouvrage
qu'on en doit mesurer le prix, que par son utilité et par sa matière.'[4]

To avoid misinterpretation, we should bear in mind that La Fontaine is
dealing, here, with a genre which has so far no existence of its own and
which, in the eyes of his contemporaries, is only justified by its illustrative
value as a moralizing anecdote. It is therefore conceivable that La Fontaine genuinely means not to lose sight of what was considered by so
many, to be the *raison d'être* of the fable. But it must be noted that this
remark immediately follows a detailed account of the care given by the
poet to his own style and the contrast between this precise, well sub-
stantiated literary justification and the rather vague statement, backed by
still vaguer arguments, which follows it warns the reader not to take it at
its face value. Both Haraszti and Waltz[5] have shown the subtle irony
which pervades at least one paragraph of this preface, the reference to
'l'élégance' and 'l'extrême brièveté qui rendent Phèdre recommandable'.

---

[1] *Contes*, vol. I, p. 6 (Preface to part I).
[2] *Contes*, vol. II, p. 10 (Les Oies de frère Philippe).
[3] *Contes*, vol. II, p. 255 (La Clochette).
[4] *Fables*, Preface, vol. I, p. 10.
[5] J. Haraszti, *En glanant chez La Fontaine*, pp. 37–8; R. Waltz, 'Phèdre et La Fontaine',
in *L'Information Littéraire*, VI (May–June 1954), pp. 91–2.

It seems that the next paragraph, dealing with the pre-eminence of subject-matter over style, is also to be read in that light. La Fontaine's skill in using litotes and antiphrasis often makes his humour extremely subtle and difficult to detect; the more so when he wishes to express, under cover of a smile, an unorthodox idea. Here, there is a very strong probability that he may not be taking his own reasons too seriously: all are solemn and far-fetched, although they form an amusing demonstration which, while keeping the external appearance of logical reasoning, ends in a paradox. La Fontaine himself does not seem to be altogether convinced by his own argument: 'Ce que je dis n'est pas tout à fait sans fondement'; indeed, we might almost wonder whether this remark does not reflect his surprise at being able, after all, to produce at least one plausible argument in favour of such an idea. Moreover, another paragraph of the same preface gives what is probably a much more personal view of the relative importance of artistic form and moral purpose in the fable:

'L'Apologue est composé de deux parties, dont on peut appeler l'une le corps, l'autre l'âme. Le corps est la Fable, l'âme, la Moralité. Aristote n'admet dans la Fable que les animaux; il en exclut les hommes et les plantes. Cette règle est moins de nécessité que de bienséance, puisque ni Esope, ni Phèdre, ni aucun des Fabulistes ne l'a gardée: tout au contraire de la Moralité dont aucun ne se dispense. Que s'il m'est arrivé de le faire, ce n'a été que dans les endroits où elle n'a pu entrer avec grâce, et où il est aisé au lecteur de la suppléer. On ne considère en France que ce qui plaît; c'est la grande règle, et pour ainsi dire la seule.'[1]

When in the Fable *Le Bûcheron et Mercure*[V,1] La Fontaine meditates on his craft, he dwells with a certain pleasure on the discussion of the style adopted by him for the first four books, but dismisses the question of the moral in two lines:

Quant au principal but qu'Esope se propose,
J'y tombe au moins mal que je puis.

Thus, we may safely conclude, La Fontaine's preoccupation in the *Fables* is primarily aesthetic and the paragraph about the importance of the moral aim mere lip-service paid to the supporters of the traditional conception of the genre whom La Fontaine did not want to alienate unnecessarily.

[1] *Fables*, Preface, vol. I, p. 12.

His reference to Patru's mistrust of the rhymed fable shows that he was fully aware of the controversial character of his innovations.[1]

2. THE RELATIVITY OF BEAUTY

La Fontaine's main aim is the same as that acknowledged by all the great French classicists of the century: *plaire*.[2] To conform to the predominant taste and fashion of the day is the surest means of attaining this goal:

> 'Mon principal but est toujours de plaire: pour en venir là, je considère le goût du siècle.'[3]

> 'Je m'accommoderai s'il m'est possible, au goût de mon siècle, instruit que je suis par ma propre expérience, qu'il n'y a rien de plus nécessaire. En effet, on ne peut pas dire que toutes saisons soient favorables pour toutes sortes de livres.'[4]

This feeling for the opportune moment is present everywhere in La Fontaine: if he writes light and short verse, it is because 'menus vers sont en vogue à présent'[5]; if he hurries to issue the first volume of his *Contes*, it is because 'quelques personnes m'ont conseillé de donner dès-à-présent ce qui me reste de ces bagatelles; afin de ne pas laisser refroidir la curiosité de les voir qui est encore en son premier feu'.[6] If he mentions the style of Malherbe's *Odes*, it is to say that it is no longer in favour.[7] When he publishes *Psyché*, he notes the conformity of his natural taste for *galanterie* and *plaisanterie* with that of his contemporaries.[8] It is the public's loss

---

[1] *Fables*, Preface, vol. I, p. 7: 'Ce n'est pas qu'un des maîtres de notre éloquence n'ait désapprouvé le dessein de les mettre [les fables] en vers.' La Fontaine's original attitude towards the didactic importance of his work contrasts with that of La Bruyère:

> 'On ne doit parler, on ne doit écrire que pour l'instruction; et s'il arrive que l'on plaise, il ne faut pas néanmoins s'en repentir, si cela sert à insinuer et à faire recevoir les vérités qui doivent instruire. Quand donc il s'est glissé dans un livre quelques pensées ou quelques réflexions qui n'ont ni le feu, ni le tour, ni la vivacité des autres, bien qu'elles semblent y être admises pour la variété, pour délasser l'esprit, pour le rendre plus présent et plus attentif à ce qui ce va suivre, à moins que d'ailleurs, elles ne soient sensibles, familières, instructives, recommandées au simple peuple, qu'il n'est pas permis de négliger, le lecteur peut les condamner et l'auteur les doit proscrire: voilà la règle.' *Les Caractères*, in *Œuvres* vol. II, p. 18.

[2] *Fables*, Preface, vol. I, p. 12.

[3] *Psyché*, Preface, *O.D.*, 121.

[4] *Contes*, vol. I, p. 3 (Preface to part I).

[5] *Je vous l'avoue* . . ., *O.D.*, p. 495.

[6] *Contes*, vol. I, p. 3 (Preface to part I).

[7] *Clymène*, *O.D.*, p. 32.

[8] *Psyché*, Preface, *O.D.*, p. 121.

of interest in lyrical and heroic poetry that makes him hesitate to publish *Adonis*[1] and leave the *Songe de Vaux* unfinished.[2]

This feeling for the requirement of a period, in art, this determination to be modern, does not blind La Fontaine to the beauty of other ages. On the contrary, it is his frank acceptance of changes in taste which enables him to perceive the relativity of beauty, an important factor in literary criticism which very few seventeenth-century critics ever acknowledged. He admires Marot and Saint-Gelais,

'quoique les ouvrages de ces derniers soient presque tout pleins de ces mêmes fautes qu'on nous impute. On dira que ce n'étaient pas des fautes en leur siècle et que c'en sont de très grandes au nôtre'.[3]

and later, writes:

'Il y a bien plus de gloire à Platon d'avoir trouvé le secret de plaire dans les endroits même qu'on reprendra; mais on ne les reprendra point si on se transporte en son siècle.'[4]

The humble and at the same time perfectly natural and almost businesslike attitude of the artist towards his public and the taste of the day is certainly one reason for the undisputed success which La Fontaine had with his contemporaries. It was not, on his part, a mere principle, it was as we have seen, a matter of experience.

Again and again he reaffirms his wish to submit his work to the readers' verdict:

'Je me suis souvenu d'une ballade qui pourra encore trouver sa place parmi ces Contes. . . . Je l'abandonne donc ainsi que le reste au jugement du public.'[5]

'Je pense avoir justifié suffisamment mon dessein; quant à l'exécution, le public en sera juge.'[6]

Thus, before venturing to write more *contes*, he first tries *Joconde* and *Le Cocu battu et content*, each representing a different kind of verse and style, on the public in 1664. When, in 1671, La Fontaine publishes, with his *Fables nouvelles*, fragments of a poem he had begun at the request of

[1] *Adonis, Avertissement, O.D.*, p. 1.
[2] *Le Songe de Vaux*, I, *Avertissement, O.D.*, p. 76.
[3] *Contes*, vol. I, p. 60 (Preface to part II).
[4] *Ouvrages de prose et de poésie des Sieurs de Maucroix et de La Fontaine, Avertissement, O.D.*, p. 653.
[5] *Contes*, vol. I, p. 53 (Les Amours de Mars et de Vénus).
[6] *Fables*, Preface, vol. I, p. 9.

Fouquet in 1659, he makes the public the sole judge whether the original plan is to be completed or abandoned. Aware of a change in the taste of his contemporaries, he gives them samples of the different kinds of style to be used in his intended work, so that they may make an informed choice:

> 'La poésie lyrique ni l'héroique . . . ne sont plus en vogue comme elles étaient alors. J'expose donc au public trois morceaux de cette description. Ce sont des échantillons de l'un et l'autre style: que j'aie bien fait ou non de les employer tous deux dans un même poème, je m'en dois remettre au goût du lecteur plutôt qu'aux raisons que j'en pourrais dire. Selon le jugement qu'on fera de ces trois morceaux, je me répondrai: si la chose plaît, j'ai dessein de continuer; sinon, je n'y perdrai pas de temps davantage.'[1]

And further on, he adds:

> 'C'est assez de ces deux échantillons pour consulter le public sur ce qu'il y a de sérieux dans mon songe; il faut maintenant que je le consulte sur ce qu'il y a de galant; et, selon le jugement qu'il fera de l'un et de l'autre, je me règlerai, si je continue cet ouvrage.'[2]

Admittedly, deference towards the reader was the rule in a century when literature depended so much on wealthy and noble patrons. The tone of La Fontaine's prefaces and even that of his dedications is, at the same time, technical and informal. In them, he shows his concern for the right choice of style and form and he associates his reader with the discussion. Not infrequently, his sensitivity to adverse criticism makes him firmly refute the possible objections of an impatient reader[3] or discuss a friend's suggestion in a footnote, in a letter or even in his poems,[4] thereby showing his respect for constructive criticism.[5] But, although La Fontaine

---

[1] *Le Songe de Vaux*, I, *Avertissement*, *O.D.*, p. 76.
[2] *Le Songe de Vaux*, III, *Avertissement*, *O.D.*, p. 95.
[3] See *L'Eunuque*, *Avertissement*, *O.D.*, p. 262; *Contes*, vol. I, p. 15 (Joconde), *l.* 287 sqq.; ibid. p. 144 (La Fiancée du roi de Garbe), *l.* 179 sqq.; ibid., vol. II, p. 10 (Les Oies de frère Philippe), *l.* 28 sqq.; ibid., p. 99 (Le Petit chien), *l.* 511 sqq. and footnote p. 100; ibid., p. 237 (La Matrone d'Éphèse), *l.* 3 sqq.; *Fables*, II, 1; V, 16; and variant of XII, 12, *l.* 35 sqq.:

> Je change un peu la chose. Un peu? J'y change tout:
> La critique en cela va me poursuivre à bout,
> Car c'est une étrange femelle;
> Rien ne nous sert d'entrer en raison avec elle. . . .

[4] See La Fontaine's notes to fables I, 15–16 and II, 3; see also fable VIII, 13; and letter to Fouquet, January 30th 1663, *O.D.*, p. 532; also, undated note to Maucroix, *O.D.*, p. 587, III.
[5] La Fontaine's own judgements on other writers are precise and outspoken; on Ronsard, Letter to Racine, June 6th 1686, *O.D.*, p. 655; on a 'certain auteur', *A Mgr. l'évêque de Soissons*, *O.D.*, p. 646; on Goibeau du Bois, letter to Maucroix, October 26th 1693, *O.D.*, pp. 726–7.

considers himself as bound by the ultimate decision of the public, he does not hesitate to try out new or avowedly anachronistic genres, and even experiments, on this very public. That his attitude is not passive is shown by the range of his work and his introduction of a new genre, the rhymed fable, into the literary field. That he himself was conscious of the originality of his creation can be inferred from the prefaces to the *Fables* and incidental comments of the type:

> Si mon œuvre n'est pas un assez bon modèle,
> J'ai du moins ouvert le chemin.[1, XI, *Epilogue*]

3. THE PRACTICE OF TECHNIQUES

While submitting to the verdict of popular favour, he is fully aware of the literary problems which have to be solved in order to gain and to retain this favour. Just as he turns to the work of some classical model for thematic inspiration, so he is guided by the prevailing taste of the moment in his choice of tone and, to a certain extent, of genre. But the essential aesthetic problem remains for him to solve: how to combine a traditional theme, a fashionable tone, and the resources of style and language so as to make a work of art? La Fontaine knew what he was doing, why he was doing it and how it was to be done: we find in his work ample evidence of a permanent awareness of literary problems and a constant effort to solve them. At an early stage in his career, he showed enough independence of judgement to be able to assess the value of Malherbe's poetry and measure its cramping influence upon his own style. Throughout his work, La Fontaine comments on his own attempts, achievements and experiments: we know, from the *Avertissement* of *Adonis*[2] and from *Psyché*,[3] that he tried his hand at a variety of styles: epic, heroic, *galant*. He seems to delight in self-imposed stylistic exercises: the *Avertissement à l'inscription tirée de Boissard*[4] shows La Fontaine polishing concurrently a prose and a verse translation of a Latin inscription for art's sake and out of sheer interest in literary technique:

> 'Le principal motif qui m'a attaché à l'inscription dont il s'agit, c'est la beauté que j'y ai trouvée ... J'ai traduit cet ouvrage en prose et en vers, afin de le rendre plus utile par la comparaison des deux

[1] See also II, 1.
[2] *Adonis, Avertissement, O.D.*, p. 1.
[3] *Psyché, O.D.*, pp. 121–257, passim.
[4] *Inscription tirée de Boissard, Avertissement, O.D.*, pp. 763–4.

genres. J'ai eu, si l'on veut, le dessein de m'éprouver en l'un et en l'autre: j'ai voulu voir, par ma propre expérience, si en ces rencontres les vers s'éloignent beaucoup de la fidélité des traductions, et si la prose s'éloigne beaucoup des grâces ... J'ajouterai seulement que ce n'est point par vanité, et dans l'espérance de conserver tout ce qui part de ma plume, que je joins ici l'une et l'autre traduction; l'utilité des expériences me l'a fait faire.'

And La Fontaine adds:

'Platon dans Phaedrus, fait dire à Socrate qu'il serait à souhaiter qu'on tournât en tant de manières ce qu'on exprime, qu'à la fin la bonne fût rencontrée. Plût à Dieu que nos auteurs en voulussent faire l'épreuve, et que le public les y invitât!'[1]

This is exactly what La Fontaine himself does. *Clymène* is an *Ars Poetica* in the form of a sequence of stylistic variations on a given theme; the fables *Contre ceux qui ont le goût difficile*[II,1] and *Le Cierge*[IX,12] contain, in a lesser degree, similar exercises on style.[2] What cannot fail to strike the reader is the pleasure which the poet takes in these exercises pursued conscientiously as long as enthusiasm drives him and shelved when the joy of creation begins to fade:

'Je n'ai eu pour but que de m'exercer en ce genre de comédie ou de tragédie mêlé de chansons, qui me donnait alors du plaisir. L'inconstance et l'inquiétude qui me sont si naturelles m'ont empêché d'achever les trois actes à quoi je voulais réduire le sujet. Si l'on trouve quelque satisfaction à lire ces deux premiers, peut-être me résoudrai-je à y ajouter le troisième.'[3]

This introduction to the opera *Galatée* is the perfect formulation of this happy, leisurely and yet elaborate creation which is at the origin of La Fontaine's masterpieces.

The interest of the seventeenth century in rhetoric undoubtedly played a part in this aesthetic consciousness and this realistic approach to the problem of style. Georges Couton, in his *Poétique de la Fontaine*[4], stresses the importance of the manuals of Latin rhetoric in the formation of the

[1] *Inscription tirée de Boissard, Avertissement, O.D.*, pp.763-4.
[2] See also XII, *A Mgr le Duc de Bourgogne* and XII, 5, I, 15-16, XII, 12, XII, 15, fables in which the apologue is narrated in different tones. The *fables doubles*, i.e. II, 11-12 and VII, 4 offer a similar scope for stylistic variations; so do many others containing deliberate pastiches which will be studied later.
[3] *Galatée, O.D.*, 405.
[4] Paris, 1957.

poet. The study of Latin rhetoric was then an essential part of the schools' curricula and although we are not sure which school he attended, there is no doubt that La Fontaine underwent the traditional initiation into rhetoric, as described in the *Ratio Studiorum* of the Jesuits or in the *De Scholasticorum Officiis*, written by Mercier, from the *Collège de Navarre*.[1] Couton limits himself to the Latin textbooks on the subject but there was, at the time, a profusion of manuals of formal rhetoric written in French, together with a large number of works dealing with linguistic, grammatical and stylistic problems.[2] The works of La Fontaine as well as his letters to Huet, Bouhours and Maucroix,[3] his friendship with Boileau, Patru and Chapelain,[4] provide evidence of his awareness of the questions debated in these books and, in the course of our study, we shall often be led to compare and contrast their views with those of La Fontaine. All these treatises had a common source of inspiration: Quintilian's *Institutio Oratoria*, an Italian translation of which La Fontaine sent to Huet with his famous epistle. That Quintilian had written a manual for public orators and not for poets is irrelevant: in the seventeenth century, the study of style as such hardly emerged yet from that of eloquence and the principles formulated by Quintilian were those of universal common sense and good taste. La Fontaine remained constant in his admiration for him[5] and for rhetoric in general, but the poet seemed to be more impressed by its remarkable power of persuasion rather than by its aesthetic potentialities.[6] The *Préface* to the *Recueil de poésies chrétiennes et diverses* makes serious reservations with regard to rhetoric and treatises on poetry.[7] Although often attributed to La Fontaine, this text is apocryphal and La Fontaine

---

[1] See H. Lantoine, *Histoire de l'enseignement secondaire en France au XVIIème et au début du XVIIIème siècle*, Paris, 1874.

[2] F. Brunot, in *Histoire de la langue française*, vol. IV, part 2, pp. 1093 sqq., mentions the birth and subsequent development of a French rhetoric in the middle of the century. István Sőtér, in *La Doctrine stylistique des rhétoriques du XVIIème siècle*, Budapest, 1937, a thesis marred by a large number of misprints and misquotations, follows this development of French rhetoric from its origins, when it was still closely related to eloquence, to the ultimate outcome of stylistic theory. See also Le Hir, *Rhétorique et stylistique*, Paris, 1960.

[3] *A Monseigneur l'Évêque de Soissons en lui donnant un Quintilien de la traduction d'Oratio Toscanella*, O.D., pp. 645–7; Letter to Bouhours, undated, ibid., pp. 659–60; P. Clarac, 'Six pages inédites de La Fontaine', in *Revue d'Histoire Littéraire de la France*, 1951, pp. 61–8.

[4] Jules Brody in *Boileau and Longinus*, pp. 29–31, has proved that La Fontaine had access to Boileau's translation of Longinus six years before its publication. See also *Psyché*, O.D., pp. 182 and 825 n. 54.

[5] *Contes*, vol. I, p. 59 (Preface to part II); *Fables*, Preface, vol. I, p. 10. La Fontaine's friend, Maucroix, made a fragmentary translation of Quintilian, *L'Instruction de Quintilien sur la manière de composer tirée de sa Rhétorique*, to be found in Maucroix's *Œuvres posthumes*, Paris, 1710. Several translations found in this volume are to be attributed to d'Olivet. See M. Rat, *Grammairiens et amateurs de beau langage*, Paris, 1963, p. 113.

[6] *Fables*, VIII, 4; *Le Songe de Vaux*, II, O.D., p. 93; also G. Couton, *La Poétique de la Fontaine*, pp. 36–7.

[7] *Recueil de poésies chrétiennes et diverses*, Preface, O.D., p. 779.

can only be considered responsible for the judgements it contains in so far as he collaborated in its editing. He probably approved of the texts selected for inclusion, and the mistrust of rhetoric and treatises, the acute sense of the relative value of rules in art are consistent with the ideas of our poet and his attitude towards the set framework of art forms. This last provides the writer with a whole range of literary exercises through which to practise the technique of his art. Once the author masters this technique, it should become subservient to the subject-matter and the general tone of the passage. In other words, it should provide the only instrument adequate to the expression of a particular idea. It is taste which points out the *ornements* and *traits* to be borrowed from the arsenal of rhetoric and used in a given instance.

4. PROFESSIONAL CONSCIENCE

The stress laid by La Fontaine on the importance of conscious effort in poetic creation is another argument in favour of his artistic maturity. Far from being an inspired and irrepressible *fablier*, La Fontaine often complains of the slow rhythm of his work, due to his efforts to reach the high standard he had set himself. Prose and verse demand from him the same amount of attention and care:

> 'J'ai trouvé de plus grandes difficultés dans cet ouvrage qu'en aucun autre qui soit sorti de ma plume. Cela surprendra sans doute ceux qui le liront. On ne s'imaginera jamais qu'une fable contée en prose m'ait tant emporté de loisirs ... et d'amener de la prose à quelque point de perfection, il ne semble pas que ce soit une chose fort malaisée: c'est la langue naturelle de tous les hommes. Avec cela je confesse qu'elle me coûte autant que les vers.'[1]

He writes 'à force de temps' owing to his careful corrections and alterations:

> 'J'ai corrigé les derniers vers que vous avez lus, et qui ont eu l'honneur de vous plaire; j'espère que vous les trouverez en meilleur état qu'ils n'étaient. Entre autres fautes, j'y avais mis un deux pour un trois, ce qui est la plus grande rêverie dont un nourrisson du Parnasse se pût aviser.'[2]

[1] *Psyché*, Preface, *O.D.*, p. 121.
[2] *A M.F.*, *O.D.*, p. 519.

He writes to Maucroix, in a more serious mood:

'La Fiancée du Roi de Garbe est un breuvage de longue haleine. Il y a des traits qu'il me faut revoir.'[1]

Most of his writings bear traces of these numerous corrections, sometimes spread over long periods of time, and which result in a definite artistic improvement, with one single exception: *Achille*. The manuscript of La Fontaine's unfinished tragedy reveals, through his numerous corrections,[2] not only the poet's endeavour to attain the most perfect expression, but also, in this case, his difficulties in mastering the sustained elevated style required by tragic poetry: a comparatively large number of corrections are, here, either artistically indifferent or indeed, inferior to the first draft. La Fontaine, in several instances, has crossed out his alterations and restored the original text however unsatisfactory it may have seemed to him. These hesitations, the flat and uninspired style added to the thinness of the plot, account for La Fontaine's final renunciation of a genre which required more than stylistic ability. Guisan has studied the transformations which the 1658 manuscript of *Adonis* underwent before its publication in 1669 and 1671;[3] he has shown the development and maturing of La Fontaine's artistic skill in the interval between the two versions. Wadsworth[4] reproaches Guisan with failing 'to detect the poet's many signs of haste or fatigue as he retouched the latter part of his poem'. These signs exist, and one may argue that more corrections might have brought the final version nearer to perfection; however, most of the sixty-two variants[5] result in a definite and conscious improvement of the text of 1658. La Fontaine's letters to his wife, dated from Limoges, September 12th and 19th 1663, also bear the marks of careful writing. Clarac, in the notes to the *Œuvres diverses*[6] and Caudal, in the notes to the *Lettres de La Fontaine à sa femme ou relation d'un voyage de Paris en Limousin*[7], reproduce original fragments of text subsequently altered by the poet. A comparison between them and the final version sent to Madame de La Fontaine

[1] Note to Maucroix, undated, *O.D.*, p. 587, I.
[2] Notes and variants, *O.D.*, pp. 835–61.
[3] G. Guisan, 'L'Évolution de l'art de La Fontaine d'après les variantes de l'Adonis', in *Revue d'Histoire Littéraire de la France*, April–June and July–September, 1935, pp. 161–80 and 321–43.
[4] P. A. Wadsworth, *Young La Fontaine*, p. 223.
[5] Guisan mentions sixty-three variants, but one of them, 'Rois des peuples légers', is not to be found in the manuscript. Guisan used the text of the *Les Grands Écrivains de la France* edition, (vol. VI, p. 271, n. 1), which gives 'Roi' for the 1658 version; in fact, both versions read 'Rois'.
[6] Notes and variants, *O.D.*, pp. 905–11.
[7] Unpublished thesis, Paris, 1956. Caudal, unlike Clarac, has gained access to the Conrart manuscript and his edition forms an indispensable complement to that of Clarac in *O.D.*

shows serious attempts, nearly always successful, at finding a clearer or more elegant expression, at achieving greater conciseness, more precision and, sometimes, a slightly humorous tone. Hermann Oelsner has studied the author's marginal corrections on the copy of *Psyché* which he discovered in the British Museum.[1] He classifies them into groups, according to whether La Fontaine corrected passages which he found ugly, prosaic, incorrect or redundant, or tried to make his meaning clearer, or simply suppressed sentences which were out of harmony with the rest. Only a few alterations do not fall into this classification: these are corrections of obvious misprints and minor details of spelling but they, too, illustrate the care with which La Fontaine used to revise his published works. There are also various readings for several fables; Gohin records them in the notes of his edition.[2] Rahir had already found an early version of *Le Curé et le Mort*, printed c. 1672, and containing ten readings which differ from the text of 1678.[3] La Fontaine corrected the three editions of the *Fables* published in his life-time, with the utmost care and even gave, at the end of the first volume of the third edition, a list of *errata* correcting the misprints of the second. The variants of the first collection and of Book XII are far more numerous than those of the second collection. Moreover, an early version of *Le Renard, les Mouches et le Hérisson*[XII,13] has been preserved and gives, by comparison with the final version, totally different from it, the most enlightening clue to La Fontaine's exacting method of composition. Albalat, in *Le travail du style enseigné par les corrections manuscrites des grands écrivains*,[4] has no difficulty in showing the stylistic consciousness of La Fontaine in the writing of this fable. The *Contes* also show many alterations which, though, in the main, limited to details, amount to a general improvement of the final text on the original. As for the retouching of Malherbe's poems by La Fontaine, in the *Recueil de poésies chrétiennes et diverses*,[5] both Gohin and Clarac[6] show its limited importance: the forcefulness of a few archaic terms and phrases has been sacrificed in favour of greater clarity and fluency. But

[1] H. Oelsner, 'Änderungen von la Fontaines Hand an seinen Amours de Psyché et de Cupidon', in *Archiv für das Studium der neueren Sprachen und Litteraturen*, vol. 99, 1897, pp. 389–94.

[2] See also F. Gohin, *L'Art de La Fontaine*, pp. 34–6 and G. W. Rosen, *Style and Morality in La Fontaine*, pp. 188–9.

[3] E. Rahir, 'L'Édition originale d'une fable de La Fontaine', in *Revue des Livres Anciens*, 1917, vol. II, pp. 159–62. P. Clarac, 'Variations de La Fontaine dans les six derniers livres des Fables', in *L'Information Littéraire*, January-February 1951, pp. 1–9. The early version of *Le Curé et le Mort*[VII,10] is given in a postscript to this article.

[4] Paris, 1923, pp. 178–87.

[5] *Extrait des endroits changés dans les ouvrages de M. de Malherbe, O.D.*, pp. 779–83.

[6] F. Gohin, *La Fontaine, études et recherches*, Paris, 1937, p. 197; Notes and variants, *O.D.*, pp. 1079–80.

the fact that La Fontaine thought this exercise necessary and profitable is, in itself, of some significance for an appreciation of his interest in the technical aspect of literature.[1]

5. THE VIRTUE OF CONCISENESS

The exacting demands made on La Fontaine by his artistic ideal as well as his punctilious efforts to attain perfection give his appreciation of conciseness as the great virtue of style, the stamp of authority. Even if the poet referred ironically to Phaedrus' *brièveté* in the preface of the first *recueil* of fables, he considered this quality to be necessary to his own work. It was a matter of temperament:

> Les longs ouvrages me font peur
> Loin d'épuiser une matière,
> On n'en doit prendre que la fleur,[VI, *Epilogue*]

as well as a safe course to take for an author always conscious of his limitations: 'Je pourrais tout gâter par de plus longs récits'.[XII, *À Mgr le Duc de Bourgogne*] Moreover, in the *Fables*, the very genre required this approach:

> Nombre de gens fameux en ce genre ont écrit
> Tous ont fui l'ornement et le trop d'étendue.
> On ne voit point chez eux de parole perdue.[VI,1-2]

La Fontaine also sensed, in his readers, a general and permanent taste for conciseness:

> 'Mais outre que je puis m'être trompé dans mon choix, il ne sera
> pas difficile de donner un autre tour à celles-là même que j'ai choisies;
> et si ce tour est moins long, il sera sans doute plus approuvé.'[2]

To these practical reasons, he adds others involving artistic principles and reflecting a more subtle approach to aesthetic problems:

> Cent exemples pourraient appuyer mon discours;
> Mais les ouvrages les plus courts
> Sont toujours les meilleurs. En cela j'ai pour guides
> Tous les maîtres de l'art et tiens qu'il faut laisser
> Dans les plus beaux sujets quelque chose à penser.[3, X,14]

---

[1] La Fontaine's detailed examination and criticism of Maucroix's *Astérius* also shows his precise and technical approach to the problems of style. See P. Clarac, 'Six pages inédites de La Fontaine'.

[2] *Fables*, Preface, p. 9; also ibid., XII, 23.

[3] See also *A Son Altesse Sérénissime Mgr le Prince de Conti, O.D.*, p. 709:
> J'aime mieux garder avec soin
> La loi que l'on se doit prescrire
> D'être court et ne pas tout dire.

Thus, he acknowledges the part played by the imagination of the public in the completion of a work of art. This restraint recommended and practised by the poet as an effective device of creative technique is the sign of a mature talent. It is not an attempt to evade difficulty but, on the contrary, a pretext given to imagination to venture beyond the limits of what is expressed and to enrich it with individual and irreplaceable elements.

La Fontaine had experienced, recognized and analysed the illusion which is part of artistic perception when he was confronted with Michelangelo's unfinished slaves at Richelieu.[1] His readiness to let his imagination outstrip the pace of nature and give the bare and newly laid out gardens of Vaux and Versailles[2] the luxurious growth and charm of old estates also shows the poet yielding to the power of suggestion of what is still a schematic work of art. It would be hardly possible to relate La Fontaine's artistic ideas to the baroque taste still prevalent in the arts of his day and which also played on the various aspects of illusion and delusion: the Baroque tended towards the intricate and the dramatic, whilst La Fontaine's aim is, on the one hand, to stimulate the complex workings of poetic imagination in the reader and, on the other, to preserve clarity of thought and simplicity of expression in the actual text:

> Vous voulez qu'on évite un soin trop curieux
> Et de vains ornements l'effort ambitieux.
> Je le veux comme vous; cet effort ne peut plaire
> Un auteur gâte tout quand il veut trop bien faire.[V,1]

6. Grace and Beauty

Thus, he avoids 'la longueur et l'obscurité, deux défauts intolérables dans ces matières, le dernier surtout'.[3] In La Fontaine's view, clarity and simplicity are closely related to elegance, to grace; he writes to Bouhours:

> 'Une chose qui est tout à fait de mon goût, simplement et élégamment écrite, et avec beaucoup de jugement, c'est l'éloge que vous avez fait du pauvre P. Rapin. Cela me plaît fort.'[4]

In sharp contrast to the funeral *éloges* then in fashion, this *Vie du P. Rapin* has the conciseness of a *curriculum vitae*. Its style is simple indeed,

---

[1] Letter to Madame de La Fontaine, September 12th 1663, *O.D.*, p. 555.
[2] *Le Songe de Vaux, Avertissement, O.D.*, pp. 76–7; *Psyché*, Preface, *O.D.*, p. 124.
[3] *Contes*, vol. I, p. 61 (Preface to part II).
[4] Letter to Bouhours, undated, *O.D.*, p. 660.

factual and natural and only a few gradations add a touch of rhetorical elegance. The laudatory formulae are unobtrusive and distinguished in their moderation; Bouhours' peroration constitutes a good example of his style: 'Un tel homme doit être regretté de tout le monde: il vit encore dans le cœur de ses amis; et ses ouvrages, ses vertus le feront vivre dans la mémoire de tous les siècles'.[1] Lucidity about the true nature of one's own talent, 'Il est bon de s'accommoder à son sujet, mais il est encore meilleur de s'accommoder à son génie', as well as about its limitations,

> Ne forçons point notre talent
> Nous ne ferions rien avec grâce,[IV,5]

is essential to procure ease and achieve naturalness. Indeed, La Fontaine considers these elements conducive to poetry; he writes of Plato:

> 'Parmi tout cela ... [Platon] sait mêler des grâces infinies. Les circonstances du dialogue, les caractères des personnages, les inter-locutions et les bienséances, le style élégant et noble et qui tient en quelque façon de la poésie: toutes ces choses s'y rencontrent. ... On se laisse amuser insensiblement comme par une espèce de charme.'[2]

'La grâce plus belle encor que la beauté'[3] is the supreme achievement of art. Pre-eminence of grace and charm over beauty is the criterion by which, in *Psyché*, Ariste judges tragedy superior to comedy and King Philocharès, Myrtis to Megano.[4] Grace implies a certain irregularity and movement which contribute to the concealing of artistic perfection and provide an element of mystery more stimulating for the imagination than the contemplation of naked beauty:

> 'Le principal point qui est d'attacher le lecteur, de le réjouir, d'attirer malgré lui son attention, de lui plaire enfin. Car, comme l'on sait, le secret de plaire ne consiste pas toujours en l'ajustement ni même en la régularité: il faut du piquant et de l'agréable si l'on veut toucher.'[5]

---

[1] *La vie du Père Rapin par le P.B*** in R. *Rapini S. J. Hortorum libri IV*, Paris 1723, pp. lxxxi–lxxxiv.

[2] *Ouvrages de prose et de poésie des Sieurs de Maucroix et de La Fontaine, Avertissement*, O.D., pp. 652–3. We find here a detailed analysis of what La Fontaine calls elsewhere (letter to Racine, June 6th 1686, ibid., p. 615):
'Des Grecs et des Latins les grâces infinies'.

[3] *Adonis*, O.D., p. 4; also *L'Eunuque*, V, 4, ibid., p. 335:
'J'estime sa beauté, mais j'admire sa grâce.'

[4] *Psyché*, O.D., pp. 182 and 222–3.

[5] *Contes*, vol. I, pp. 59–60 (Preface to part II).

C

La Fontaine, who, in this respect, departed from the taste prevalent in his time,[1] could appreciate the lack of symmetry in architecture; he writes of the château of Blois:

> 'Il y a en face un corps de logis à la moderne, que feu Monsieur a fait commencer: toutes ces trois pièces ne font, Dieu merci, nulle symétrie, et n'ont rapport ni convenance l'une avec l'autre; l'architecte a évité cela autant qu'il a pu. Ce qu'a fait faire François I, à le regarder du dehors, me contente plus que tout le reste: il y a force petites galeries, petites fenêtres, petits balcons, petits ornements, sans régularité et sans ordre; cela fait quelque chose de grand qui plaît assez.'[2]

Clarac finds in the description of the town of Richelieu, composed only two days later, 'une note toute différente'.[3] This variation seems to be purely superficial and does not reflect any substantial change in the poet's taste: if he mentions the symmetry of the town buildings, it is as a redeeming feature for an ill-chosen location, and if he assumes that his wife would approve of these impressive buildings, it is only to add that he found them, as well as the streets, empty of inhabitants:

> Il m'en déplut; j'aime aux cités
> Un peu de bruit et de cohue.[4]

To perfect but lifeless beauty, the poet prefers the variety, the movement, the irregularity of life and their unpredictable developments, just as he prefers the suggestive to the exhaustive. Glaring beauty would be overwhelming, too rigid, fatal to imagination; the artist will therefore conceal technical perfection and ingeniousness under the veil of apparent ease and simplicity. The illusion, if successfully contrived, will increase the poet's freedom as well as the enjoyment of his public:

> Qui pense finement et s'exprime avec grâce
> Fait tout passer; car tout passe.[5]

This subtle analysis of the essence of art and this distinction between formal beauty and grace may be related to a whole trend of thought then predominant throughout Europe. Men of letters, painters and art critics

---

[1] La Fontaine, however, is by no means unique. Cf. Marolles and Sorbière's judgements on Paris quoted by Borgerhoff, *The Freedom of French Classicism*, pp. 144, n. and 239, n.
[2] Letter to Madame de La Fontaine, September 5th 1663, *O.D.*, p. 544.
[3] P. Clarac, *La Fontaine par lui-même*, pp. 109–10.
[4] Letter to Madame de La Fontaine, September 5th 1663, *O.D.*, pp. 550–1.
[5] *Contes*, vol. II, p. 229 (Le Tableau).

commonly referred to the distinction made by the ancients between τὸ καλόν and ἡ χάρις;[1] but, when trying to define the latter, most of them resorted to the vague notion of '*le je ne sais quoi*.'[2] La Fontaine, as we shall see, went further than most of them towards an identification of the operative components of grace. It is remarkable that he himself never used this phrase in his numerous reflexions on art, aesthetics and technique, but always chose more explicit terms of criticism which are to be found only in the most perceptive of his contemporaries[3] and precisely when these attempt to explain what they mean by '*le je ne sais quoi*'. Thus, Bouhours writes:

'Il est du je ne sais quoi comme de ces beautés couvertes d'un voile, qui sont d'autant plus estimées qu'elles sont moins exposées à la vue, et auxquelles l'imagination ajoute toujours quelque chose. De sorte que, si par hasard on venait à apercevoir ce je ne sais quoi qui surprend et qui emporte le cœur à une première vue, on ne serait peut-être pas si touché ni si enchanté qu'on est; mais on ne l'a point découvert et on ne le découvrira jamais apparemment, puisque si l'on pouvait le découvrir, il cesserait d'être ce qu'il est. ... Les pièces délicates en prose et en vers ont je ne sais quoi de poli et d'honnête qui en fait presque tout le prix et qui consiste dans cet air du monde, dans cette teinture d'*urbanité*, que Cicéron ne sait comment définir. Il y a de grandes beautés dans les livres de Balzac; ce sont des beautés régulières qui plaisent beaucoup, mais il faut avouer que les ouvrages de Voiture, qui ont ces charmes secrets, ces grâces fines et cachées dont nous parlons, plaisent infiniment davantage.'[4]

A few lines of *Le Songe de Vaux* state this artistic ideal, though La Fontaine denies, with traditional humility, that he ever achieved it:

Vous ne trouverez point chez moi cet heureux art
Qui cache ce qu'il est et ressemble au hasard:
Je n'ai point ce beau tour, ce charme inexprimable
Qui rend le dieu des vers sur tous autres aimable:
C'est ce qu'il faut avoir, si l'on veut être admis
Parmi ceux qu'Apollon compte entre ses amis.[5]

[1] See Samuel Holt Monk, 'A Grace beyond the Reach of Art', in *Journal of the History of Ideas*, vol. V, April 1944, pp. 131–50.
[2] See Vaclav Cerny, 'Le "Je ne sais quoi" de Trissotin', in *Revue des Sciences Humaines*, Fascicule 103, July–September 1961, pp. 367–78. Also Pierre-Henri Simon, 'Le "je ne sais quoi" devant la raison classique', in *Cahiers de l'Association Internationales des Études Françaises*, No. 11. May 1959, pp. 104–17.
[3] E.g. Méré.
[4] D. Bouhours, *Entretiens d'Ariste et d'Eugène*, Paris, 1920, pp. 204 and 210.
[5] *Le Songe de Vaux*, II, *O.D.*, p. 82.

7. *Style enjoué* AND *Gaieté*

Grace and subtlety, such are the characteristics of the *style enjoué*, this light tone in which Marot and Voiture excelled and which had a particular attraction for La Fontaine. In the lighter poetic genres, the poet did not find a pretext for a lowering of aesthetic standard or for a relaxation of his efforts to reach technical perfection. In *Clymène*, Erato assures Apollo that, in order to succeed at what he calls '*un jeu*',

Il y faut plus de temps que le monde ne croit.[1]

It seems that La Fontaine was aware of the suspicion which this style roused among the most serious-minded readers; these, like himself, would be satisfied only by achievements of unquestionable quality:

On cherche les rieurs et moi je les évite.
Cet art veut sur tout autre un suprême mérite
Dieu ne créa que pour les sots
Les méchants diseurs de bons mots.[VIII,8]

The poet was, by temperament, irresistibly attracted by what he calls '*la bagatelle, le galant, les badineries, la plaisanterie, la gaieté*'.[2] In *Psyché*, Poliphile, who is generally accepted as voicing La Fontaine's opinions, declares:

'J'ai déjà mêlé malgré moi de la gaieté parmi les endroits les plus sérieux de cette histoire; je ne vous assure pas que tantôt je n'en mêle aussi parmi les plus tristes. C'est un défaut dont je ne me saurais corriger, quelque peine que j'y apporte.'

As for Gélaste, he is all too ready to excuse such a breach of the *bienséances*:

'Défaut pour défaut, . . ., j'aime beaucoup mieux qu'on me fasse rire quand je dois pleurer, que si l'on me faisait pleurer lorsque je dois rire.'[3]

In a letter to the Prince de Conti, in which he proposes to celebrate, in his manner, the misadventure which befell Mademoiselle de La Force, La Fontaine remarks maliciously:

---

[1] *Clymène, O.D.*, p. 37.
[2] Ibid., *O.D.*, p. 37; *Le Songe de Vaux, Avertissement*, ibid., pp. 78 and 95; *Psyché*, Preface, ibid., pp. 121–2; *Fables*, Preface, vol. I, pp. 9–10.
[3] *Psyché, O.D.*, p. 173.

'Je commence par une espèce de *lamentabile carmen*, à la manière des anciens; et, comme l'aventure est tragi-comique je me laisse bientôt entraîner à ma façon d'écrire ordinaire.'[1]

In the poem which follows this introduction, we find all the elements characteristic of the *bagatelle*, which represent the poet's usual and most successful manner of writing:

Rarement pour les pleurs mon talent réussit.[XII,28, *l.* 300]

Here again, we must admire La Fontaine's lucidity with regard to his own talent. Nevertheless, if his sense of propriety and his acceptance of the taste of his day prevented him from introducing his favourite style into any genre, he complained of the strict rules then in force, which made diversity difficult within a given work: 'L'uniformité de style est la règle la plus étroite que nous ayons'.[2] To an artist as sensitive to the requirements of the contemporary taste and genres, as lucid in the analysis of his own temperament and ability, as eager to please his public as La Fontaine, the technical problem thus set was almost insoluble. Only the most fastidious balancing of seemingly contradictory elements, the most complete pervasion of one's whole work by a predominant tone of lightness and fantasy could harmoniously combine the poet's taste and temperament with the specific quality of contemporary art forms and the particular nature of the subject-matter. The technical achievement of *Psyché* had proved to be beyond the legitimate and modest expectation of its author: 'Il est bon de s'accommoder à son sujet; mais il est encore meilleur de s'accommoder à son génie.'[3] In this work, however, this dual aim was reached through the congenial medium of the *style enjoué*.

An anonymous manuscript of the *Bibliothèque Nationale*, recording some alleged conversation with La Fontaine, quotes him as emphasizing the superiority of French poetry over the ancient and the foreign ones on account of the variety of the French meters and prosody, and saying: 'Notre poésie est enjouée, les anciens étaient assez sérieux.'[4] Not only was La Fontaine convinced that *enjouement* was an original feature in French poetry, he remarked that he considered it also to be one of the necessary components of a successful piece of writing, the aim of which is 'd'attacher le lecteur, de le réjouir, d'attirer malgré lui son attention, de lui plaire

[1] *A Son Altesse Sérénissime Mgr le Prince de Conti*, O.D., pp. 697–8.
[2] *Psyché*, Preface, O.D., p. 121.
[3] Ibid., p. 173.
[4] O.D., p. 931.

enfin.'[1] In the preface to the first collection of fables, where La Fontaine, in a semi-humorous manner praises Phaedrus' brevity, he writes:

'Comme il m'était impossible de l'imiter en cela, j'ai cru qu'il fallait en récompense égayer l'ouvrage plus qu'il n'a fait. ... C'est ce que j'ai fait avec d'autant plus de hardiesse que Quintilien dit qu'on ne saurait trop égayer les narrations. ... J'ai pourtant considéré que ces Fables étant sues de tout le monde, je ne ferais rien si je ne les rendais nouvelles par quelques traits qui en relevassent le goût. C'est ce qu'on demande aujourd'hui: on veut de la nouveauté et de la gaieté. Je n'appelle pas gaieté ce qui excite le rire, mais un certain charme, un air agréable qu'on peut donner à toutes sortes de sujets même les plus sérieux.'[2]

Just as he distinguished between grace and beauty, La Fontaine now makes a distinction between *gaieté* and the comic. Here again, we find our poet, if not completely original, ranking, at least, among the most perceptive of his contemporaries. This notion of *gaieté* is not without analogies with that defined by the author of the '*Lettre sur le Misanthrope*', the effect of which was to '*faire rire dans l'âme*'.[3] Monchesnay writes of Boileau:

'Monsieur Despréaux ... me disait qu'il y avait deux sortes de rire, l'un qui vient de surprise, et l'autre qui réjouit l'âme intérieurement, et fait rire plus efficacement, parce qu'il est fondé sur la raison. Car, disait-il, l'effet naturel de la raison, c'est de plaire.'[4]

Mademoiselle de Scudéry comments:

'Il y a bien de la différence entre divertir et faire rire. Cependant il y aura plusieurs poètes qui confondront la poésie galante et enjouée avec la poésie burlesque. ... Il y a pourtant une grande distinction à faire de l'une à l'autre.'[5]

According to Guez de Balzac, 'il y a une certaine gaieté de style éloignée en distance égale de la bouffonnerie et de la tristesse.'[6] Voiture, writes Pellisson, had struck this happy medium:

[1] *Contes*, vol. I, p. 60 (Preface to part II).
[2] *Fables*, Preface, vol. I, pp. 9–10.
[3] In Molière, *Œuvres*, Grands Écrivains de la France, Paris, 1912, vol. V, p. 440. The attribution of this letter either to Donneau de Visé or to Molière himself is still disputed. See R. Robert, 'Des Commentaires de première main sur les chefs-d'œuvres les plus discutés de Molière', in *Revue des Sciences Humaines*, Fascicule 81, January–March 1956, pp. 19–55.
[4] Monchesnay, *Bolœana*, Amsterdam, 1742, pp. 86–8.
[5] Mademoiselle de Scudéry *Clélie*, part IV, book II, quoted by F. Bar, in *Le Genre burlesque en France au XVIIème siècle*, Paris, 1960, p. xxvi.
[6] Guez de Balzac, *Socrate chrétien*, *Avant-propos*, in *Œuvres*, Paris, 1854, vol. II, p. 12.

'Cette sorte de poésie que Monsieur de Voiture avait introduite, qui renonçant à la gravité sans s'abaisser jusqu'à la bouffonnerie est plus propre que pas une autre à divertir les honnêtes gens.'[1]

To understand what La Fontaine means by *la gaieté*, it is necessary, first, to define the elements which, in his eyes, were its chief components. Diffused *gaieté* is necessary to *poésie enjouée* or *galante*, the effect of which is to *réjouir* and *divertir* the reader in a subtle manner, causing him to *rire dans l'âme*. It is distinct from other tones, such as the heroic and the idyllic which La Fontaine once cherished but abandoned as they fell from the public's favour. Both these styles thrive on an abundance of *ornements*, whilst the *poésie enjouée* prefers *traits*. The vagueness of seventeenth-century terminology of criticism and the lack of comprehensive study on the subject,[2] make it necessary for us to give a definition of these two terms as used by La Fontaine:

Ornement belongs to the vocabulary of the criticism of poetry:

'Il serait véritablement à souhaiter que d'autres mains que les miennes y eussent ajouté les ornements de la poésie'[3]

'Ce n'est pas qu'un des maîtres de notre éloquence n'ait désapprouvé le dessein de les mettre [les fables] en vers. Il a cru que leur principal ornement est de n'en avoir aucun.'[4]

It also refers more particularly to the noble poetic genres, the heroic and the idyllic:

---

[1] Pellisson, *Discours sur les œuvres de M. Sarasin*, in Sarasin, *Œuvres*, Paris, 1656, p. 55. See also Méré, Letter LXVIII, to Balzac, quoted by Borgerhoff, *The Freedom of French Classicism*, p. 94: 'Il me semble que cette urbanité n'est point ce qu'on appelle de bons mots, et qu'elle consiste en je ne sais quoi de civil et de poli, je ne sais quoi de railleur et de flatteur tout ensemble.' See also Letter CLXXI, ibid., pp. 98–9: 'Si vous me demandez ce que j'entends par ces choses rares, je vous réponds que celles que j'aime le mieux et qui me touchent le plus vivement ce sont les subtiles, les hautes et les tendres; ... Je mets encore en ce nombre une raillerie honnête, qui réjouit sans choquer personne; elle procède d'un esprit agréable et d'une humeur enjouée,' Some theorists have an altogether broader conception of *la gaieté*: e.g. the anonymous author of *Le Parterre de la Rhétorique française*, Lyon, 1659, pp. 13–14, places against the following passage: 'Les beaux adverbes donnent de la force et de l'énergie aux verbes. ... Il est glorieusement occupé, aimer passionnément, pleurer inconsolablement, se présenter effrontément, les lions rugissent épouvantablement. ...', the marginal note 'gaieté du style'. See also Furetière, *Dictionnaire Universel*: 'Enjouement se dit aussi des pensées gaies, des descriptions fleuries qui se rencontrent dans quelque ouvrage de prose, ou de vers. ... On le dit aussi en peinture et en musique, des manières de peindre ou de chanter qui sont égayées'.
[2] With the exception of I. Sőtér, *La Doctrine stylistique des rhétoriques de XVIIème siècle*, Le Hir, *Rhétorique et stylistique*, Q.M. Hope, *Saint-Evremond, The Honnête Homme as Critic*, Bloomington, USA, 1962, ch. VI, 'Keywords'. N. Hepp, 'Esquisse du vocabulaire de la critique littéraire de la querelle du Cid à la querelle d'Homère', in *Romanische Forschungen*, vol. LXIX, 1957, 3–4, pp. 332–408; and G. Couton, *La Poétique de La Fontaine*.
[3] *Fables*, *A Mgr le Dauphin*, vol. I, p. 3.
[4] *Fables*, Preface, vol. I, p. 7.

'Je m'étais toute ma vie exercé à ce genre de poésie que nous
nommons héroique; c'est assurément le plus beau de tous, le plus
fleuri, le plus susceptible d'ornements et de ces figures nobles et
hardies qui font une langue à part, une langue assez charmante pour
mériter qu'on l'appelle la langue des dieux.'[1]

The word *ornement* is sufficiently vague and general to cover a variety of
rhetorical devices whose effect is to give the poem the formal, lofty and
dignified tone required by tradition: allegory, anaphora, antonomasion,
gradation, hyperbole, proem, repetition, prosopopoeia etc. The poet's own
invention plays only a minor part in their choice and has little bearing
on the treatment of the subject-matter: strict conformity with universally
recognized models and uniformity of tone are the rigid rules of the *genre
orné* in which Malherbe, 'qui louait ses héros en un style superbe',[2] excelled.
Professor Couton sees in *ornements* a term usually endowed with a pejorative nuance,[3] this judgement would require some qualification: the
example given above does not imply such a nuance because the word is
used with reference to high poetry. Boileau makes this point very clear.

D'un air plus grand encor la poésie épique
Dans le vaste récit d'une longue action,
Se soutient par la fable et vit de fiction.
Là pour nous enchanter tout est mis en usage;
Tout prend un corps, une âme, un esprit, un visage.

Ainsi, dans cet amas de nobles fictions,
Le poète s'égaye[4] en mille inventions,
Orne, élève, embellit, agrandit toutes choses,
Et trouve sous sa main des fleurs toujours écloses.

Sans tous ces ornements le vers tombe en langueur,
La poésie est morte, ou rampe sans vigueur.[5]

On the contrary, when the word is used with reference to the *Fables* the
pejorative sense is obvious, implying that *ornements* are out of place in
minor genres:

Nombre de gens fameux en ce genre ont écrit.
Tous ont fui l'ornement et le trop d'étendue.
On ne voit point chez eux de parole perdue.[VI,1-2]

[1] *Adonis, Avertissement, O.D.*, p. 1.   [2] *Clymène, O.D.*, p. 32.
[3] G. Couton, *La Poétique de la Fontaine*, p. 34.
[4] *S'égayer*, 'On dit qu'un homme, un auteur s'égaye, lorsqu'il dit quelque chose d'agréable
qui n'est pas tout à fait de son sujet'. (*Dictionnaire de l'Académie française*, Paris, 1694.) Cf.
Fables, Preface, vol. I, pp. 9-10.
[5] Boileau, *Art poétique*, III, in *Œuvres complètes*, vol. II, pp. 352-6.

Vous voulez qu'on évite un soin trop curieux,
Et des vains ornements l'effort ambitieux.
Je le veux comme vous; cet effort ne peut plaire.[V,1]

In the fable, and, more generally, in middle style, *ornements* give way
to *traits*:

Un auteur gâte tout quand il veut trop bien faire.
Non qu'il faille bannir certains traits délicats:
Vous les aimez, ces traits, et je ne les hais pas.[V,1]

Patru was right when he warned La Fontaine against the use of the
ornements of poetry in the fable: 'Il a cru que leur principal ornement est
de n'en avoir aucun.'[1] The problem was, on the one hand, to avoid the
terseness of the ancients and, on the other, to use *ornements* in a minor
genre. La Fontaine thus resorted to '*quelques traits*' well in keeping with
the middle style required by the fable. *Trait* is a vague term covering a
variety of devices and effects; Georges Couton has defined the nature and
function of the *traits familiers*, which he identifies with *éthopée*[2], the
figure used to elaborate the characters and 'pour peindre nos mœurs'.[IV,18]
This elucidation contributes greatly to our understanding of La Fontaine's remarks[3] and indeed these *traits*, situated on a lower plane than the
ornements, belong to the fable. The acceptation of the word could be
extended still further to cover another meaning also recorded in contemporary texts: Littré's definition: 'Trait, particulièrement. Pensée vive,
brillante, imprévue', is justified, among other quotations, by La Fontaine's allusion to 'certains traits délicats'[4] and by Madame de Sévigné's
remark to Madame de Grignan:

'Vous parlez de mes lettres, je voudrais que vous vissiez les traits
qui sont dans les vôtres, et tout ce que vous dites en une ligne.'[5]

In *Clymène* Uranie sees in *traits* an indispensable component of true
poetry, ranking with 'ce langage divin, ces charmantes figures'.[6] When,
after writing *La Mort et le Malheureux*[I,15], La Fontaine, on Boileau's
advice, returned to the Latin original and composed *La Mort et le
Bûcheron*[I,16], he introduced the latter fable in the following terms: 'Je

[1] *Fables*, Preface, vol. I, p. 7.
[2] G. Couton, *La Poétique de La Fontaine*, p. 34.
[3] *Fables*, Preface, vol. I, p. 10; ibid., *Avertissement*, vol. II, p. 9; *A Mgr le Prince de Conti*, O.D., p. 588.
[4] *Fables*, V, 1; cf. *Contes*, vol. II, p. 229, *ll.*4–7 (Le Tableau).
[5] Madame de Sévigné, Letter to Mme de Grignan, September 27th 1684, in *Lettres*, vol. III, (1957), p. 18.
[6] *Clymène*, O.D., p. 39.

laissais passer un des plus beaux traits qui fût dans Esope'. This *trait* is the wood-cutter's ingenious justification of his appeal to Death:

> C'est, dit-il, afin de m'aider
> A recharger ce bois. . . .

It is at the same time an *éthopée*, a *sermocinatio*, which lays human nature bare, and—in this context—an unexpected witticism. In the words of Gamaches:

> 'Les traits nous causent . . . cette espèce de surprise qui sert à soutenir ou à réveiller notre attention; ils offrent toujours à notre esprit quelque chose d'inattendu.'[1]

Thus, a *trait* would be the ingenious expression of an ingenious idea and it seems to be the adequate means to achieve the ideal of our poet:

> 'J'ai pourtant considéré que ces fables étant sues de tout le monde, je ne ferais rien si je ne les rendais nouvelles par quelques traits qui en relevassent le goût.'[2]

Good taste remains the sole criterion in the choice of *traits* and we may trust La Fontaine's discernment to reject the superficial brilliance of the purely gratuitous:

> Je pris certain auteur autrefois pour mon maître;
> Mais ses traits ont perdu quiconque l'a suivi.[3]

If 'trop d'esprit, antithèses, concetti'[4] are the components of these unworthy *traits*, it is among the more moderate forms of these elements that we must look for equivalents to acceptable *traits*. Boileau would confirm this view:

> Que de traits surprenants sans cesse il [l'auteur] nous réveille,
> Qu'il coure dans ses vers de merveille en merveille.
> Et que tout ce qu'il dit, facile à retenir,
> De son ouvrage en nous laisse un long souvenir.[5]

Egayer l'ouvrage, relever le goût, to impart *un certain charme, un air agréable*,[6] such is the part played by the *traits* in the fable and such are,

---

[1] E. S. de Gamaches, *Les Agréments du langage réduits à leurs principes*, Paris, 1718, p. 338.
[2] *Fables*, Preface, vol. I, p. 10.
[3] *A Monseigneur l'Evêque de Soissons*, *O.D.*, p. 646.
[4] Ibid., La Fontaine's own footnote.
[5] Boilean, *Art poétique*, III, in *Œuvres complètes*, vol. II, p. 351.
[6] *Fables*, Preface, vol. I, pp. 9–10.

for La Fontaine, the requirements of the *gaieté* which radiated from Voiture's poetry:

> Et puis maître Vincent, qui même aurait loué
> Proserpine et Pluton en style enjoué.[1]

Here again, La Fontaine's judgement and the terminology he uses coincide with those of contemporary critics; Bouhours writes of Voiture:

> 'C'est un écrivain enjoué, qui dans une petite débauche d'esprit dit des folies de gaieté de coeur pour se réjouir et pour réjouir les autres.'[2]

Phérotée de La Croix writes of him:

> 'On ne voit rien dans notre langue, qui soit plus fin, plus délicat et plus enjoué que ses Lettres: ses vers ne sont pas si exacts, mais le tour en est heureux et singulier. Cette urbanité qu'il admirait dans les ouvrages de l'antiquité se rencontre dans tous les siens; le sel attique y est répandu partout et jamais on n'a mieux entendu l'art de badiner noblement et agréablement.'[3]

Pellisson's analysis of Voiture's peculiar charm is even more subtle and already hints at the *gaieté* 'qu'on peut donner à toutes sortes de sujets, même les plus sérieux':

> 'Monsieur de Voiture, qui pourrait lui refuser cette louange? vint alors avec un esprit très galant et très délicat et une mélancolie douce et ingénieuse, de celles qui cherchent sans cesse à s'égayer. Il se souvenait de la liberté de notre ancienne poésie, il avait devant les yeux celle de quelques italiens, et les finesses des plus polis auteurs de Rome et de Grèce. De tout cela ensemble ne suivant personne, mais éclairé, il se fit lui-même un genre d'écrire qui ne charma pas moins par ses grâces que par sa nouveauté.'[4]

It is remarkable that this judgement could also be applied to La Fontaine without qualifications.[5] We may complete it by a remark of Gamaches which may account for the success met with by the *style enjoué*:

[1] *Clymène*, O.D., p. 32.
[2] D. Bouhours, *Remarques nouvelles sur la langue française*, Paris, 1675, p. 32.
[3] Phérotée de La Croix, *L'Art de la poésie française et latine avec une idée de la musique*, Lyon, 1694, p. 402.
[4] Pellisson, *Discours sur les œuvres de M. Sarasin*, in Sarasin, *Œuvres*, p. 58.
[5] Even 'jusqu'au sombre plaisir d'un cœur mélancolique'.

'Les grâces de la nouveauté dans quelque genre que ce soit, sont toujours celles auxquelles on est le plus sensible.'[1]

The novelty of the *Fables* resides not only in La Fontaine's choice of the genre but, above all, in the creation of a style admirably suited to this genre. More than a limited framework for his inspiration which, he admitted, soon flagged, the poet was to find, in the fable, free scope for his experiments in matters of tone and technique, and to enjoy the freedom which only a medium neglected by the theorists could provide. His innovation was to make the fable poetic and follow in Horace's tentative steps, in spite of the reservations of Quintilian[2] and Patru.[3] It gave La Fontaine an opportunity and a pretext to break the strictest, and, to him, the most thwarting rule of his time; that of the uniformity of style within any given genre.[4] The fable was not a poetic genre and was to become, in his hands, 'a repository for all genres',[5] a repository of half a century of poetry which, in the words of Renée Winegarten, had been 'a maze of cross-currents and under-currents.'[6] The blending of varied and sometimes opposed tones constituted the ideal language of the fable as viewed by La Fontaine, a composite genre thriving on the interplay of human beings, animals and plants, didactic intentions, philosophical reflexions and personal confidences. The aesthetic value of variety had not escaped the contemporaries of La Fontaine. Pellisson had praised

> 'la variété qui est utile et louable en toute sorte d'ouvrages, mais absolument nécessaire en ceux qui ne se proposent pour but que le plaisir',[7]

and Boileau was to write, after Horace:

> Heureux qui, dans ses vers, sait d'une voix légère
> Passer du grave au doux, du plaisant au sévère.
> Son livre aimé du ciel et chéri des lecteurs,
> Est souvent chez Barbin entouré d'acheteurs.[8]

But La Fontaine shows himself conscious of the danger for such a

---

[1] E. S. de Gamaches, *Les Agréments du langage*, p. 87.
[2] 'Horatius ne in poemate quidem humilem generis huius usum putavit in illis versibus quod dixit. . . .' Quintilian, *Institutio Oratoria*, V, XI, 20, vol. II, p. 282.
[3] *Fables*, Preface, vol. I, p. 7.
[4] *Psyché*, Preface, *O.D.*, p. 121.
[5] C. W. Rosen, *Style and Morality in La Fontaine*, p. 114.
[6] R. Winegarten, *French Lyric Poetry in the Age of Malherbe*, Manchester, 1954, p. XII.
[7] Pellisson, *Discours sur les œuvres de M. Sarasin*, in Sarasin, *Œuvres*, pp. 18–19.
[8] Boileau, *Art poétique*, I, in *Œuvres complètes*, vol. II, p. 291.

composite style to become the target of cross-fire criticism when he asks M. de Barillon:

> La qualité d'ambassadeur
> Peut-elle s'abaisser à des contes vulgaires?
> Vous puis-je offrir mes vers et leurs grâces légères?
> S'ils osent quelquefois prendre un air de grandeur,
> Seront-ils point traités par vous de téméraires? VIII,4

As an artist sensitive to the peculiar qualities of the different styles, who had practised them all and pondered over the question of matching subject-matter and form throughout his works, he shows, in the *Fables*, a remarkable mastery of technique in the happy blending of the most various elements. Supremely at ease in this delicate art form of his own invention, he gives his *style enjoué*, irregular by nature, this sprightly grace which he preferred to formal beauty. It would be very wrong to imagine that this creation was the result of one single deliberate successful attempt on the part of the poet: the progressive evolution of certain types of fables from 1668 to 1693, the technical discussions found in the prefaces, *avertissements*, and also the very text of some fables[1] reveal the preoccupations, the hesitations and the constant searchings of La Fontaine. The genre thus created is always adaptable and open to experiments and accretions which give the whole work a pleasant variety, the artistic as well as the practical value of which is acknowledged by the poet:

> 'Voici un second recueil de fables que je présente au public; j'ai jugé à propos de donner à la plupart de celles-ci un air et un tour un peu différent de celui que j'ai donné aux premières, tant à cause de la différence des sujets que pour remplir de plus de variété mon ouvrage.'[2]

Yet this permanent artistic consciousness and elaboration is completely unobtrusive and the general impression given by a work of art must be one of perfect naturalness and propriety. This *naïveté* which, according to Vaugelas, ranks first among the qualities of style,[3] has been defined by many theorists:

---

[1] *Fables*, II, 1; III, 1; V, 1; VIII, 4; IX, 1, etc.
[2] *Fables*, *Avertissement*, vol. II, p. 9. La Fontaine's awareness of the value of variety is obvious throughout his work: i.e. *Clymène*, *O.D.*, p. 19; *Contes*, vol. I, p. 9 (Preface to Part I); ibid., vol. II, p. 200 (Le Pâté d'anguilles), etc.
[3] Vaugelas, *Remarques sur la langue française*, Paris, 1934, p. 104.

'On parle toujours bien quand on parle naturellement: tout le secret consiste à choisir les termes proportionnés à la matière dont on traite. Si le sujet est grand, il faut des expressions plus nobles: s'il est petit, il ne faut employer que des expressions simples. Les paroles sont à peu près à l'égard des pensées comme les habits à l'égard des personnes: il serait ridicule de donner à un nain l'habit d'un géant.'[1]

Our poet was not only aware of the technical propriety of style, he also sensed a more subtle form of propriety: that of temperament[2] and feeling:

Ce qu'on n'a point au coeur, l'a-t-on dans ses écrits?[3]

Naturalness, then, is achieved through sincerity and the style thus gains a personal touch which, in Pascal's words, surprises and charms the reader:

'Quand on voit le style naturel, on est tout étonné et ravi, car on s'attendait de voir un auteur et on trouve un homme.'[4]

Nevertheless, La Fontaine's devotion to sincerity does not make him reveal the favourite device by which he so often achieves this naturalness; indeed, the poet made but a few comments on the use and the value of studied negligence.[5] The very nature of the device required discretion: is it not:

... Cet heureux art
Qui cache ce qu'il est et ressemble au hasard[6]

which, like grace, surpasses beauty?[7]

8. SELECTIVE IMITATION

The poet is far more explicit about the question of imitation which preoccupied almost all his contemporaries and came to a head towards the end of the century, in the quarrel between the supporters of the ancients and those of the moderns. In the seventeenth century, most writers

---

[1] J.-B. Morvan de Bellegarde, *Réflexions sur l'élégance et la politesse du style*, Amsterdam, 1706, p. 13.
[2] *Psyché, O.D.*, p. 173.
[3] *Clymène, O.D.*, p. 18.
[4] Pascal, *Pensées*, ed. Brunschvicg, Paris, 1946, p. 330, Pensée 29.
[5] *Contes*, vol. I, p. 59 (Preface to part II); *Fables*, V, 1.
[6] *Le Songe de Vaux*, II, *O.D.*, p. 82.
[7] Tallemant des Réaux writes of Gomberville: 'Il a fait quelques vers: ils sont plus beaux que naturels.' *Historiettes*, Paris, 1932–34, vol. VI, p. 47.

were, at the same time, competent and widely read scholars; their attitude towards the heritage of ancient and foreign literature reveals, on the one hand, serious doubts about their own ability to discover any new field of inspiration or any new material for literary compositions[1] and to surpass or even equal the masters in original creation. On the other hand, they approached the works of the ancients with an uninhibited freedom, the result of a long familiarity:[2] the border line between the free translations known as *belles infidèles* and literary imitations is sometimes difficult to trace. Nevertheless, imitation is considered by all to be absolutely necessary as a schooling in taste for the writer and this formative method is simply the continuation, on a higher plane, of the rhetorical and literary training received in schools.[3] La Fontaine, in the *Avertissement* of *Adonis*, refers to the stock of topologies he had gathered 'soit par la lecture des anciens, soit par celle de quelques uns de nos modernes'[4] and which he almost exhausted in the composition of his poem. He is only too willing to name all those whom he acknowledges as his masters, as well as the sources of his writings and sometimes, of occasional

---

[1] 'C'est une sotte ambition de dire des choses qui surprennent par leur nouveauté.' J.-B. Morvan de Bellegarde, *Réflexions sur l'élégance et la politesse du style*, p. 83. 'Tout est dit, et l'on vient trop tard depuis plus de sept mille ans qu'il y a des hommes, et qui pensent.' La Bruyère, *Les Caractères*, in *Œuvres*, vol. II, p. 25.

[2] See R. W. Ladborough, 'Translation from the Ancients in XVIIth-Century France', in *Journal of the Warburg Institute*, vol. II, 1938–39, pp. 85–104.

[3] This formative imitation is, by no means, limited to the ancients. See Preface to the *Recueil de poésies chrétiennes et diverses*, *O.D.*, p. 777:

> 'Il est donc visible que, pour former les personnes à la poésie, il faut leur former le sentiment et le goût. Or pour cela il n'y a qu'une méthode, qui est de lire quantité de bons vers et de n'en lire point de mauvais. En lisant d'excellents vers, on s'en imprime l'idée, et en n'en lisant point de mauvais, on empêche que cette idée, ne s'obscurcisse et ne se corrompe. . . . De sorte que ce qui fait que les uns parlent mieux et plus agréablement que d'autres, c'est que leur esprit est rempli d'idées, de tours et de manières plus agréables. . . . On n'a pas besoin d'un grand raisonnement pour conclure de là qu'un recueil d'excellents vers est le meilleur art poétique qu'on se puisse imaginer.'

Cf. Guillaume du Vair, in *De l'éloquence française*, in *Œuvres*, Paris, 1625, p. 437:

> 'Apprendre par préceptes est un chemin bien long, pour ce que nous avons de peine à les entendre, après les avoir entendus à les retenir, et après les avoir retenus à les mettre en usage . . . Mais l'exemple et imitation nous apprennent sur l'ouvrage même, nous invitent avec beaucoup plus d'ardeur et nous promettent quasi semblable gloire que celle de ceux que nous prenons à imiter. L'accoutumance et familiarité a une merveilleuse force, pour conduire la disposition à ce qui lui est familier.'

Cf. also *La Rhétorique de l'honnête homme*, by an anonymous author, Amsterdam, 1699, p. 139:

> 'Il faut choisir un petit nombre de livres approuvés, comme les œuvres de Malherbe, de Balzac, de Vaugelas, d'Ablancourt, de Pellisson, de Voiture, de Patru, de Costar, de Bouhours, de Fléchier, de Saint-Evremond et de quelques autres. Après, il faut prendre garde aux plus beaux endroits de leurs écrits et à leurs expressions les plus élégantes; les repasser souvent dans l'esprit et tâcher de les retenir afin de pouvoir les employer dans les occasions et s'acquérir en même temps la facilité de bien parler.'

[4] *Adonis, Avertissement, O.D.*, p. 1.

imitations or simple phrases borrowed for their picturesque quality, their vigour or their humour. 'Que n'imitait-il point, et quel genre de poésie n'a-t-il point imité?'[1] Le Verrier's exclamation about La Fontaine is more than a rhetorical question; it is a tribute to the poet's knowledge of literature. La Fontaine's originality lies, to a certain extent, in the fact that he did not limit imitation to the ancients: medieval and modern French and foreign writers, even oriental ones, rank among his creditors. The range and the sheer amount of his acknowledged reading are really impressive and make him one of the most widely cultured writers of his century.[2] Enthusiasm in his investigations of new reading matter and a close attachment to old favourites are the amiable characteristics of his attitude to books, summarized by two well-known anecdotes. The unconventional—and unsuitable—seminarist who read profane literature more readily than theology and admitted that, at the Oratory 'Desmares s'amusait à lire son Saint Augustin et moi, mon Astrée',[3] was, in later life, able to enthuse over a minor prophet of the Old Testament to the point of greeting new acquaintances with the question: 'Avez-vous lu Baruch?'[4] It is significant that La Fontaine's work bears obvious traces of both specific reminiscence and the diffused influence of his reading; it shows that imitation, on his part, was, as he so often claimed, selective and creative:

> Mon imitation n'est point un esclavage.[5]

This selective imitation is a valuable training for the poet, since it follows discriminating readings from which he retains only the best elements, be it a whole episode, or a choice of effective phrases, or simply some observations concerning technical devices to be re-used, imitated, or adapted independently at any time when their aesthetic superiority over all the other possible original renderings is clear:

> Je ne prends que l'idée et les tours et les lois
> Que nos maîtres suivaient eux-mêmes autrefois.[6]

---

[1] Le Verrier, *Commentaire sur les Satires de Boileau*, in *Les Satires de Boileau commentées par lui-même*, Le Vésinet. Courménil, 1906, p. 91.

[2] There is evidence, too, that La Fontaine imitated many more writers than he mentioned; e.g. Du Bartas, Théophile de Viau, François Maynard, Saint-Amant, Tristan L'Hermite, etc.

[3] Le Verrier, *Commentaire sur les Satires de Boileau* in *Les Satires de Boileau commentées par lui-même*, p. 110.

[4] Louis Racine, *Mémoires sur la vie de Jean Racine*, in *Œuvres de J. Racine*, Grands Ecrivains de la France, Paris, 1865–73, vol. I, p. 326.

[5] *A Monseigneur l'Evêque de Soissons*, O.D., pp. 645–6; cf. also *Psyché*, ibid., p. 122; *Contes and Fables*, passim. See Colbert Searles, 'La Fontaine's Imitation', in *Philological Quarterly*, vol. I, 1922, pp. 56–70.

[6] *A Monseigneur l'Evêque de Soissons*, O.D., p. 646.

In this context, the word *tour*, which puzzled Faguet,[1] requires elucidation. This word became very popular in the second half of the seventeenth century and acquired new figurative meanings. Bouhours and Bellegarde[2] listed these new acceptations, stressing their novelty; among these, we find: *tour d'esprit agréable*, *tour d'expression* and *tour de l'expression*, *tour galant*, *des vers bien tournés* and *tourner bien un vers*. These, obviously, belong to the vocabulary of literary criticism and it is to the theorists that we shall turn in order to elucidate their meaning. A *tour* is the turn of phrase used in the expression of an idea; it usually implies a special regard for effectiveness, clarity, elegance and a conciseness exempt of oversimplification; in the words of Maucroix:

> 'Peu importe qu'on écrive lentement, pourvu que ce soit exactement. Ne nous contentons pas de ce qui se présente d'abord, cherchons ce qu'il peut y avoir de meilleur. Il faut faire choix de ses pensées et les mettre dans l'ordre qui leur convient. Il faut ensuite peser toutes ses paroles et les arranger de telle sorte qu'elles donnent au discours un nombre et une cadence qui frappe agréablement l'oreille. Pour attraper aisément ce tour harmonieux, il est bon de répéter la phrase qui précède ce qu'on a écrit à l'instant même.'[3]

This technical acceptation of the word occurs again and again in contexts which bear it out unmistakably: these are precise discussions of the respective value of sentences quoted in full, followed by possible alternatives. Their comparative merits reside in the different arrangement of their components, every arrangement being referred to as *tour* by the critics.[4] These word-arrangements often result in the formation of figures of speech; hence the definition of the latter given by Bretteville:

> 'Les figures ne sont autre chose que certains tours d'expression et de pensée dont on ne se sert point communément.'[5]

[1] 'Je ne comprends pas ce qu'il veut dire ici par les tours car s'il est original par quelque côté, c'est bien par la forme'. In *Revue des Cours et Conférences*, 1897, quoted by Haraszti, *En glanant chez La Fontaine*, p. 14, n. 1.
[2] D. Bouhours, *Entretiens d'Ariste et d'Eugène*, p. 83. J.-B. Morvan de Bellegarde, *Réflexions sur l'élégance et la politesse du style*, pp. 259–60.
[3] F. de Maucroix, *Traduction de l'Instruction de Quintilien sur la manière de composer*, tirée de sa *Rhétorique*, in *Œuvres posthumes*, pp. 335–6.
[4] Andry de Boisregard, *Réflexions sur l'usage présent de la langue française*, Paris, 1689, pp. 668–72; 677; 680–2. Leclerc, *Bibliothèque universelle et historique de l'année MDCLXXXVIII* Amsterdam, 1688, vol. VII, pp. 191–2. Le Verrier, *Commentaire sur les Satires de Boileau*, p. 76. Claude Irson identifies *tours* and style and sees in them the specific features of an author's manner. See *Nouvelle méthode pour apprendre facilement les principes et la pureté de la langue française*, Paris, 1656, p. 86.
[5] Bretteville, *L'Eloquence de la chaire et du barreau selon les principes les plus solides de la rhétorique sacrée et profane*, Paris, 1689, III, 1, quoted by C. Chesneau du Marsais, *Des Tropes*, Paris, 1766, p. 2.

D

which is conformable to the etymological meaning of the word *trope*, also
used as a synonym of figure of speech.[1] Gamaches restricts the meaning
of *tour* even more and reserves the term for the figures which tend to
imply more than their literal sense expresses:

> 'Le tour ainsi que le mot semble le porter, est une manière
> détournée de faire entendre ce qu'on affecte de ne point déclarer.'[2]

This definition does not seem to represent the general usage of the word
but reflects the notion of ingenuity and subtlety which it implies.
At any rate, *tour* is different from *trait*; it refers to the technical presentation of the statement whilst the latter insists on the quality of its content.
A *trait* may be presented more or less effectively according to the *tour*
chosen from among the many possible ones to express it.

When La Fontaine admits that he imitates *les tours*, he probably
suggests that he imitates some of his models' figures of speech and also
stylistic patterns which are neat, pleasant, and effective. The fable *La
Belette entrée dans un grenier*[III,17] provides a clear example of this type
of imitation. Horace had written:

> Macra cavum repetes arctum quem macra subisti.[3]

In La Fontaine, the line becomes:

> Vous êtes maigre entrée, il faut maigre sortir.

The poet has retained the figures and patterns which made Horace's line
distinctive: the repetition of the keyword and its significant position in
front of the verbs, the parallelism combined with an antithesis; but French
syntax did not enable La Fontaine to link both clauses by a relative, a
tour which gave the original conciseness; the French poet replaced sub-
ordination by juxtaposition, enriching his rendering with a striking
asyndeton consecutivum. All these figures and patterns, these *tours*, are,
when borrowed, well in keeping with La Fontaine's usual style and blend
harmoniously. The best formulation of this selective imitation comes from
our poet's pen:

> Si d'ailleurs quelque endroit plein chez eux [les anciens]
> d'excellence

---

[1] Τρόπος, tour, from τρέπειν, tourner.
[2] E. S. de Gamaches, *Les Agréments du langage*, p. 154, and passim; the whole volume is
a *traité des tours*.
[3] Horace, *Epistles*, I, 7, l. 33, Loeb Classical Library, London, 1961, p. 296.

Peut entrer dans mes vers sans nulle violence,
Je l'y transporte, et veux qu'il n'ait rien d'affecté,
Tâchant de rendre mien cet air d'antiquité.[1]

It echoes Balzac's statement:

'Je prends l'art des Anciens, comme ils l'eussent pris de moi si j'eusse été le premier au monde; mais je ne dépends pas servilement de leur esprit ni ne suis pas né leur sujet, pour ne suivre que leurs lois et leur exemple. Au contraire, si je ne me trompe, j'invente beaucoup plus heureusement que je n'imite.'[2]

Imitation and borrowings must remain discreet, well integrated into the fabric of the modern text, thus maintaining the smooth effect of naturalness. In the words of La Mothe Le Vayer:

'Quelque peine que nous prenions à copier ces beaux originaux de l'antiquité, ou ceux de ce temps que nous jugerons dignes d'être imités, il le faut faire avec beaucoup de discrétion et se souvenir que le plus grand artifice de tous, consiste à bien cacher celui dont on se sert.'[3]

The author of *La Rhétorique de l'honnête homme* writes on the same subject:

'Quand on prendra d'un auteur quelque belle expression, il faut tâcher de la déguiser avec tant d'adresse qu'on la rende sienne ou meilleure. En un mot, on doit cacher le larcin qu'on fait, aussi finement que les Lacédémoniens cachaient les leurs. On leur permettait de dérober; mais on les punissait rigoureusement s'ils étaient assez maladroits pour se laisser surprendre en dérobant.'[4]

Those who do not succeed in achieving this smooth and complete integration are mere plagiarists and remain outside the humanistic tradition. La Fontaine keeps for them his rare sarcasms:

C'est un bétail servile et sot à mon avis
Que les imitateurs; on dirait des brebis
Qui n'osent avancer qu'en suivant la première
Et s'iraient sur ses pas jeter dans la rivière.[5]

---

[1] *A Monseigneur l'Evêque de Soissons*, *O.D.*, p. 646.
[2] Guez de Balzac, Letter to Boisrobert, February 11th 1624, in *Œuvres*, vol. I, p. 444.
[3] La Mothe Le Vayer, *Considérations sur l'éloquence française de ce temps*, Paris, 1638, pp. 180–1.
[4] Amsterdam, 1699, p. 140.
[5] *Clymène*, *O.D.*, p. 32; cf. also *Fables*, IV, 9.

Quelques imitateurs, sot bétail, je l'avoue,
Suivent en vrais moutons le pasteur de Mantoue:
J'en use d'autre sorte; et, me laissant guider,
Souvent à marcher seul j'ose me hasarder.[1]

Balzac was not more kindly disposed towards those whom he called 'des
frippiers et des ravaudeurs' who 'traduisaient mal au lieu de bien imiter.'[2]
Indeed, tasteful imitation is in no way incompatible with originality.
Thus, Pellisson praises Sarasin in these terms:

'Quand un homme est reconnu pour avoir l'esprit grand, noble,
fertile comme M. Sarasin, ce reproche d'avoir emprunté d'autrui ce
qu'il pouvait trouver en soi-même, et préféré des richesses étrangères
aux siennes propres, ce reproche, dis-je, ne tient guère plus du
blâme que de la louange,'[3]

and Bouhours writes of Voiture:

'En imitant les autres, il s'est rendu inimitable. Il savait admirable-
ment l'art de mettre en œuvre et de faire valoir les belles pensées
des auteurs. Les traits qu'il emprunte quelquefois de Térence et
d'Horace semblent faits pour son sujet et sont bien plus beaux dans les
endroits où il les met que dans ceux d'où il les a pris, de même que
les pierres précieuses sont plus belles dans les bagues où on les
enchasse que dans les rochers d'où on les tire.'[4]

On this point, as on many others, we find La Fontaine, as a critic, in
excellent company.

Cotin, in his *Discours satirique au cynique Despréaux*, protesting to
Boileau against what he thought was an attack on 'Maucroix . . . qui doit
être de vos amis puisqu'il l'est de ceux qui vous gouvernent', implied that
Boileau owed much to La Fontaine.[5] Not the least merit of the fabulist is
that he ranks among the most explicit and competent theorists of literature of his time. His knowledge, his taste and his critical approach make
his contribution to the theory of writing almost as comprehensive and
illuminating as that of the professional critics, of Bouhours, Rapin, Méré,
Boileau. Moreover, his remarks in prose or in verse have the authority of
the practitioner and their formulation, the charm and simplicity of his
familiar style.

[1] *A Monseigneur l'Evêque de Soissons, O.D.*, p. 648.
[2] Guez de Balzac, *Entretien XXI*, in *Œuvres*, vol. II, p. 458; see also J.-B. Morvan de
Bellegarde, *Réflexions sur l'élégance et la politesse du style*, pp. 91–2.
[3] Pellisson, *Discours sur les œuvres de M. Sarasin*, in Sarasin, *Œuvres*, p. 16.
[4] D. Bouhours, *Entretiens d'Ariste et d'Eugène*, p. 159.
[5] Quoted by Adam, *Les Premières satires de Boileau*, Lille, 1941, pp. 35 and 202.

CHAPTER II

THE STYLE OF THE *FABLES*—RICHNESS, VIGOUR AND FREEDOM

THE most striking quality of La Fontaine's style in the *Fables* is its vigour. No one can fail to marvel at the strength, the precision, the richness and the variety of the means of expression displayed in these short poems, which, technically speaking, belonged to a minor genre. The language is not without analogies with that of earlier or contemporary poetic trends such as *galanterie*, neither is it, at first sight, substantially different from that of La Fontaine's other works; yet its composition, its range, its expressive and picturesque value make it an exceptional achievement worthy of study.

1. La Fontaine's Attitude to Language

As there is ample evidence of La Fontaine's interest in style, there are also, in his work and correspondence, many indications of his interest in linguistic questions. The Preface of the *Recueil de poésies chrétiennes et diverses*[1] of 1671 discusses problems of poetical composition and gives a very interesting glimpse of the workings of the creative imagination: some poets, the author suggests, write a first draft in poetic prose and subsequently versify it. The author of the Preface, and La Fontaine himself, do not seem to have adopted this method as the tone of the remark and, in the case of La Fontaine, the evidence of early rhymed versions of a few fables prove. The Preface goes on to analyse another method of creation; the apologetic way in which it is introduced and the warm enthusiasm which gradually pervades the explanation show clearly that it has the author's favour:

'Ceux qui d'ailleurs ont de l'esprit et du discernement et qui ne sont pas habitués à cette façon de composer [i.e. the drafting, in

---

[1] *O.D.*, pp. 773 sqq. The authorship of the Preface is still the subject of controversial speculation. It has been attributed successively to Nicole, Lancelot, Dodart and even to La Fontaine. Jules Brody, in 'Platonisme et classicisme', in *Saggi e Ricerche di Letteratura Francese*, Milan, 1961, vol. II, p. 22, n. 30, claims to have solved the problem: 'J'ai eu le bonheur de découvrir tout récemment la copie d'un premier brouillon de la Préface (Sorbonne Ms. 764, fos. 296–300), portant des corrections de la main de Nicole. Les données de ce manuscrit permettront, comme j'espère pouvoir le montrer dans un proche avenir, de revendiquer pour Nicole, sans réserve aucune, la paternité de la Préface.'

prose, of the poem to be rhymed] ne laisseront pas de réussir fort
bien en ne la pratiquant pas; parce que la rime leur fournissant des
pensées, leur discernement leur fera rejeter les mauvaises et ne
choisir que les bonnes.'[1]

The importance of this statement as a definition of the poet's attitude
towards language and poetry cannot fail to strike the reader: inspiration,
in some poets, is awakened and guided by rhyme, that is by a word and
the various echoes which prolong it. The word comes first, unavoidable,
exacting, leading to thought, 'fournissant des pensées'. This analysis of
the mechanism of poetic creation, which emphasizes the essential part
played by the word in an art based on the word, fits in well with La
Fontaine's ideas on technique and style. La Fontaine's friend, Maucroix,
also formulated the poet's dependence on words imposed by rhyme when
he wrote to Boileau: 'Pour nous, ce n'est rien que de faire un vers, il faut
en faire deux, et que le second ne paraisse pas fait pour tenir compagnie
au premier.'[2] This approach to poetry recalls that of Malherbe, who,
according to Racan, 's'étudiait fort à chercher des rimes rares et stériles
sur la créance qu'il avait qu'elles lui faisaient produire quelques nouvelles
pensées',[3] and that of Boileau, who, according to Brossette, 'faisait
ordinairement le second vers avant le premier. C'est un des plus grands
secrets de la poésie, pour donner aux vers beaucoup de sens et de force.
Il conseilla à Mr. Racine de suivre cette méthode.'[4]

La Fontaine's interest in words is present throughout his work and
often the poet refers to his irrepressible curiosity about linguistic phenomena in the humorous tone of an amateur discussing his pet subject with
non-specialists: 'Est-ce Montléry qu'il faut dire, ou Montlehéry?', 'Bouts
de navires ne vous plaît guère, et peut-être aimeriez-vous mieux le terme
de pointes ou celui de becs; . . . je doute fort que pas un ne soit propre;
mais j'aime autant m'en servir que d'appeler cela colonnes rostrales.'
'Sans esprit, c'est la phrase et non sans de l'esprit.'[5] Just as he plays with
different kinds of style in the fables *Contre ceux qui ont le goût difficile*[II,1] and

---

[1] Ibid., *O.D.*, p. 775.
[2] Maucroix, Letter to Boileau, May 23rd 1695, in Maucroix, *Œuvres Diverses*, vol. II,
pp. 226–8.
[3] Racan, *Vie de Mr. de Malherbe*, in Malherbe, *Œuvres*, Grands Ecrivains de la France,
Paris, 1862, vol. I, p. lxxxiii.
[4] Brossette, 'Remarques sur la Satire II de Boileau', in *Œuvres de Mr. Boileau Despréaux
avec des éclaircissements historiques donnés par lui-même*, Geneva, 1716, vol. I, p. 29 (4° ed.),
p. 39 (12° ed.).
[5] Letter to Madame de La Fontaine, August 30th 1663, *O.D.*, p. 536; to the same, September
12th 1663, ibid., p. 553; *A. M. Girin*, *O.D.*, ibid., p. 656. See also Letter to Madame de La
Fontaine, September 3rd 1663, *O.D.*, p. 544; '. . . la levée ne nous quitta point, ou nous ne
quittâmes point la levée; l'un vaut l'autre.'

Le Cierge[IX,12] or in *Clymène*,[1] he draws amusing effects from the substitution of the language of romance for plain everyday French:

> Et s'il me plaisait de dire
> Au lieu d'Anne Sylvanire,
> Et pour Messire Thomas
> Le grand Druide Adamas
> Me mettrait-on à l'amende?
> Non; mais tout considéré
> Le présent conte demande
> Qu'on dise Anne et le curé.[2]

When he mentions 'les Jeannetons', he adds:

> 'Comme il ne coûte rien d'appeler les choses par noms hono-
> rables, et que les Nymphes de delà les monts, les bergers mêmes,
> pourraient s'offenser de celui-ci, je leur dirai que j'ai voulu d'abord
> les qualifier de Chloris; mais ma rime m'a fait choisir l'autre nom. . . .
> > Je me contente à moins qu'Horace
> > Quand l'objet en mon cœur a place,
> > Et qu'à mes yeux il est joli,
> > *Do nomen quodlibet illi.*'[3]

His enjoyment, in the *Contes*, at expressing the unmentionable unmistakably, at ignoring the taboos of decency and respectability, derives from
the same vein. La Fontaine exercises his verbal virtuosity, confident in the
issue of the *gageure*:

> Qui pense finement, et s'exprime avec grâce
> > Fait tout passer; car tout passe:
> > Je l'ai cent fois éprouvé
> > Quand le mot est bien trouvé
> Le sexe en sa faveur à la chose pardonne.[4]

Everything, in such a delicate matter, depends on the right choice of
words:

> Dites au dieu des vers que dans mon entreprise
> > Il est bon qu'il me favorise
> > Et de mes mots fasse le choix
> > Ou je dirai quelque sottise.[5]

---

[1] *Clymène, O.D.*, pp. 18–44.
[2] *Contes*, vol. II, pp. 153–4 (Le Cas de conscience).
[3] *A Son Altesse Sérénissime Mgr le Prince de Conti, O.D.*, p. 706.
[4] *Contes*, vol. II, p. 229 (Le Tableau).
[5] Ibid.

But this fear was unnecessary and Perrault acknowledged the success of La Fontaine's attempts when he wrote that no one had ever 'parlé plus honnêtement des choses déshonnêtes.'[1] When, in an even lighter mood, La Fontaine lets his imagination run wild, his facetiousness assumes the form of pseudo-philological variations on *la gale*.[2]

The quality of La Fontaine's linguistic knowledge has seldom been questioned and, indeed, in a century when most masterpieces were scrutinized by purists whose observations concerning language usually appeared in print together with remarks on genre, *bienséances*, etc., it is noteworthy that there are very few discordant notes in the critics' almost unanimous praise of our poet. One comes from the *Second factum* of Furetière[3] whose spite and partiality, after his eviction from the Academy, against the Academicians in general, and La Fontaine in particular, make his anecdotes concerning the poet, if not altogether worthless, at least very questionable. Accused of not knowing, in spite of his office of *Maître Particulier des Eaux et Forêts*, the meaning of *bois de grume* and *bois de marmenteau*, La Fontaine answered by a witty and caustic epigram, giving the matter no more attention than it deserved.[4] The anecdote told by Richelet in his dictionary, under the item *Tousselle*, also requires little comment.[5] According to Richelet, La Fontaine knew nothing about *tousselle* or *touzelle* beyond the fact that it was *une herbe*, though he had borrowed the word from Rabelais and used it in his *Contes*.[6] O. Servan and S. Pitou[7] have proved by textual evidence that La Fontaine knew the meaning of this word. According to Monchesnay, Boileau made some reservations about Molière and La Fontaine:

'Selon lui [Boileau], Molière pensait toujours juste; mais il n'écrivait pas toujours juste parce qu'il suivait trop l'essor de son premier feu, et qu'il lui était impossible de revenir sur ses ouvrages. Il avait cela de commun avec La Fontaine, chez qui l'on trouve beaucoup de négligences et de termes hasardés, qui auraient pu être réparés par une lime attentive et laborieuse: mais Molière fuyait la peine. . . '[8]

[1] Charles Perrault, *Des Hommes illustres*, Paris, 1696–1701, vol. I, p. 179.
[2] *Sur la gale*, O.D., pp. 769–72.
[3] *Recueil des Factums d'Antoine Furetière contre quelques uns de cette Académie*, Paris, 1859, vol. I, pp. 183 and 227.
[4] *Épigramme contre Furetière*, O.D., p. 645.
[5] P. Richelet, *Dictionnaire français*, Geneva, 1680.
[6] *Contes*, vol. II, p. 159 (Le Diable de Papefiguière).
[7] O. Servan, 'A propos de La Fontaine et de Rabelais', in *Revue du XVIème Siècle*, vol. XIV, 1927, pp. 170–6; S. Pitou, 'Rabelais, La Fontaine, Richelet and la touselle', in *Modern Language Notes*, vol. LXV, 1950, pp. 399–403.
[8] Monchesnay, *Bolœana*, pp. 31–2.

All that we know about La Fontaine's approach to his work and other more favourable judgements attributed to Boileau by the same Monchesnay tend to minimize this reservation.[1] These references are, so far as we know, the only adverse criticisms made by the poet's contemporaries, of his knowledge and use of the language,[2] and they do not amount to any positive castigation.

2. LA FONTAINE'S LANGUAGE

It is this linguistic interest and skill, and the scope which the freedom of the genre offered them, which account for the originality of the language of the *Fables*. This language, 'c'est la langue même que La Fontaine a créée, langue conforme aux sujets traités, aux personnages mis en scène'.[3] All the critics agree on this point:

> 'Il l'a créée à son usage, telle qu'il la lui fallait non pour représenter les choses à notre esprit, mais pour nous en donner la sensation même.'[4]

> 'Il écrit en artiste qui crée sa langue.'[5]

The originality of this language resides in the complex combinations of its linguistic elements; they show both the extent of the author's knowledge and the freedom with which he made his choice, ignoring the traditional limitations of vocabulary set by the laws of genre, poetry and fashion. It is not the result of a systematic reaction, on the part of the poet, against the language of his time; it is a conscious and skilful use of all possible linguistic resources to produce definite aesthetic effects best suited to the particular poem he was composing, taking account of the very effect of disparity between common usage and his own. Brunot, with some exaggeration, but not without truth, has said:

> 'Aussi sa langue est-elle justement le contraire de la langue poétique de son temps; une grande partie de son charme est fait de toutes les audaces que l'on condamnait.'[6]

---

[1] Monchesnay, *Bolœana*, pp. 54–7, 114.

[2] To these, Brossette's anecdote concerning the condemnation by the Academy, on Boileau's request, of La Fontaine's use of the negative in his own epitaph, should be added although it really concerns grammar more than language as such. Le Verrier, *Commentaire sur les Satires de Boileau*, in *Les Satires de Boileau commentées par lui-même*, p. 28 and n.; and *O.D.*, pp. 496–7.

[3] F. Gohin, *La Fontaine, études et recherches*, p. 152.

[4] P. Clarac, *La Fontaine, l'homme et l'œuvre*, p. 79.

[5] A. Adam, *Histoire de la Littérature française au XVIIème siècle*, vol. IV, p. 46.

[6] F. Brunot, *Histoire de la langue française*, vol. IV, part I, p. 69.

This uninhibited attitude towards the language caused Faguet to write: 'La Fontaine a une langue très difficile et, croyez-en un vieux professeur, il n'y a pas d'auteur ou l'on fasse plus de contre-sens que dans la Fontaine.'[1] The hesitations and, sometimes, the contradictions found in serious works of criticism concerning the poet cannot but cause some misgivings to anyone undertaking a study of his style.

The richness of La Fontaine's vocabulary has been stressed by many critics,[2] but no precise estimate has yet been attempted. A rapid numerical comparison, based on the word index of the *Grands Ecrivains de la France* edition of seventeenth-century writers, clearly shows the extent of La Fontaine's vocabulary: it leaves that of the other great classicists far behind, with the exception of Molière.[3] Whilst the *Contes* bristle with archaisms and terms borrowed from the language of the church, of travel and of love, the range of vocabulary is wider in the *Fables* and covers most of the specialized activities of man, agriculture and hunting, trade and law, arts and crafts, diplomacy and warfare, etc. The comprehensiveness of this vocabulary reflects the wholeness of La Fontaine's vision as well as his determination not to resort to a predominantly abstract vocabulary to evoke it, in reaction against the contemporary tendency to over-intellectualize and restrict the language within narrow limits. Except in the rare cases when he deliberately chooses a general term or a periphrasis for a precise effect required by his subject, he always uses *le mot propre*, thus agreeing with André Renaud that

> 'Une des premières précautions à prendre, c'est d'éviter comme un écueil la fréquente répétition de ces mots généraux "choses, ceci, cela" qui sont les grands asiles de l'ignorance des termes propres ou les effets de la précipitation à parler'.[4]

and with Boileau pleading before the king in favour of the *mot propre*, 'quelque rude et bizarre que parût ce mot.'[5] Without holding such an

[1] Quoted by F. Gohin, in *Fables*, vol. I, p. lxix.
[2] T. Lorin, *Vocabulaire pour les Œuvres de La Fontaine*, Paris, 1852. Marty-Laveaux, *Essai sur la langue de La Fontaine*, Paris, 1853. H. Régnier, 'Lexique de la langue de La Fontaine', in *Œuvres de Jean de La Fontaine*, vol. X and XI. A. France, 'La langue de La Fontaine', in *Le Génie latin*, Paris, 1919, pp. 79–115. L. Arnould, *La Terre de France chez La Fontaine*, passim. F. Boillot, *Les Impressions sensorielles chez La Fontaine*, passim.
[3] The vocabulary of La Fontaine and of Molière is approximately 6,000 words; Racine's is 4,000; La Bruyère, Mme de Sévigné and Corneille's 3,000; La Rochefoucauld's 2,500. When interpreting these figures, if we take into account the size and nature of the writer's work, the richness and variety of La Fontaine's vocabulary is even more striking. So is, incidentally, the comparative size of the vocabularies of Corneille and Racine.
[4] A. Renaud, *Manière de parler la langue française selon les différents styles*, Lyon, 1697, p. 75.
[5] Monchesnay, *Bolœana*, p. 66.

extreme position, La Fontaine does not hesitate to write many words which were, at the time, excluded from any literature distinct from the *burlesque*.

> Il n'était ambre, il n'était fleur,
> Qui ne fût *ail* au prix. . . .[VII,6]

The two widows, in *L'Homme entre deux âges et ses deux Maîtresses*,[I,17] are

> L'une encore *verte* et l'autre un peu bien *mûre*,

the banker is 'tout cousu d'or'[VIII,2], the garden contains 'oseille, laitue, un maître chou, chicorée, porreaux, de quoi mettre au potage'[IV,4]. The freedom and vigour of the vocabulary are matched by those of the figures of speech, often original, always concrete and concise: 'le souper du croquant s'envole'[II,12], the cat 'fonde sa cuisine' upon the mice[VI,5].

3. TECHNICAL VOCABULARY

In the *Fables*, technical terms, though numerous, are neither obscure nor gratuitous. La Fontaine limited himself to words understood by the general public as were, for example, in those days, terms of hunting and falconry. The poet's choice is almost always justified either by the intrinsic value of the word or by the effects he derives from it. It is true, to a certain extent, that his characters, kings, courtiers, gardeners, merchants, shepherds, hunters, soothsayers, judges, etc., speak the jargon of their trade, the language of their class; when these are animals, their speech helps to complete their identification with their human counterparts; in the words of Gohin: 'Un langage technique complétait leur accoutrement.'[1] The device is effective, but elementary: we almost expect the rabbit and the weasel to use legal terms in an argument on the right of property[VII,15]. Indeed, La Fontaine uses this device with great moderation and tends to reserve the technical terms for more subtle effects, be it in the narrative or in direct speech. Sometimes, he is obviously under the charm of a word of great precision in its technical acceptation but also rich in poetic undertones: thus, when he writes of the peacock:

> Toi que l'on voit porter à l'entour de ton col
> Un arc-en-ciel nué de cent sortes de soies.[II,17]

---

[1] F. Gohin, *L'Art de La Fontaine dans ses Fables*, p. 93.

it is the words *soies* and *nué* which, with *col*, reveal the implicit comparison *arc-en-ciel - écharpe d'Iris* to which these lines owe most of their subtle poetic charm. The reader may well wonder to what extent the ease and naturalness of the metaphor are due to the juxtaposition of *arc-en-ciel* and *nué*, the latter suggesting, besides the gradation of shades in embroidery work, its homonym *nuées*. . . . When he writes *l'août* for *la moisson*[1, 1 and V,9], the poet restores all the poetic value of a hackneyed synecdoche and, by using it as a temporal reference, *avant l'août, dès qu'on aura fait l'août*, evokes the season as well as its economic significance. In *Le Philosophe Scythe*[XII,20], the technical terms, *ébrancher, émonder*, are used to describe the loving care with which the competent gardener tends his orchard; but approximate and brutal verbs will suggest the ruthless treatment given to his own orchard by the philosopher who 'coupe et taille à toute heure' and 'tronque son verger contre toute raison.' The graphic evocation of the lion's agitation in his attempt to rid himself of the fly and the contrast between his size and that of his enemy, between the formidable deployment of his ineffective means of defence and the mobility of the fly are increased by the choice of the word *quadrupède*[II,9]. The ridiculous precariousness of the duck's ill-fated invention in *La Tortue et les deux Canards*[X,2] is stressed by the technical language used to refer to it:

Nous vous voiturerons, par l'air, en Amérique

Marché fait, les oiseaux forgent une machine

In a serious context, the beaver's competence at dam-building is emphasized by the same device:

Après un lit de bois est un lit de mortier.[IX, *Discours à Mme de La Sablière, l.*101]

La Fontaine even succeeds in drawing a whole variety of effects from the use of legal jargon: for example, a satirical effect in *Les Frelons et les Mouches à miel*[I,21], the atmosphere of courts of justice in *Le Juge Arbitre, l'Hospitalier, et le Solitaire*[XII,29], the genuine flavour of a legal document in *Testament expliqué par Esope*[II,20], which not only the vocabulary but also the syntax, i.e. *chacune sœur*, reflect the peculiarities of legal style.

4. NEOLOGISMS AND PSEUDO-NEOLOGISMS

La Fontaine's thorough knowledge of the language has often led critics to credit him with the coining of many neologisms. Marty-Laveaux and Anatole France[1] have shown clearly that many of these, usually endowed with the flavour and vigorous evocative power associated with words of popular origin, had been in use long before La Fontaine's time:

> 'La Fontaine qui employa tant de mots n'en inventa guère. Il est à remarquer que les bons écrivains sont généralement fort sobres de néologismes. Le fond commun du langage leur suffit.'[2]

In spite of this *caveat*, the reduced lists of 'neologisms' given by more recent critics are still often unreliable: it has been proved that *entrouir* is not, as Boillot believed, an invention of our poet;[3] *volereau* and *daubeur* were not coined by La Fontaine, as Coppin suggested.[4] Verdun-Louis Saulnier lists *souriquois* among 'une douzaine de mots que La Fontaine semble avoir créés'; Régnier, in the first volume of the *Grands Ecrivains de la France* edition, comments in a note on this adjective: 'Mot de l'invention de notre poète'; but, later, in his *Lexique de la langue de La Fontaine*, volume XI of the same edition, he refers the readers to the *Dictionnaire de Trévoux* which gives *souriquois* as found in a sixteenth-century translation of the *Batrachomyomachia*.[5] These are only a few examples of fairly frequent errors in a field where research is infinitely delicate. A language is spoken before it is written; consequently, it is always extremely dangerous to ascribe the invention of a word to the author who is, so far as can be determined, the first to use it. Unless the new term presents unmistakable features of originality and there is clear evidence of an attempt by the writer to overcome a deficiency in the language, there always remains the possibility that the so-called neologism is, in fact, a provincialism or a popular expression which has not, so far, found its way into writing.

The seventeenth-century stylists and grammarians often associate

---

[1] Marty-Laveaux, *Essai sur la langue de La Fontaine*; A. France, 'La Langue de La Fontaine', in *Le Génie latin*.

[2] A. France, op. cit., p. 110. Unfortunately, Anatole France's own conclusion: 'Il ne reste guère que le mot Fabuliste qu'il faille considérer comme de l'invention de La Fontaine' cannot be accepted. Dauzat's *Dictionnaire étymologique*, Paris, 1947, points out that the word fabuliste, derived from the Spanish, was already known in the sixteenth century. La Fontaine only gave it renewed currency.

[3] *Contes*, vol. II, p. 223 (Le Magnifique); F. Boillot, *Les Impressions sensorielles*, p. 251; Régnier, *Œuvres de Jean de La Fontaine*, vol. V, p. 564, n. 1; Littré, *Dictionnaire de la langue française*.

[4] J. Coppin, 'La Fontaine', in J. Calvet, *Histoire de la Littérature française*, vol. IV. p. 168. *Volereau*, *Fables*, II, 16, is traced back, by Bloch and Wartburg, in their *Dictionnaire étymologique*, Paris, 1950, as early as 1651. *Daubeur*, *Fables*, VIII, 3, is used twice in *L'Impromptu de l'Hôtel de Condé*, first performed in 1663; see Montfleury, *Théatre*, Paris, 1705, vol. II, pp. 540 and 543.

[5] *Fables*, IV, 6; XII, 8; *Fables*, ed. V. L. Saulnier, vol. II, p. 407; Régnier, *Œuvres de Jean de La Fontaine*, vol. I, p. 287, n. 4 and vol. XI, p. 354.

neologism and archaism in their observations and are equally suspicious of both.[1] To a neologism, they prefer a word from a provincial idiom 'car ce mot de province sera toujours plus français que celui que l'on prendra ailleurs.'[2] Thus, archaisms of popular or rural origin become acceptable to writers in search of expressive terms and reluctant to coin them. 'On sait que les paysans sont essentiellement conservateurs en fait de langage';[3] it is this conservative tendency which preserved a traditional and exclusively oral language, rich in words of ancient, unrecorded origin and spontaneous formation, likely to arouse the interest of such a connoisseur as La Fontaine. Thus, Anatole France writes about the word *besacier*:

> 'On ne le trouve que chez notre fabuliste mais tout bon villageois voyant un mendiant porteur de besace . . . put nommer ce gueux un besacier avant que le mot ne fût écrit et allât chez l'imprimeur.'

It has been ascertained now that this word existed long before La Fontaine used it, but even though modern linguistics has proved Anatole France to be wrong on a point of fact, it entirely justifies his reservations with regard to neologism.[4]

There remain, in La Fontaine, a number of words which have, so far, not been traced to any earlier writer. The fact that a humorous effect is obtained by the use of these neologisms in the majority of cases, tends to prove that La Fontaine used them consciously for artistic reasons; but since he often obtains the same effect through the use of terms of popular origin, no definite conclusion whether he coined them himself or borrowed them from the vernacular, can be drawn from this observation. In any case, his approach to word formation is not different from that of his contemporaries: ordinary suffixes, direct derivations from verbs, obvious analogies, in fact, most of the phenomena associated with the formation and development of popular speech, give La Fontaine's neologisms the appearance of vigorous words resulting from a free and regular linguistic evolution. Chamfort's comment on the word *épongier* 'mot créé par La Fontaine, mais employé si heureusement qu'on croirait qu'il existait

---

[1] D. Bouhours, *Entretiens d'Ariste et d'Eugène*, p. 85; A. Renaud, *Manière de parler la langue française selon les différents styles*, p. 515.
[2] Frain du Tremblay, *Traité des langues*, Paris, 1703, p. 145.
[3] L. Arnould, *Racan*, Paris, 1896, pp. 661–2.
[4] *Fables*, I, 7; A. France, 'La Langue de La Fontaine', in *Le Génie latin*, pp. 108–10. *Besacier* is already in Cotgrave, *A Dictionarie of the French and English Tongues*, London, 1632: 'Besacier, m. The bagge-bearer, or wallet-bearer of a begging, or beggarly companie'. M. des Prez, a character in Chasles's *Les Illustres françaises*, Paris, 1959, vol. I, p. 244, (1st ed. 1713), calls mendicant monks *besaciers*; but the author clearly indicates that the word is used in a derogatory manner. Tallemant des Réaux also calls a judge *soutanier* because of his robes; *Historiettes*, vol. VI, p. 38.

déjà avant lui,'[1] accounts for the success of the poet's rare neologisms: they are, at the same time, artistically indispensable and linguistically familiar. La Fontaine derives *épongier* from *éponge*, using a suffix often found in the names of officials: *chancelier*, *argentier*, *aumônier*, etc.[2] A humorous flavour is thus given to the text through this neologism which evokes official dignity, whilst referring to such an unworthy character as a donkey already compared with a *courrier* at the beginning of the fable.[3] Madame de Bouillon was following a similar pattern of derivation when she called La Fontaine her *fablier*.[4]

The composition of the agent noun by the addition of the suffix-*eur* to the verbal root was a very popular device in the seventeenth century. Guez de Balzac had an unfortunate tendency to resort to it, thus multiplying such platitudinous periphrases as *les violateurs de la franchise de nos ports*, *les peintres faiseurs de paysages*, etc.[5] The Academy had defended Corneille's use of *offenseur* against Scudéry's contention that 'ce mot d'offenseur n'est point français'.[6] Frain du Tremblay praised Ménage for coining the word *prosateur*,[7] but Bellegarde reacted against such word-formations:

> 'Il n'est pas permis de faire des mots selon son caprice ni de se servir de ceux qui ne sont pas encore bien établis. Je doute que

---

[1] 'Camarade épongier', i.e. the donkey carrying a load of sponges. *Fables*, II, 10; Chamfort, Notes sur les Fables de La Fontaine, in Gail, *Les Trois fabulistes, Esope, Phèdre, La Fontaine*, Paris, an V (1796), vol. III, p. 229.

[2] Indeed, the function existed already: 'Porte-éponge i. un jeune page'; 'porter l'éponge i. être jeune page d'une dame'. A. Oudin, *Curiosités françaises*, 1656, reprinted in La Curne de Sainte-Palaye, *Dictionnaire historique de l'ancien langage français*, Paris, 1882, vol. X, pp. 267 and 335.

[3] Alphonse Daudet, in *Lettres de mon moulin*, Charpentier, Paris, 1934, p. 89, 'La Mule du Pape', creates the amusing title of *Premier Moutardier du Pape*, by giving the old word *moutardier*, *pot à moutarde*, 1323, and *fabricant de moutarde*, 1311, (Bloch and Wartburg, op. cit.), the new meaning 'qui présente la moutarde'.

[4] 'Comme l'arbre qui porte les pommes est appelé pommier, elle [Mme de Bouillon] disait de M. de La Fontaine, c'est un fablier, pour dire que ses fables naissaient d'elles mêmes dans son cerveau.' D'Olivet, in Pellisson and D'Olivet, *Histoire de l'Académie Française*, Paris, 1858, vol. II, p. 300. There is little originality in the very form of this remark: Tallemant des Réaux relates that Brunier, physician to Gaston d'Orléans, once said to his master who was telling him about his frequent misdemeanours: 'Monsieur, les aliziers font les alizes, et les sottisiers font les sottises' and adds: 'C'est un proverbe.' *Historiettes*, vol. II, p. 175. Antoine de La Sablière was known as *le madrigalier* 'parce qu'il fait bien des madrigaux et qu'il ne fait guères que cela'. M. Conrart en riant lui en expédia des lettres.' Maucroix's note to his own *Madrigal à l'occasion du mariage de M. de La Sablière*, quoted by L. Roche, in *Vie de J. de La Fontaine*, Paris, 1913, p. 49. n. 3. See also P. Richelet, *Les Plus belles lettres des meilleurs auteurs français*, Lyon, 1689, p. 4.

[5] G. Guillaumie, *J.-L. Guez de Balzac et la prose française*, Paris, 1927, pp. 304–5.

[6] Corneille, *Le Cid*, I, 7, l. 300. Scudéry, *Observations sur Le Cid*, in P. Corneille, *Œuvres*, Les Grands Ecrivains de la France, Paris, 1862, vol. XII, p. 457. *Les Sentiments de L'Académie Française sur la tragi-comédie du Cid, Remarques sur les vers*, ibid., p. 487.

[7] Frain du Tremblay, *Traité des langues*, pp. 137–41.

rendeur, preneur, loueur, soupireur et une infinité de mots de cette nature dont quelques auteurs se servent impunément soient français. Quoique *rendre, prendre, louer, soupirer*, soient en usage; ce n'est pas une conséquence que l'on puisse former de ces mêmes verbes des substantifs, ni l'usage ne l'approuve.'[1]

However, it is reassuring to find Voiture, Racine, La Bruyère and La Fontaine among these authors accused of imperilling the French language.[2] Indeed, La Fontaine uses many words of the kind[3] and, at times, seems to revert to the original verbal form to coin or to revive a forgotten doublet instead of using a term already in existence. Thus, he forms *machineur*[X,9], *émoucheur*[VIII,10], *pondeur*[VIII,6], *devineuse*[VII,14] from *machiner, émoucher, pondre, deviner*, ignoring *machinateur, esmoucheteur* which he must have read in Rabelais, the traditional feminine *pondeuse* and, for variety's sake, the familiar *devineresse*.[4] So simple a method of composition gives the words vigour since their derivation is made obvious and the verbal element remains apparent in the agent noun. This stress on action, on verb, on verbal derivations is a characteristic feature of La Fontaine's style, combining economy of speech with forcefulness of expression.

La Fontaine did not depart much from the contemporary language when he coined the word *grimacerie*[VI,6], probably not so much for the sake of the rhyme, as Gérusez suggested, as for that of the parallelism it makes with *singerie*.[5] *Grimacerie*, it would seem, has been formed from

---

[1] J.-B. Morvan de Bellegarde, *Réflexions sur l'élégance et la politesse du style*, p. 369. La Fontaine uses *preneur* in the *Fables*, V, 5.

[2] E.g.:   .... l'affligé cocher ....
Le trop hardi *meneur* ne savait pas
De Phaéton l'histoire et piteux cas.'

Voiture, *Œuvres*, Paris, 1855, vol. II, p. 426.

'Là l'on voit la biche légère,
Loin du sanguinaire *aboyeur*.'

J. Racine, *Le Paysage ou promenade de Port-Royal des Champs*, Ode III, *Œuvres*, Les Grands Ecrivains de la France, Paris, 1865–73, vol. IV, p. 29.

'Depuis trente années on prête l'oreille aux *rhéteurs*, aux *déclamateurs*, aux *énumérateurs*.' La Bruyère, *Les Caractères*, in *Œuvres*, Vol. III, p.222.

[3] E.g., *croqueur, Fables*, V, 5; *daubeur*, VIII, 3; *gobeur*, IX, 9; *enfouisseur*, X, 4.

[4] Littré quotes a XIVth century example of the very rare *machineur*; *esmoucheteur* is found in *Pantagruel*, book II, ch. XV. See Rabelais, *Œuvres*, ed. Moland, Paris, n.d. p. 153. The encounter of the unusual masculine *pondeur* is no more surprising than that of equally unusual persons of the verb *pondre* in Palsgrave, *L'Eclaircissement de la langue française* (1st ed. 1530) Paris, 1852, p. 601, 'Je pons, nous ponnons, je ponny, j'ay ponnu, je pondray, que je ponne,' etc.

[5] *Grimacerie*, 'Ne se trouve que dans cette fable de notre poète et il est si bien placé qu'on oublie qu'il a été inventé pour la rime.' Gérusez, quoted by Régnier, *Œuvres de J. de La Fontaine*, vol. II, p. 20, n. 4.

grimacer by analogy with *criaillerie*, a derivation from *crier*, then in usage.[1]

La Fontaine's bold approach to language is reflected in his use of new, rare and unexpected forms of existing words, more than in scanty neologisms. Only a few examples of the figurative use of the word *préciosité*[2] had been recorded before it found its way into the *Fables*[VII,4]. The use of the rare feminine *opératrice*[3] is entirely justified by the vividness and the conciseness which this word enables the author to give his vision, to stress, along with other devices, the rapidity of the action:

Il lui fait signe; elle accourt
Voilà l'opératrice aussitôt en besogne.[III,9]

One word is enough to turn the stork into a female surgeon at work; and the choice of this agent noun makes the elliptic demonstrative construction possible, whilst it still evokes the specific action described by the now missing verb. *Pèlerine* is, by the seventeenth century, an already unusual feminine, both with its popular, pejorative meaning of shady and cracked-brained character and the more general meaning of traveller,[4] which La Fontaine combines in his reference to the tortoise 'à la tête légère'[X,2].

Marty-Laveaux who, like Anatole France, stressed the rarity of neologisms in La Fontaine, suggested nevertheless that La Fontaine's style 'tire bien plus souvent son originalité de la nouvelle conception d'un mot que de la création d'un terme.'[5] These extensions of meaning remain rare and when they occur, take the form of a return to the etymological meaning. Thus, *parleur*[XI,7] is rid of its pejorative implications and simply means speaker. *Nagée*[II,10] loses its technical meaning of 'contenance d'un bateau', to take that of a stroke in swimming; La Fontaine ignores *nageure* and *nagement* listed in Cotgrave and Nicot.[6]

Most of the generic adjectives of the type *la dindonnière gent*[XII,18],

---

[1] E.g. Molière, *Tartuffe*, V, 7, *l*. 1897.   [2] Régnier, vol. II, p. 117, n. 13.

[3] See *Mémoires du Maréchal de Bassompierre*, in Collection des Mémoires relatifs à l'Histoire de France, vol. XXI, Paris, 1823, p. 396. 'Mais Dieu m'envoya de bonne fortune la connaissance d'une *opératrice*, nommée Giot, mère du premier sergent de la Bastille, qui commença ... à me mettre des emplâtres ... qui ont réduit cette grande cicatrice à si petit point, que l'on dirait que ce n'a été qu'un coup d'épée.' (Written between 1631 and 1640, first published in 1665.)

[4] Cotgrave, *A Dictionarie of the French and English Tongues*: 'Pélerin, m. -ine, fem. Peregrine, forraine, strange, wayfaring, wandering', and 'Pélerin, a pilgrim palmer, wanderer, wayfaring man; a traveller in a strange country; also a fantasticall, giddie, hare-braind or odde-humored fellow'.

[5] Marty-Laveau, *Essai sur la langue de La Fontaine*, p. 43.

[6] See *nagée* in Godefroy, *Lexique de l'Ancien Français*, Paris, 1901; *Nageure*, in Cotgrave, op. cit.; *nagement*, in Nicot, *Trésor de la langue française*, Paris, 1621.

E

which have often been considered as creations of La Fontaine, are, in fact, sixteenth-century terms relegated by the seventeenth to the minor genres of the *galant* and the *burlesque*. The collection of epithets, compiled by La Porte in 1571, lists, among many other adjectives of the same kind, *marescageuse* under the item *grenouille*, and *moutonnière* under *bergerie*.[1] Similar word formations are to be found in Odet de La Noue's *Amas d'épithètes recueilli dans l'œuvre de G. de Salluste, Seigneur Du Bartas*, compiled in 1624.[2] When he writes about *Sa Majesté lionne*[VII,6] and *la rateuse Seigneurie*[Appendix II, la Ligue des Rats], La Fontaine follows the example of Marot's free and amusing use of word derivation in his *Epître à son ami Lion*:

> Mais dépita chats, chattes et chatons
> Et prisa fort rats, rattes et ratons. . . .
> Secouru m'as fort lionneusement
> Or secouru seras rateusement.[3]

It would be more difficult to find other examples of the use of *marcassine*[III,6] or *escarbote*[II,8] but even if we are inclined to consider these adjectives as amusing neologisms, we should not overlook the fact that such derivations were very common[4] and often resulted in baroque or *burlesque* clichés: Scarron, for example, writes of

> . . . ces langues vipérines
> Qui mordent plus fort que vermines.[5]

One of Thomas Corneille's heroes declares:

> Quand mon coeur est lion, j'ai l'ame léoparde
> Délionnez le vôtre. . . .[6]

---

[1] M. de La Porte, *Les Epithètes françaises*, Paris, 1571, pp. 117 and 35. *Fables*, III, 4; II, 16.

[2] Odet de La Noue, *Le Dictionnaire des rimes françaises (. . .) plus un amas d'épithètes recueilli des œuvres de G. de Salluste Seigneur Du Bartas*, Cologne, 1624. The attribution of this work to Odet de La Noue remains controversial. Here, we also find the rare *cloîtrière*, *Contes*, vol. II, p. 231, given as an epithet for *nonnain* and *nonne*.

[3] Marot, *Œuvres complètes*, Garnier, Paris, n.d., vol. I, p. 141.

[4] E.g. Jean de La Ceppède, *Les Théorèmes sur le sacré mystère de notre Rédemption*, 1613, in Eluard, *Première anthologie vivante de la poésie du passé*, Paris, 1951, vol. II, p. 164:

> 'Ce noir matin rassemble au Conseil nos galants
> Pour vomir le venin que presse leur poitrine,
> Et là tous les plus vieux et les plus insolents
> Donnent ainsi carrière à leur rage *tigrine*.'

Also, Maucroix, *Lettre cochonne à Mesdemoiselles . . .*, in *Œuvres diverses*, vol. II, p. 68.

[5] Scarron, *La Seconde légende de Bourbon*, in *Poésies diverses*, Paris, 1948, vol. I, p. 167.

[6] Thomas Corneille, *Le Geôlier de soi-même*, III, 3, quoted by F. Bar in *Cahiers de l'Association Internationale des Etudes Françaises*, Nr. 9, June 1957, p. 237. Cf. also Du Bartas, *La Seconde sepmaine*, Premier jour, Eden, in *Works*, Chapel Hill, USA, 1935–40, vol, III, p. 16, l. 446.

It is La Fontaine's merit to have succeeded in retaining the picturesqueness and the humorous flavour of this archaic device, without letting it become tiresome or ridiculous. These adjectives are usually found with a noun such as *gent* or *peuple*, giving the phrase a mock-epic touch:

> Son frère . . .
> Fut le premier César que la gent chienne ait eu.[VIII,24]

Although neologisms as such play only a very small part in the *Fables*, La Fontaine's imagination and subtle feeling for language enabled him to extend the meaning of existing words, to recast colloquial phrases in order to give them a new power of evocation; thus he preserves simplicity and conciseness of vocabulary whilst broadening the field of meaning. These daring new usages are introduced with perfect naturalness and are always justified by their effective contribution to the artistic quality of the style. Thus, *dévorer des yeux* becomes *avaler des yeux*[IX,9] when an oyster is concerned; *compter par ses doigts* becomes *compter par ses ongles*[I,6] when the subject of this verb is a lion; the stag *broute sa bienfaitrice*[V,15] and when we hear that the poor maids sleep *de tout leur appétit*[V,6] we know that they are not only extremely tired but also famished.

5. ARCHAISMS

Archaisms play a very important part in the language of the Fables. Contemporaries were not, as a rule, opposed to their use so long as they remained confined to the lower genres outside the field over which the purists claimed absolute jurisdiction and so long as they were acknowledged with a tolerant smile. Callières writes:

> 'Les mots qui ont vieilli ne sont pas propres à être employés dans les discours ordinaires et sérieux; mais on peut s'en servir par forme de raillerie dans les conversations libres et enjouées.[1]

The same was true of the written language. A whole tradition of artistic and linguistic freedom remained unbroken throughout the century, from Théophile de Viau to the Abbé Claude Cherrier, thanks to poets who, like La Fontaine, chose to limit themselves to the minor genres rather than force their talent and their speech to attempt what were considered

---

[1] F. de Callières, *Du Bon et du mauvais usage dans les manières de s'exprimer. Des façons de parler bourgeoises et en quoi elles sont différentes de celles de la cour*, Paris, 1693, p. 139.

to be more noble achievements; in doing so, they availed themselves of the full resources of an incomparably richer language than that of the purists. Towards the close of the century, several prominent contemporaries of La Fontaine became aware of the restriction of the French language since the successive expurgations to which it had been submitted since the sixteenth century. Le Clerc complains of the limitations of *le beau langage*:

> 'Ceux qui écrivent s'aperçoivent souvent qu'ils auraient besoin de ces mots qui ont vieilli, ou qui vieillissent, quoique dans la conversation on ne s'en aperçoive point, parce qu'on ne fait pas difficulté de redire plusieurs fois le même mot.'[1]

Andry de Boisregard opens the door to possible additions to the present language in the form of a few unobtrusive archaisms:

> 'On peut ... se servir quelque fois de vieux mots, et pourvu qu'on en use sobrement, ils donnent aux discours une force et une noblesse que les nouveaux n'y sauraient donner.'[2]

Many are the writers who, in the second half of the century, refer to the *vieux langage d'Amyot* as being the very model of a rich, colourful and powerful means of expression.[3] Imitations of Marot had always been considered a pleasant literary exercise and even La Bruyère quotes as authentic Marotic verse two poems which, in fact, were pastiches probably composed at the beginning of the century.[4]

La Fontaine, who had read most of the sixteenth-century authors and some late medieval ones as well, felt a great admiration for the expressive and picturesque value of their language. In the *Contes*, he found an opportunity to use it and, for twenty years, went on composing tales in a style bristling with archaisms. In the *Fables*, however, the old language is used with far more discrimination: their comparative shortness, their subject matter, their tone, called for much more variety than did the *Contes*. Here, each archaism is the result of a deliberate choice, on the part of the poet, to endow his verse with a specific quality. This artistic consciousness is reflected in La Fontaine's regret at the loss of an old expressive term which would hardly be understood by his readers. In

---

[1] Le Clerc, *Bibliothèque universelle et historique*, vol. VII, p. 189.

[2] Andry de Boisregard, *Réflexions sur l'usage présent de la langue française*, Preface.

[3] E.g. Racine, Preface to *Mithridate*, in *Œuvres*, Grands Ecrivains de la France, vol. III, p. 19. Le Clerc, *Bibliothèque universelle et historique*, Vol. VII, pp. 189–90. Fénelon, *Lettre sur les occupations de l'Académie Française*, Paris, 1908, pp. 8–9. 'Il avait [le vieux langage] je ne sais quoi de court, de naïf, de hardi, de vif et de passionné.'

[4] La Bruyère, *Les Caractères*, *Œuvres*, vol. III, part I, pp. 216–19. Voiture also wrote verse 'en vieux langage'. Cf. *Œuvres*, vol. II, pp. 415–20.

La Grenouille et le Rat, he quotes an old proverb in which the verb *engeigner* is used twice and he comments:

J'ai regret que ce mot soit trop vieux aujourd'hui;
Il m'a toujours semblé d'une énergie extrême.[(IV,11)1]

This remark is of particular significance since it shows at the same time La Fontaine's fondness for the older language and his lucid appreciation of its artistic and practical value: he cannot resist the temptation to give the medieval proverb in full, even if only to add that he rejects it. Significant also is the word *énergie* used in connexion with this archaism, for picturesqueness and vigour are precisely the two major aesthetic effects usually created by archaisms in his verse; as Royère wrote, 'Chez lui, l'archaïsme est une figure.'[2]

These archaisms have often been listed and traced back to their probable sources, a task which the extent of the poet's reading and his technique of selective imitation render most intricate; but their artistic value has not hitherto been assessed.[3] A discreet use of *le vieux langage* cannot but add charm to a collection of fables. These are, for the most part, apologues transmitted through a very long tradition. Linguistic archaisms link the up-to-date literary version with the original popular tales and their successive, now archaic, adaptations; they also enable the fables to retain the naïve quality of old tales whilst remaining perfectly intelligible to the modern reader. Here, words no longer in use are remarkably well integrated into the text. La Fontaine does not limit his use of the older language to vocabulary but often adopts syntactical and structural archaisms as well, so that the archaic tonality of the work is discreetly and evenly spread. It is not so much a question of vocabulary, as one of style. For example, Rabelais's 'c'est un tour de vieille guerre.'[4] becomes in La Fontaine 'c'est tour de vieille guerre'[III,18]; the ellipsis of the

---

[1] F. Bar, in *Le Genre burlesque en France au XVIIème siècle*, p. 225, points out that Furetière, who excluded this word from his *Dictionnaire*, used it in his *Énéide travestie*.

[2] J. Royère, *Le Musicisme*, p. 45.

[3] See Arnould, *La Terre de France*, A. France, 'La Langue de La Fontaine', in *Le Génie latin*, pp. 79–115, Gudra, *Die Sprache La Fontaines in seinen Fabeln*, Marty-Laveaux, *Essai sur la langue de La Fontaine*, Potthoff, *La Fontaines Stil mit besonderer Berücksichtigung der syntaktischen Archaismen*, Régnier, 'De la Langue de La Fontaine', in *Œuvres de J. de La Fontaine*, vol. X, pp. LI–LII, Siegert, *Die Sprache La Fontaines mit besonderer Berücksichtigung der Archaismen*. Also, A. Cavens, 'La Fontaine et Rabelais', in *Revue du XVIème Siècle*, 1922, pp. 175–9 and in *La Renaissance d'Occident*, XXVI, 1928, pp. 177–216, N. Edelman, *Attitudes of XVIIth Century France towards the Middle Ages*, New York, 1946; W. P. Fischer, *The Literary Relations between La Fontaine and L'Astrée of Honoré d'Urfé*, Philadelphia, 1913; W. de Lerber, *L'Influence de Clément Marot aux XVIIème et XVIIIème siècles*, Lausanne, 1920, pp. 56–7.

[4] Rabelais, *Pantagruel*, in *Œuvres*, book IV, ch. VIII, p. 370.

article gives the phrase the more authentic aspect of an old saying. The old possessive *un mien, un sien,* the impersonal *il est* for *il y a,* belong to the familiar style of old tales as does the indefinite *certain*.[1] La Fontaine's choice of words seems to be guided by an acute sense of their aesthetic value: *chevance*[IV,20 and VII,5], *déduit*[IV,20], *duire*[IX,16], *géniture*[V,18 and VIII,16], *matineux*[VI,11], *noise*[IX,14 and X,7], *parentage* and *lignage*[IV,1 and X,2], *pensers*[III,1, IV,18 and VIII,26], *prouesses*[III,14 and VI,7], *semondre* and *semonce*[V,7 and XII,1], *souvenance*[VII,1], have the charm and the distinction of nearly extinct terms which present, as yet, no difficulty of understanding. Most of them are border-line cases, words which contemporary lexicographers and grammarians describe as 'un peu vieux' or reserve either for poetry or for the *style bas,* but which are still understood by all. Thus, for example, La Fontaine often uses *maint* but never the already forgotten *moult,* whilst La Bruyère made no difference between the two and regretted that they had become archaic: the contrast between the point of view of the amateur and that of the practitioner is striking.[2]

Unobtrusive, fairly widely distributed, these archaisms contribute to the general tone of the *Fables*; moreover, their use in any given instance is seldom or never gratuitous and is, indeed, usually justified by the additional effects which the poet derives from them. Old words have often the advantage of being shorter than their modern equivalents and thus, may conveniently fulfil the requirements of prosody: *detteur*[XII,7], *s'éjouir*[IV,21], *lôs*[XII,1], *miellé*[X,10], *partant*[I,17, II,20, VII,1 and IX,3], may fit in where *débiteur, se réjouir, louange, melliflu,* and *par conséquent* would prove unsuitable, the substitution of *un fol*[IX,8] for *un fou* may result in the suppression of a hiatus. La Bruyère pointed out the practical value of archaisms,[3] and La Fontaine sometimes uses them, too, to avoid repeating a word. In such cases, the meaning of the old word is, if need be, explained by the modern term. Thus, in the same fable[X,6], we find both *aragne* and *araignée*; *loyer* in the sense of reward is used in three different fables[VI,13, X,1 and XII,25] and, each time, closely followed or preceded by *salaire*.

Archaisms are sometimes found in fables where they contribute to

---

[1] See *Fables,* IV, 7; VIII, 8; etc. V, 6; VII, 5; X, 2; X, 3; XII, 19, etc. V, 15; VII, 8; XI, 4; XII, 9, etc.

[2] La Bruyère, *Les Caractères,* in *Œuvres,* vol. III, pp. 206–7.

[3] La Bruyère, *Les Caractères,* in *Œuvres,* vol. III, pp. 206 and 210: 'Maint est un mot qu'on ne devrait jamais abandonner, et par la facilité qu'il y avait à le couler dans le style, et par son origine. ... Heur se plaçait où bonheur ne saurait entrer.' Cf. Louis-Auguste Alemand, *Nouvelles observations ou guerre civile des Français sur la langue,* Paris, 1688, pp. 319–23: 'M. de Vaugelas, M. Ménage et on peut dire, en un mot, tous nos grammairiens généralement condamnent pourtant cependant que. ... On le peut pourtant mettre encore en poésie ... pour remplir la mesure d'un vers ... puisque nous avons d'excellents modernes ... qui le prennent volontiers'. See *Fables,* I, 22.

evoke more precisely a remote or legendary past, as a background to the action. In *Le Lion amoureux*[IV,1], the archaisms of language (*parentage*), of syntax (ellipsis of the article), as well as the comparison 'comme place démantelée', help to conjure up the atmosphere 'du temps que les bêtes parlaient'. The old language is particularly effective, in *Le Renard, le Singe et les Animaux*[VI,6], to describe the ancient rite of the coronation:

Dans une chartre un dragon la gardait [la couronne],

and, in *Le Lion malade et le Renard*[VI,14], in the royal edict

De par le roi des animaux. . . .

Archaisms are also found in the speech of rustic and uncouth characters of the *Fables*: it is the ox who answers *nenni*[I,3], 'mot ancien et barbare' according to Marguerite Buffet;[1] when we read 'le meunier n'en a cure'[III,1], we feel sure that it is the very phrase used by the miller to express his indifference.[2] It is significant that *semondre*, which, according to Richelet, 'ne se dit encore que parmi les gens de certaines provinces et encore n'a-t-il cours que parmi ceux qui parlent le plus mal',[3] is used with reference to the Satyre described as 'le sauvage'[V,7] and a paragon of ignorance and rusticity. In *Les Animaux malades de la peste*[VII,1], the humble donkey's naïve confession 'j'ai souvenance . . .' contrasts significantly with the fox's subtle casuistry; his ridiculous old-fashioned speech makes him a figure of derision, a perfect scapegoat. *Le Chien maigre*[IX,10] begins his defense with *jà*, 'mot vieil et qui ne s'use qu'entre les paysans.'[4] Elsewhere, it is a knight errant, 'au pays des romans', who declares with diffidence:

On nous veut attraper dedans cette écriture.[X,13]

Sometimes, an old term helps to make a bold and impertinent metaphor go down:

L'éteuf[5] [la fille] passant à celui-là,
Il la renvoie . . .[IX,7]

or adds a humorous touch through indirect reference to a more recent acceptation of the word:

[1] M. Buffet, *Nouvelles observations sur la langue française*, Paris, 1668, p. 82.
[2] La Bruyère, *Les Caractères*, in *Œuvres*, vol. III, pp. 211–2.
[3] P. Richelet, *Dictionnaire français*, Geneva, 1680.
[4] Malherbe, *Commentaire sur Desportes*, in Desportes, *Les Amours d'Hippolyte*, Paris, 1960, sonnet XXVI, p. 54, n. 5.
[5] *Éteuf*, 'petite balle dont on joue à la longue paume', *Dictionnaire de l'Académie*.

Ce dernier [médecin] espérait, quoique son camarade
Soutînt que *le gisant*[1] irait voir ses aïeux.[V,12]

La Fontaine often draws subtle and amusing effects from the interplay of
the various meanings of a single archaism richer in implications than its
modern equivalent: thus, in the line

Chiens, chevaux et valets, tous gens bien endentés,[IV,4]

the epithet is to be understood in its metaphorical sense with all three
nouns, but also in its concrete sense with the first two. When, in *L'Homme
entre deux âges et ses deux Maîtresses*[I,17], the poet explains the exact
meaning of *testonner*:

L'allaient quelquefois testonnant,
C'est à dire ajustant sa tête,

he does not, by doing so, restrict the meaning of the word, but on the
contrary, draws the reader's attention to the possible ambiguity involving
the second sense of *testonner*, *battre*, also acceptable here as is borne out
by the rest of the fable.[2] Whilst in the lines

. . . On vit presque détruit
L'ost des Grecs; et ce fut l'ouvrage d'une nuit,[XI,3]

the archaic word conjures up an evocation of ancient and medieval epic
poetry, in the following:

L'ost au peuple bêlant crut voir cinquante loups,[XII,9]

also introduced by a mock-epic comparison drawn from Greek literature,
the effect of the old word is made more complex by the fact that *ost* is not
only an army, but also, in the Picard dialect, a flock of sheep.[3]

In a more serious context, La Fontaine's treatment of archaisms shows
clearly that he was fully aware of their evocative power, often conducive
to a rich poetic vision: the choice of words in the description of the lion

Chargé d'ans et pleurant son antique prouesse[III,14]

accounts for the dignity and the moving quality of the line. Just as
enlightening is the study of La Fontaine's use of *cheminer*, of which

---

[1] *Gisant*, which, according to Richelet, in his *Dictionnaire français*, was, at one time, used
substantivally to refer to a man lying down, in the XVIIth century, only referred to a corpse.

[2] Oudin, *Curiosités françaises*, p. 361 and P. de La Noue, *Synonyma et æquivoca gallica*,
Lyon, 1618, p. 477.

[3] Godefroy, *Dictionnaire de l'ancienne langue française et de tous ses dialectes*, Paris, 1881–
1902. See also Littré.

Richelet writes: 'Mot un peu vieux, néanmoins il y a des endroits où il a bonne grâce'.[1] We find it in the *Fables* with its ordinary, concrete meaning in *Les deux Mulets*[1,4], and *Le Coche et la Mouche*[VII,8]; yet, in the latter, it reflects a deliberate choice on the part of the poet, since this verb makes the alliteration *char-chemine* possible and recalls the *chemin montant, sablonneux, malaisé*, of the opening line. Its figurative acceptation provides La Fontaine with a particularly evocative and poetic image to describe the sower's action[1,8], the rotation of the earth[VII,17], and, by means of a synecdoche, the progress of a watch hand:

> Telle est la montre qui chemine
> A pas toujours égaux, aveugle et sans dessein.   IX, *Discours à Mme de la Sablière, I.33*

Here, older language and poetic idiom are one; the critics and lexicographers of the time constantly assimilate these, but it is not so much the archaic flavour of the word which makes it poetic as the graphic quality of its metaphorical meaning as understood by La Fontaine. The figurative meaning generally accepted at the time was far more abstract and less poetical. The controversy between Andry de Boisregard who rejected any figurative acceptation of the word and Bouhours who accepted it is illuminating:

> 'L'auteur des *Remarques nouvelles* [Bouhours] ... prétend que cheminer se dit dans le figuré, mais je ne sais quelle autorité il en a. Un tel cheminera ..., s'avancera, poussera sa fortune, il a cheminé fort vite, il est parvenu en peu de temps à quelque chose de considérable. Il veut qu'on dise encore d'un discours uni et coulant, que le discours chemine bien; mais je doute que les gens polis s'accommodent de ce langage.'[2]

La Fontaine's taste for vigorous expression accounts for the picturesque archaic phrases found in the *Fables*. These were no longer accepted by the purists, but very probably remained in use in popular speech which so often preserves expressive and irreplaceable idioms. Anatole France and Louis Arnould[3] warned readers of La Fontaine against the danger of wrongly labelling archaisms words and phrases which had only disappeared from the speech of the cultured circles of the capital and survived elsewhere. Indeed, it has even been argued that La Fontaine

---

[1] P. Richelet, *Dictionnaire français.*
[2] Andry de Boisregard, *Suite des Réflexions sur l'usage présent de la langue française*, Paris, 1693, pp. 35–6.
[3] A. France, 'La Langue de La Fontaine', in *Le Génie latin*, p. 94; L. Arnould, *La Terre de France chez La Fontaine*, p. 348.

prolonged the literary life of many terms which would have otherwise disappeared altogether from the written language.[1] They can therefore only be considered as relative archaisms and La Fontaine's merit is to have used them in literary compositions based on tales of popular origin, which thus retain their pristine flavour. *A Dieu ne plaise*[VII,4], *à qui mieux mieux*[I,14], *faire la figue*[II,5], *fils de bonne mere*[I,14], *se prélasser*[III,1], *se ruer en cuisine*[IV,4], *savant jusques aux dents*[VIII,9], to take but a few examples, evoke Rabelais and also a long tradition of anonymous rustic story-tellers. La Fontaine could not but be aware of his contemporaries' reservations concerning Rabelais of whom Girac wrote:

> 'Rabelais ... a pu passer autrefois pour un excellent bouffon, maintenant il fait rire bien peu de personnes: ses railleries sont aussi glacées que ces paroles dont il parle quelque part et vouloir les remettre en usage, c'est présenter des viandes froides et réchauffées, c'est rappeler dans le bal la volte et la pavane, c'est ramener la mode des fraises et des vertugadins.'[2]

In La Fontaine's borrowings, the literary reference is, often, only incidental, it is the expressive value and the picturesque quality of the phrases in their new context which justify them.

6. POPULAR SPEECH

That La Fontaine resorted to popular speech can easily be ascertained by consulting such contemporary collections of phrases and proverbs as those of Pierre de La Noue, Jean Nicot, Antoine Oudin and Fleury de Bellingen:[3] they contain a large number of colourful elements which were to find their way into the *Fables*. Most of them are classified as vulgar and we are warned that 'il faut entendre que ce ne sont pas des phrases dont on se doive servir qu'en raillant'. Old language, popular speech and comic tone are closely related: La Fontaine's taste for old idioms enabled him to give the *Fables* an additional touch of humour. Many of these phrases, he used almost without alteration, e.g.: *affiner*[III,18], *bon apôtre*[VII,15 and X,3], *arpenter*[VI,10], *bien et beau*[II,16 and IX,16], *chape-*

[1] F. Brunot, *Histoire de la langue française*, vol. IV, part I, pp. 238-9.
[2] P. T. de Girac, *Réponse à la défense des œuvres de M. de Voiture faite par M. Costar*, Paris, 1655, p. 92. See also Rapin, *Les Réflexions sur la Poétique*, in *Les Réflexions sur l'Eloquence, la Poétique, l'Histoire et la Philosophie*, Amsterdam, 1686, vol. II, p. 205.
[3] Pierre de La Noue, *Synonyma et æquivoca gallica ...*, Jean Nicot, *Trésor de la langue française ...*, Antoine Oudin, *Curiosités françaises*, Fleury de Bellingen, *Etymologie des proverbes français*, The Hague, 1656.

chute[IV,16], *jurer comme un chartier embourbé*[VI,18], *bonne commère*[III,9], *croquant*[II,12], *déloger sans trompette*[IV,22], *enfiler la venelle*[XII,17], *escornifleur*[IX], *Discours à Mme de la Sablière*, *faire fête*[I,17], *troubler la fête*[I,9], *faire la folie*[IV,13], *franche lippée*[I,5], *avoir part au gâteau*[VIII,7], *gros et gras*[VII,15], *crier haro*[VII,1], *cela m'est hoc*[V,8], *des plus huppés*[XII,12], *jeu de princes*[IV,4], *Martin bâton*[IV,5 and V,21], *se panader*[IV,9], *papelard*[IV,15], *de deux paroisses*[XII,11], *planter le piquet*[III,8], *ruer en cuisine*[IV,4], *saigner du nez*[X,13], *testonner*[I,17], *tirer le long*[II,12], *tomber dans les pattes de qqn.*[III,9], *trousser son paquet*[VIII,1], *faire la vie*[I,9] are listed in Oudin; *y laisser les houseaux*,[XII,23] is in Bellingen, etc.

Many proverbs used in the *Fables* are also to be found in these contemporary collections: *chien hargneux a toujours l'oreille déchirée*[X,8], *Ce n'est rien ce n'est qu'une femme qui se noie*[III,16], *il vaut mieux un tiens que deux tu l'auras*[V,3], are listed in Oudin; *le chien de Jean de Nivelle*[VIII,21], *belle tête si elle avait de la cervelle*[IV,14], in Bellingen; *tirer les marrons du feu avec la patte du chat*[IX,17], *bâtir des châteaux en Espagne*[VII,9], *l'œil du maître engraisse le cheval*[IV,21], in both Oudin and Bellingen. *Croire en Dieu par bénéfice d'inventaire*[IV,19], *il ne faut pas vendre la peau de l'ours qu'on ne la tienne*[V,20], *un trompeur trouve qui le trompe*[II,15 and X,4], *la défiance est mère de sûreté*[III,18], are listed in La Noue; *aide-toi Dieu t'aidera*[VI,18], in Nicot; *mieux vaut plier que rompre*[I,22] and *à l'œuvre on connait l'artisan*[I,21] in both La Noue and Nicot.

Although seventeenth-century theorists deprecate the use of proverbs, they tolerate them in the *style enjoué*. Bouhours writes:

> 'On serait ridicule d'user aujourd'hui de ces sortes de proverbes dans un discours sérieux, et dans des compositions relevées. On ne peut guère les employer qu'en riant et dans la conversation, encore le faut-il faire sobrement, de peur qu'on ne nous accuse de parler proverbe. ... Un proverbe peut trouver sa place dans une pièce comique, et dans un ouvrage burlesque. Ce n'est pas que certains proverbes ne puissent entrer quelquefois dans des lettres ingénieuses, et dans des discours délicats; mais il faut un grand art pour les mettre bien en œuvre, et c'est en quoi M. de Voiture a excellé.'[1]

Bellegarde comments:

> 'Les proverbes sont de certaines façons de parler familières et triviales ... fades et dégoûtantes parce qu'elles sont usées et que les oreilles en sont rebattues. Afin que les proverbes plaisent aux gens

---

[1] D. Bouhours, *Remarques nouvelles sur la langue française*, pp. 587–8.

de bon goût, il faut qu'ils soient fins et piquants. . . . Tout le secret consiste à les bien mettre en œuvre.'[1]

Some apparently proverbial expressions in the *Fables* are probably La Fontaine's own creation. It would be extremely difficult to distinguish them from those which were already in use and Arnould's attempt at listing them remains inconclusive.[2] However, such lines as

> Fille se coiffe volontiers
> D'amoureux à longue crinière,[IV,1]

and

> Volontiers gens boiteux haïssent le logis[X,2]

are so perfectly integrated into the context of the fable and so typical of La Fontaine's wit and manner that it seems safe to credit him with their invention. His success in avoiding discrepancy between the language, tone and contents of the genuine proverbs and those of his own creation is no mean achievement.[3]

The impression of informality given by the *Fables*, their tone of familiarity, are due to this complete freedom from all theoretical classification of words, to the poet's marked preference for vigorous, picturesque and evocative words and phrases rejected by the purists: *laitière ainsi troussée*[VII,9], *épouse de la sorte bâtie*[IX,15], *chien qui porte au logis la pitance*[VIII,7], *héron au long bec emmanché d'un long cou*[VII,4], *belette grasse, maflue et rebondie*[III,17], the skylark's young *voletant, se culbutant*[IV,22], kick from a horse *qui vous lui met en marmelade les mandibules et les dents*[V,8], *peuple en liesse noyant son souci dans les pots*[VI,12], Frenchmen fearing *qu'on ne nous mette toute l'Europe sur les bras*[VIII,4], such is the familiar idiom of the story-teller speaking in his own name. The same language is, of course, whenever suitable, attributed to the characters:

> Cornes cela? Vous me prenez pour cruche,[V,4]

the cricket says to the hare; and the hare to the tortoise:

> Ma commère, il vous faut purger
> Avec quatre grains d'ellébore.[VI,10]

---

[1] J.-B. Morvan de Bellegarde, *Réflexions sur l'élégance et la politesse du style*, pp. 306–7.
[2] L. Arnould, *La Terre de France chez La Fontaine*, p. 365. Some of the 'creations' listed by Arnould are, in fact, to be found in La Noue, Nicot, Oudin or Bellingen.
[3] There are also, in the *Fables*, references to popular songs. See L. Roche, *La Vie de Jean de la Fontaine*, p. 65; G. Michaut, *La Fontaine*, vol. I, p. 252 and vol. II, p. 287, n. 2; V. Lugli, *Il Prodigio di La Fontaine*, pp. 241–2. Lugli notes that, at times, the poet even gives a popular flavour to literary borrowings: 'Anche la sagezza che era nei libri prende l'aspetto di sentenza popolare'.

... Il suffit qu'a la fin
J'attrape le bout de l'année.
Chaque jour amène son pain,[VIII,2]

replies the cobbler to the financier. Even Hercules 'veut qu'on se
remue'[IV,18]. The moral, too, is often couched in informal style, whether
it takes the form of a comment made by a character:

> Si tu n'avais servi qu'un meunier, comme moi,
>   Tu ne serais pas si malade,[I,4]

or of a reflexion made by the fabulist:

> Quelque accident fait-il que je rentre en moi-même,
>   Je suis gros Jean comme devant,[VII,9]

or of a proverb:

> A l'œuvre, on connaît l'artisan,[I,21]

or even of a proverb in dialect:

> Biaux chires leups, n'écoutez mie
> Mère tenchent chen fieux qui crie.[IV,16]

What is of particular significance is the vividness and the forcefulness
of these popular expressions to which La Fontaine often gives renewed
evocative power or additional humorous implications. The technical
devices he uses for this purpose are often very simple, but their effect is
subtle and complex. Many popular phrases, although not always found
textually, are, in the *Fables*, referred to indirectly by allusions, now lost,
but probably clear to the seventeenth-century reader. Although it is
difficult to estimate the meaning a work of art had for its contemporaries
three hundred years ago, we may venture to indicate some of these
multiple allusions. The repeated warnings of the purists tend to prove
that the picturesque flavour of popular speech was generally appreciated
by the literary public, whilst the same characteristic may account for the
early success of the *Fables* as a moral treatise for children. In any case, it
should be made clear that, if some understanding of these possible
allusions contained in the text increases our intellectual pleasure, the text
itself always remains perfectly intelligible and satisfactory when taken at
its face value. Thus, reading *Le Meunier, son Fils et l'Ane*[III,1], La Fontaine's contemporaries would probably recall the phrase 'mener l'âne',
i.e. 'être exposé à la risée d'autrui'.[1] In *Le Savetier et le Financier*[VIII,2], the

[1] Oudin, p. 215.

remark 'On nous ruine en fêtes' is obviously a realistic reference to a well-known grievance of craftsmen of the *Ancien Régime*. We may however wonder whether contemporaries would not see, here, an ironical intention on the part of La Fontaine, since it is voiced, of all people, by a cobbler, at a time when cobblers' idleness was proverbial: 'Faire le lundi des savetiers', i.e. 'ne point travailler, vulg.'[1] When La Fontaine calls his *citoyen du Mans* 'Le Normand et demi'[VIII,21], he accounts for the latter's exceptional cautiousness by a reference to the saying 'Un Manceau vaut un Normand et demi'.[2] The stork which 'vivait de régime et mangeait à ses heures'[VII,4] has much in common with *la Mule du Pape*, according to the popular simile 'Il est complexionné comme la mule du Pape, qui ne boit qu'à ses heures'.[3] In *Le Renard et la Cigogne*[I,18], the reader, aware that *assaisonner un bon brouet* means *préparer un mauvais tour*, has reasons to suspect that premeditation, and not mere thoughtlessness, on the part of the fox, is responsible for the stork's embarrassment when confronted with the *brouet* prepared by the former.[4] When La Fontaine names the magpie *Caquet-bon-bec*[XII,11] after the proverb 'Caquet bon bec la poule à ma tante', i.e. 'une cajoleuse, vulg.',[5] his choice is most appropriate since, in the fable concerned, the magpie attempts to cajole the eagle by its ceaseless chatter. In *Le Chat et un vieux Rat*[III,18], the full meaning of the line

Ce bloc enfariné ne me dit rien qui vaille

can only be grasped with reference to the phrase: 'La gueule enfarinée', i.e. 'avec un grand désir, avec une grande envie d'attraper quelque chose'. Here, the concrete and the figurative meanings are not mutually exclusive.[6]

The poet often stresses the picturesqueness or increases the forcefulness of a popular word by setting it in a particularly well chosen context: hence, for example, the complex effect of the two lines:

Fille se coiffe volontiers
D'amoureux à longue crinière[IV,1]

---

[1] Oudin, p. 300.
[2] Cf. note by Gidel, in Boileau, *Œuvres*, vol. II, p. 157, n. 2.
[3] P. de La Noue, *Synonyma et æquivoca gallica* . . ., p. 346. Also, Littré, item *mule*: 'Il est quinteux comme la mule du Pape qui ne mange et ne boit qu'à ses heures'.
[4] Huguet, *Le Langage figuré au XVIème siècle*, Paris, 1933, p. 51.
[5] Oudin, p. 230. Caquet bon bec la poule à ma tante was a character of Benserade's *Mascarade en forme de ballet dansé par le Roi au Palais Cardinal en 1651*. Benserade, *Œuvres*, Paris, 1697, vol. II, p. 3.
[6] Oudin, p. 262.

in which *se coiffer de*, used in its popular figurative sense, is sufficiently near *longue crinière* not to lose altogether its original meaning and thus, provides an amusing connotation, whilst *crinière* itself is particularly effective as a metaphor since the suitor is a lion.[1] In *Le Meunier, son Fils et l'Ane*[III,1], the lines

> Tandis que ce nigaud, comme un évêque assis
> Fait le veau sur son âne et pense être bien sage

contain a jumble of words and images well suited to the absurd situation. To write *faire le veau sur un âne* is to draw the reader's attention and give a new life to an old and probably worn out phrase, *faire le veau*;[2] unless it recalled Louis XIII's facetious remark on Bassompierre's entering Madrid riding a mule: 'Oh! la belle chose que c'était de voir un âne sur une mule', and Bassompierre's quick and impertinent answer: 'Tout beau, sire, c'est vous que je représentais'.[3] The comparison miller-bishop did not sound as bold as it does nowadays, to ears accustomed to the then common phrase: 'Il est devenu d'évêque meunier'.[4]

The *Fables* also contain adaptations of popular phrases modified by the poet for greater effectiveness. Thus, 'Rossignol d'Arcadie, i. un âne'[5] becomes *roussin d'Arcadie*[VI,19 and VIII,17] when there is no need to refer directly to the braying of the donkey. Whilst one commonly referred to an ignoramus as *un âne à courtes oreilles*,[6] La Fontaine calls donkeys 'coursiers à longues oreilles'[II,10] an upgrading metaphor, well in keeping with the humorous comparison he draws of their master to a Roman emperor and of his whip to a sceptre.

Sometimes, a popular expression has, in the *Fables*, beside its figurative meaning, the value of a graphic illustration; for example, when the poet writes:

> Capitaine Renard allait de compagnie
> Avec son ami Bouc des plus haut encornés:
> Celui-ci ne voyait pas plus loin que son nez
> L'autre était passé maître en fait de tromperie,[III,5]

the phrases *haut encorné* and *ne pas voir plus loin que son nez* are ambivalent: they both suggest physical features characteristic of the he-goat, but they also figuratively refer to the gullibility of the fox's companion.

---

[1] Oudin, p. 241.
[2] Oudin, p. 368.
[3] Tallemant des Réaux, *Historiettes*, vol. III, p. 208.
[4] P. de La Noue, *Synonyma et æquivoca gallica*, p. 133.
[5] Oudin, p. 348.
[6] Oudin, p. 214.

La Fontaine does not even reject the most realistic elements of vocabulary: *crasseux*[V,6], *crotte*[II,8], *goulée*[IV,4], *malotru*[VII,4], *pécore*[I,3], *pétarade*[VI,16], *rogneux*[X,5], *tripotage*[III,6], have, among others, found their way into the *Fables*. *Excrément*, as well as these, belonged to the language of the *burlesque*, as the following lines of Saint-Amant prove:

> La garce qui naquit de l'excrément de l'onde
> Pour courir l'aiguillette en tous les lieux du monde
> Vénus, la bonne cagne aux paillards appétits,
> Sachant que ses pigeons avaient fait des petits,
> En fit faire un pâté que la grosse Euphrosine,
> Qui se connaît des mieux à ruer en cuisine
> Elle même apporta plein de culs d'artichaud. . . .[1]

Malherbe had used the word in an Ode:

> Va-t-en à la malheure, excrément de la terre[2]

and brought upon himself Balzac's reprobation:

> 'En tout le poème il n'y a qu'un mot qui ne me plaît pas, et que je voudrais avoir changé pour un autre. Excrément de la terre me semble trop bas pour un tyran . . . Le mot d'excrément est d'ailleurs assez vilain et d'assez mauvaise odeur: en sa plus honnête signification il ne peut signifier que les rats, les mouches, les vermisseaux et autres créatures imparfaites qui se forment de la corruption de la terre.'[3]

One cannot but admire La Fontaine's skill when, in *Le Lion et le Moucheron*[II,9], he succeeds in expressing the lion's wrath by this vigorous apostrophe, whilst, at the same time, parodying Malherbe's controversial line and using the metaphor in its appropriate sense according to Balzac, since it refers precisely to a *moucheron*.

These are only a few examples of the complex effects obtained through the skilful use of the most vigorous and picturesque elements of popular speech. La Fontaine also succeeds in giving vigour and significance to the most innocuous words. Never has the word *chat* had such a formidable and haunting quality as in *Le Chat, la Belette et le petit Lapin*:[VII,15]

> C'était un chat vivant comme un dévot hermite,
>   Un chat faisant la chattemite,
>   Un saint homme de chat. . . .

---

[1] Saint-Amant, *Le Melon*, in *Œuvres poétiques*, Paris, 1930, p. 107.
[2] Malherbe, *Prophétie du dieu de Seine*, in *Œuvres*, Vol. I, p. 239.
[3] Guez de Balzac, *Socrate chrétien* 'Dixième discours', in *Œuvres*, Paris, 1854, vol. II, pp. 90-1.

Repetitions, alliteration and a very bold *alliance de mots, saint homme de chat*, contribute to throw the noun *chat* into relief most effectively. Such an obvious enjoyment of language on the part of our poet cannot but bring to one's mind Barbey d'Aurévilly's judgement on Maurice de Guérin: 'Il suçait les mots comme les abeilles pompent les fleurs; voilà pourquoi il aimait tant et s'était tant assimilé La Fontaine.'[1]

7. ELLIPSIS

To his thorough knowledge of archaic and popular French, La Fontaine owes more than a remarkably comprehensive and picturesque vocabulary. Their syntactical and structural features also provide him with many devices which give his style energy and vividness. Nowhere in the *Fables* do we find the systematic use of Marotic style which makes some of the *Contes* rather tedious; here, the poet retains only those elements of this style which, skilfully blended with many other devices of varied origins, are capable of giving his work its striking dynamic quality.

The vividness of his evocations is often due to the use of all the standard elliptical devices. Thus, whilst his use of the indefinite and of the definite article is worthy of attention, the ellipsis of the article has almost always a particular artistic significance. The indefinite article introduces a character as yet unnamed and undescribed, whereas the definite article is reserved for one already silhouetted or given an exemplary personality:

> Entre les pattes d'un lion
> Un rat sortit de terre assez à l'étourdie.[II,11]

> Un jour sur ses longs pieds allait je ne sais où
> Le héron au long bec emmanché d'un long cou.[VII,4]

Ellipsis of the article had become a regular feature of Marotic style and, as Scarron pointed out, it offered practical advantages:

> Ils font des vers en vieux Gaulois,
> N'en pouvant faire en bon François,
> Et disent que c'en est la mode.
> Quand l'article les incommode,
> Ils le coupent sans hésiter.[2]

---

[1] Barbey d'Aurevilly, Letter to Trebutien, quoted by B. d'Harcourt, in *Maurice de Guérin et le poème en prose*, Paris, 1932, p. 297.

[2] Scarron, *Poésies diverses*, Paris, 1947, vol. I, pp. 471–2.

F

If such a utilitarian explanation cannot be altogether ruled out, it seldom stands out as the only justification of ellipsis in the *Fables*. Indeed, it would be most unjust to credit the poet with mere skill in the handling of *chevilles*, where he displays stylistic sensitiveness resulting in an increased vividness of evocation. Thus, in the line:

Je suis roi: deviendrai-je un citadin d'Ithaque,[XII,1]

the omission and the use of the article cannot be explained adequately in terms of mere prosody. It is true, on the one hand, that the article is optional with the attribute, but, on the other, it would be unjust to the artist not to take the aesthetic value of his option into consideration: the antithesis between the unique dignity of kingship and the common quality of citizen is greatly stressed by the absence of the article in front of *roi* and the presence of the indefinite in front of *citadin*. The reasons for the lion's refusal to be changed back into a man are thus made clearer and, at the same time, more forceful.

Ellipsis often contributes to give one of the poet's own statements the archaic flavour, the exemplary value and the universal appeal of a well-tried proverb:

Fille se coiffe volontiers
D'amoureux à longue crinière.[IV,1]

Volontiers gens boiteux haïssent le logis.[X,2]

Often, the absence of the article in front of the direct object gives the phrase the familiar sound of an old idiom: *lacs à prendre loups*[VI,1], *montrer patte blanche*[IV,15], *chercher femme*[VII,2], *faire voyage*[VIII,4], *tirer marrons du feu*[IX,17], *faire châteaux en Espagne*[VII,9], etc. Other effects are sometimes added; thus, when La Fontaine writes:

Il se faut entraider; c'est la loi de nature[VIII,17]

the ellipsis of the article suggests a personification of law-giving Nature as well as a traditional saying.[1] Elsewhere, a common noun without the article becomes a proper noun, an inanimate object becomes personified as well as animated, as is the custom in fables:

Pot de fer son camarade
Se met droit à ses côtés.[V,2]

However, the use of the article is still uncertain in the seventeenth century and the contemporary grammarians, as Brunot has shown,[2] are

---

[1] Cf. also 'Leur malade paya le tribut à Nature'.[V,12]
[2] F. Brunot, *Histoire de la langue française*, vol. IV, part 2, pp. 766–72.

far from agreeing about it; this allows the poet great freedom of expression. In many cases, the ellipsis can hardly be considered archaic, as when La Fontaine increases the intensity of his evocations by using the natural tendency of the language to omit the article in the coupling of nouns or in longer enumerations:

> ... Ils eurent bonne année,
> Pleine moisson, pleine vinée[VI,4]

> Et mon homme d'avoir chiens, chevaux et carrosses.[VII,13]

The article, on the contrary, makes an enumeration longer, more ponderous, as can be seen in the woodcutter's complaint:

> Sa femme, ses enfants, les soldats, les impôts,
> Le créancier, et la corvée
> Lui font d'un malheureux la peinture achevée,[I,16]

or in:

> La faim, l'occasion, l'herbe tendre. ...[VII,1]

A collective pronoun often precedes or rounds off such enumerations; in this case, the suppression of the articles, legitimate since the nouns are in apposition, makes these nouns stand out more vividly:

> C'est à dire environ le temps
> Que tout aime, et que tout pullule dans le monde:
> Monstres marins au fond de l'onde,
> Tigres dans les forêts, alouettes aux champs.[IV,22]

> Facteurs, associés, chacun lui fut fidèle.[VII,13]

The omission of the article may also stress the rapidity of the action described, the surprise it causes:

> Il avait vu sortir gibier de toute sorte.[IV,16]

> La sœur de Philomèle, attentive à sa proie,
> Malgré le bestion happait mouches dans l'air.[X,6]

> Créanciers et voisins reviennent aussitôt.[IV,18]

> Tandis que coups de poing trottaient. ...[I,13]

> Aussitôt qu'il faisait un pas,
> Ambassades croassantes
> Allaient dans tous les états.[Appendix I, *Le Soleil et les Grenouilles*]

Sometimes the noun, without an article, acquires a new importance, imposes itself on the reader's mind, and, placed in an emphatic position, assumes the value of a generalization:

> Médecins au lion viennent de toutes parts.[VIII,3]

The ellipsis of the pronoun subject also produces similar effects of archaic flavour, accumulation, rapidity, vividness, etc.:

> .... Et vraiment si ferai.[IX,16]

> De tous côtés [il] lui vient des donneurs de recettes.[VIII,3]

> Même j'ai vu dans mon voyage
> Gens experts et savants, leur ai dit la langueur
> Dont Votre Majesté craint à bon droit la suite.[Ibid.]

In fact, one may say that what was originally an elliptical turn of Marotic style became one of the characteristic features of that of La Fontaine. Ellipses of article and pronoun are found even in his correspondence and casual notes to friends, to which they lend an air of informality:

> 'Adieu, mon cher ami; t'en dirais beaucoup davantage si j'avais l'esprit tranquille présentement . . .'[1]

8. USE OF VERBS

La Fontaine's use of verbs also deserves some mention; these abound in the *Fables* and are comparatively the most important element of the poet's language. Virolle has counted thirty-six verbs for five adjectives in one fable and this ratio is by no means exceptional in La Fontaine.[2] His style is dynamic and few are the fables where the first verb is not to be found in the first couplet. To begin *in medias res* ensures the early appearance of the verb: the scene is set in a few words, the characters are named and immediately seen in action:

> Le chêne un jour dit au roseau. . . .[I,22]

> Un lièvre en son gîte songeait. . . .[II,14]

> Une souris tomba du bec d'un chat-huant. . . .[IX,7]

> Un octogénaire plantait. . . .[XI,8]

---

[1] Letter to Maucroix, September 10th 1661, *O.D.*, p. 528.
[2] R. Virolle, 'Explication de texte: l'amitié selon La Fontaine', in *L'Ecole*, vol. XLVII, 1956, p. 252; *Fables*, VIII, 11.

Often, the characters are not described but rather seen; thus, we are not told that the cobbler[VIII,2] is gay but that he sings all day. In the narrative, as well as in the descriptive passages, the accumulation of juxtaposed verbs gives the style rapidity and movement well in keeping with the subject-matter:

Après qu'il eut brouté, trotté, fait tous ses tours. . . .[VII,15]

Cependant on fricasse, on se rue en cuisine, [IV,4]

or evocative intensity:

Après qu'on eut bien contesté,
Répliqué, crié, tempêté. . . .[II,3]

Une [huître] s'était ouverte, et baillant au soleil,
Par un doux zéphyr réjouie,
Humait l'air, respirait, était épanouie.[VIII,9]

Juxtaposition of short clauses produces a similar effect:

Etranglent la moitié des agneaux les plus gras,
Les emportent aux dents, dans les bois se retirent.[III,13]

In the words of Andry de Boisregard,

'Lorsque le sujet qu'on traite demande un peu de feu et de mouvement, les périodes coupées sont à propos; car elles ont je ne sais quoi de fort et de mâle qui est peut-être un des plus grands ornements du langage; au lieu qu'en aplanissant toutes choses par le moyen des liaisons, on tombe dans une petite afféterie qui n'a ni pointe, ni aiguillon.[1]

La Fontaine also draws many effects from the value of verb tenses: in a narration in the past, the historic present always adds intensity to a dramatic climax; the action is shown vividly as if taking place under our very eyes:

A la porte de la salle
Ils entendirent du bruit.
Le rat de ville détale,
Son camarade le suit.[I,9]

Il vit son éléphant couché sur l'autre rive.
Il le prend, il l'emporte, au haut du mont arrive,
Rencontre une esplanade et puis une cité.[X,13]

[1] Andry de Boisregard, *Réflexions sur l'usage présent de la langue française*, pp. 608–9.

As soon as the point is made, the narration is resumed in the more
leisurely past tense:

> On écorche, on taille, on démembre
> Messire Loup. Le monarque en soupa.[VIII,3]

> A ces mots le serpent, se laissant attraper,
> Est pris, mis en un sac, et ce qui fut le pire,
> On résolut sa mort. . . .[X,1]

Many are the grammarians who recommended this device: Chiflet wrote:

> 'Les narrations historiques ont bonne grâce au temps présent,
> principalement quand on raconte une suite d'actions, ou d'événe-
> ments impétueux. . . . Mais il est bon de finir en reprenant le temps
> passé par lequel on avait commencé la narration.[1]

Andry de Boisregard agreed that

> 'Il est souvent à propos de changer le prétérit en présent, et de
> parler d'une chose déjà faite, comme si elle se faisait à l'heure qu'on
> en parle: ce changement donne de la force au discours, et met la
> chose comme devant les yeux.'[2]

Gamaches commented on Fénelon's use of the historic present in *Télé-
maque*:

> 'Les narrations ont aussi leurs images ou leurs peintures ce qui est
> passé, on le rappelle quelquefois au présent. . . . Vous voyez que ce
> n'est plus ici une narration: vous devenez vous-mêmes témoins de ce
> qu'on vous dit. On ne vous apprend pas ce qui s'est passé: on vous
> montre ce qui se passe.'[3]

Vaugelas had already insisted on the importance of reverting to the past
in the continuation of the narrative:

> 'Il y en a qui tiennent que dans le style historique, il ne faut pas
> narrer le passé par le présent . . . Il est vrai que pour diversifier et
> rendre le style plus agréable, il se faut servir tantôt de l'un et tantôt
> de l'autre, et savoir passer adroitement et à propos du prétérit au
> présent et du présent au prétérit; autrement on ferait une faute que
> plusieurs font de commencer par un temps et de finir par l'autre, qui
> est d'ordinaire un très grand défaut.'[4]

---

[1] L. Chiflet, *Nouvelle et parfaite grammaire française*, Paris, 1722, (1st ed. 1659), pp.
144–5.
[2] Andry de Boisregard, *Réflexions sur l'usage présent de la langue française*, p. 659.
[3] E. S. de Gamaches, *Les Agréments du langage*, pp. 130–1.
[4] Vaugelas, *Remarques sur la langue française*, pp. 458–9.

La Fontaine goes a step further when he introduces the historic present into a sequence of sentences in the future tense:

> . . . Une demi-douzaine
> Mettra la mer à sec, et tous ses habitants.
> Adieu joncs et marais: notre race est détruite.
> Bientôt on la verra réduite
> A l'eau du Styx . . .[VI,12]

Nominal clauses, too, produce vivid effects:

> Voilá mon âne à l'eau. . . .[II,10]

When *voici* or *voilà* are omitted, the construction amounts to an ellipsis of the verb.[1] This is customarily used to present the result or the consequence of an action already evoked, or a comment on this action. In the *Fables*, the device has the archaic quality and the directness of familiar speech: all syntactical and logical links between action and consequence are omitted:

> Rats en campagne aussitôt.[I,9]

> Belle leçon pour les gens chiches.[V,13]

> Autre plainte.[VI,11]

> Point de réponse, mot.[VIII,17]

The evocative intensity of this construction is shown by the fact that La Fontaine chooses it, together with repetitions, to suggest the obsession of one of his characters:

> Miroirs dans les logis, miroirs chez les marchands,
> Miroirs aux poches des galants,
> Miroirs aux ceintures des femmes.[I,11]

However, this elliptical style was not only found in familiar genres; its directness also suited formal oratory. Bellegarde writes of Fléchier:

> 'Un autre célèbre prélat dit dans une de ses Oraisons Funèbres: Entre-t-elle dans l'église? Prosternement, adoration, silence. Ces

---

[1] La Fontaine also uses impersonal verbs as personal: 'Notre homme . . . pleut, vente . . .', VI, 4. Cf. Richelet, *Dictionnaire français*, '*venter*. Ce mot entre dans quelques façons de parler figurées . . . "Ménage vente, grêle et tonne" (Cotin, *Ménagerie*), c. à d. Ménage crie. tempête et fait du bruit.' Cf. also Racan, *Bergeries*, in *Œuvres*, vol II, p. 96:
> 'Tonnez, grêlez, ventez, étonnez l'univers'
and Scarron, *Virgile travesti*, V, quoted by Littré, item *Pleuvoir*:
> Et pleuvez à bonne mesure. . . .

trois substantifs ne sont liés ni régis par quoique ce soit; mais cette irrégularité est plus éloquente et plus vive que ne serait une régularité plus exacte.'[1]

The historic infinitive, rare elsewhere in the seventeenth century, is a characteristic element of our poet's style,[2] bringing conciseness and rapidity. The traditional ellipsis of the article in front of the subject of this infinitive probably added, in the eyes of La Fontaine, to the merits of that construction: it made generalization and personification easier, whilst retaining an archaic grace. In the words of Maupas,

> 'Nous usons ... de l'infinitif non dépendant d'un autre verbe, pour signifier une soudaineté et hativité d'action ... On s'en sert assez en la langue latine. Nous mettons ordinairement la conjonction *et* devant, puis la préposition *de* avec un nominatif interposé. ... Nous chargeons brusquement l'ennemi, et lui *de reculer*, et nous *de le poursuivre*; il était ivre et se laissa tomber, et chacun *de rire*.'[3]

> Ainsi dit le renard, et flatteurs d'applaudir. [VII,1]

La Fontaine even suppresses the conjunction to increase the impression of rapidity:

> Grenouilles aussitôt de sauter dans les ondes,
> Grenouilles de rentrer en leurs grottes profonds.[II,14]

All these devices have the compelling directness of an oral account of some action taking place under the narrator's very eyes; they also add to the simplicity of the style since they tend to retain only the most significant features of the subject. In fact, as always in La Fontaine, the simplicity is only apparent: these grammatical devices are seldom used in isolation but nearly always combined with others, grammatical and rhetorical, which render analysis difficult and classification impossible. Thus, the line from *La Goutte et l'Araignée*,

> Autre toile tissue, autre coup de balais,[III,8]

no doubt, owes its evocative quality to the nominal construction and the ellipsis of the articles which restrict the vision to its essential elements,

---

[1] J.-B. Morvan de Bellegarde, *Réflexions sur l'élégance et la politesse du style*, pp. 381–2.

[2] P. B. Marcou, who, in *Das historische Infinitiv im Französischen*, Berlin, 1888, listed twenty-four historic infinitives in the *Fables*, commented: 'La Fontaine est sans comparaison possible l'auteur classique qui s'est servi le plus de l'infinitif historique.' Quoted by Alf Lombard, 'L'Infinitif de narration dans les langues romanes', in *Skrifter utgivna av Kungl. Humanistika vetenskapssamfundet i Uppsala*, vol. XXX, 1936–37, p. 167.

[3] C. Maupas, 1618, quoted by E. Winkler, *La Doctrine grammaticale française d'après Maupas et Oudin*, Halle, 1912, p. 180.

thereby increasing its intensity; but it also owes it to the past participle which enables the poet to retain a verbal element in a construction based on the ellipsis of the verb, and to the parallelism suggesting the rapid and automatic succession of the two actions.

Not only are verbs important by their frequency, they also enable the author to draw vivid effects from skilful use of tenses. In the line

Et le drôle eut lapé le tout en un moment,[1,18]

the past anterior, combined with the temporal indication *en un moment* suggests the rapidity of the action terminated almost as soon as begun. In Perrette's monologue, the incoherence of the tenses suggests the confusion of mind of the milkmaid mistaking her wishes for reality.[1]

Le porc à s'engraisser coûtera peu de son;
Il était, quand je l'eus, de grosseur raisonnable.[VII,9]

The device is reminiscent of the synesis in the lines:

Le pauvre carpillon lui dit en sa manière:

Laissez moi carpe devenir:
Je serai par vous repêchée.[V,3]

in which the *carpillon*, although not yet *carpe*, speaks in the first person feminine.

His frequent use of present and past participles also shows La Fontaine's tendency to prefer verbs to any other possible means of expression: Gohin shows, in a note, how Du Lorrens's lines:

Or ce champ ne se peut en sorte moissonner
Que d'autres après nous n'y trouvent à glaner.[2]

become, in La Fontaine,

Mais ce champ ne se peut tellement moissonner
Que les derniers venus n'y trouvent à glaner.[III,1]

The past participle sometimes stresses a state of helplessness, as the result of a completed action:

---

[1] Rabelais, in *Gargantua* (XXXIII), used a similar device: 'Vous passerez par l'estroict de Sibyle, et là erigerez deux colonnes, plus magnificques que celles de Hercules, à perpétuelle mémoire de vostre nom, et sera nommé cestuy destroict la mer Picrocholine. Passée la mer Picrocholine, voicy Barberousse qui se rend vostre esclave. ... De là prendrons Candie, Cypre, Rhodes, et les îles Cyclades, et donnerons sus à Morée. Nous la tenons.' Rabelais, *Œuvres*, pp. 65–6.

[2] Du Lorrens, *Satire XXIII*, quoted by Gohin in *Fables*, vol. I, p. 254, n. 4.

> Quel accident, tient arrêtée
> Notre compagne au pied léger?[XII,15]

With *voici* and *voilà*, it often emphasizes the rapidity of an action and the ineluctability of its consequence:

> Et voilà la guerre allumée.[VII,12]
>
> Les voilà devenus ours, lions, éléphants.[XII,1]
>
> Voilà les poissons pris.[X,10]

The chief effect produced by the absolute participles which abound in the *Fables* is one of economy; but the very conciseness of the construction and its resemblance to the anacoluthon give it a startling vigour which marks the whole sentence:

> Marché fait, les oiseaux forgent une machine. . . .[X,2]
>
> La tanche rebutée, il trouva du goujon.[VII,4]
>
> . . . Et la cherchant en vain,
> Ce fut pitié là-dessus de l'entendre.
>
> Ne sachant donc où mettre son espoir,
> Sa face était de pleurs toute baignée.[V,1]

The importance of the part played by the verb in La Fontaine's style has led Karl Ettmayer[1] to investigate the possibility of a relation between the recurrence of certain verbal forms and the repetition of structural patterns within the fables. Ettmayer shows that the stylistic elements resulting from the workings of the creative imagination are, in La Fontaine's *Fables*, associated with verbal forms and more particularly with verbal periphrases of the type *se mirent à jaser*[1,8], composed of a *verbum vicarium* (or *verbum efficiendi: laisser, faire, venir, aller, porter, se mettre à*) followed by the infinitive or gerund. La Fontaine was aware, argues Ettmayer, of the effect of their use as is shown by their frequent recurrence in the very places where there is a change from pictorial to dynamic imagination. Ettmayer divides the fables into a certain number of parts: prologue, static initial situation, starting point of the action, dynamic factors leading the action to its climax, the climax itself, the consequent situation, the 'official moral' added by the poet. According to Ettmayer, the *verba vicaria* are found more often at the beginning or at the end of each of these parts than in the middle of them. They correspond either to the

---

[1] K. Ettmayer, 'Die Rolle der Verba vicaria im poetischen Stil La Fontaines', *Hauptfragen der Romanistik*, pp. 3–36.

creation of tension (*Auftakt*) in the attentive listener about to hear a message or to the renewal of this tension (*Pointe*) through hearing the message. Thus, La Fontaine uses a verbal periphrasis whenever he wants to prepare his reader's mind for the reception of a new 'evolutive' image.

The novelty of this observation is striking and an investigation into the details of the numerous examples given by Ettmayer confirms, on the whole, the accuracy of the accumulated evidence which he offers in his thirty-six pages. However, a careful regrouping of all his observations concerning the particular fables chosen by him as examples shows that his division of the fables is sometimes questionable (e.g. p. 31, Fable III, 1) and he, himself, admits that it is more or less subjective.[1] It follows that in so far as his evidence is statistical, it rests on insecure foundations: one cannot, for instance, argue that the *verba vicaria* are found more often at the beginning and at the end of any given part of a fable than in the middle of it, unless one is quite sure where that part begins and ends. Besides, stimulating as Ettmayer's theory may be, it would be unwise, in the absence of any means of comparison with other authors of the same period, to conclude that one of the components of the stylistic perfection of the *Fables* has been identified. We must take into account the general form of the language in the seventeenth century and the remarks of contemporary grammarians and lexicographers who either recommend the use of the verbal periphrasis whenever possible as preferable to that of the simple verb,[2] or make no difference between the two forms.[3] It must, on the other hand, be recognized that although we find, in Corneille and Racine,[4] *verba vicaria* in places where there is a marked change in the nature of the appeal to the reader's imagination, their frequency does not seem to be so high in La Fontaine. The interest of Ettmayer's study lies in the fact that it reveals the stylistic potentiality of the conscious use of the *verba vicaria*. It makes a strong case for a new approach to the study of the verbal element in the *Fables* but, in its present form, concerns linguistics rather than stylistics.

9. WORD-ORDER

The vigour of La Fontaine's style is also due to effects of emphasis resulting from word-order. Often the poet arranges the components

---

1 K. Ettmayer, op. cit., p. 27.

2 Andry de Boisregard, *Réflexions sur l'usage présent de la langue française*, pp. 23–4; *Dictionnaire de l'Académie Française*, 1694, (items *aller*, *venir*), quoted by F. Brunot, *Histoire de la langue française*, vol. IV, part 2, pp. 741–2.

3 Oudin, *Curiosités françaises*, p. 369: 'Il vint à mourir, i. il mourut.'

4 E.g. P. Corneille, *Polyeucte*, IV, 2, stanzas 3 and 6; J. Racine, *Bérénice*, V, 7.

of a sentence in a manner corresponding to the sequence of sensations and
impressions received by the character in his fable rather than to the
objective logical and chronological order of the events. German critics
have compared this technique with that of Impressionist art and made
exhaustive studies of the devices involved.[1] Thus, when we read:

> Là dessus maître rat, plein de belle espérance,
> Approche de l'écaille, allonge un peu le cou,
> Se sent pris comme aux lacs: car l'huître tout d'un coup,
> Se referme. . . .[VIII,9]

our vision of the events is that of the rat himself, aware of being trapped
before realizing the cause of it. Sometimes, word-order gives an almost
graphic representation of the action;[2] the line

> Dans la gueule en travers on lui passe un bâton[X,2]

owes its evocative quality to the central position of *en travers* and to
the inversion which makes it possible. The device may be even more
subtle, as in the following lines:

> Laissez, entre la colère
> Et l'orage qui la suit
> L'intervalle d'une nuit.[VIII,20]

of which Boillot writes:

> 'Si nous nous avisons de prétendre que la construction aide à
> l'expression du sens, on ne manquera pas de nous objecter que loin
> de séparer les mots colère et orage comme le poète nous conseille de
> séparer les choses qu'ils signifient, la construction ici rapproche ces
> deux termes aussi près que possible l'un de l'autre. Pour confirmer,
> ajoutera-t-on, l'idée par l'image, pour qu'il y existât un heureux
> parallélisme entre la pensée et l'expression, le poète aurait dû
> trouver le moyen d'intercaler l'intervalle d'une nuit entre ces deux
> mots colère et orage. Il ne l'a pas fait, il ne pouvait pas le faire.
> Alors? Voici à notre sens ce qui s'est passé. Le poète a effectué une
> transposition d'effets, ou plus exactement de causes. Cet intervalle,
> dont il fallait que nous fussions conscients et que cependant il ne
> pouvait introduire à la bonne place, c'est à dire entre colère et orage,
> il l'a transposé, l'a fait figurer entre laissez et le troisième vers. A la
> lecture nous percevons cette irrégularité de construction. Nous

---

[1] H. Wiemann, J. Mousset, R. Auerbach, op. cit.
[2] Cf. 'De son étui la couronne est tirée'[VI,6].

sentons confusément, car nous n'analysons pas en lisant, qu'il y a
dans le cours de la phrase une interruption qui, sans se confondre
avec celle du sens, s'harmonise cependant avec elle et ceci suffit à
déclancher dans notre esprit cette sorte de vibration amplificatrice.'[1]

Inversion is the ideal device to produce emphasis: it enables the author to
set words into relief by placing them in an initial or a terminal position,
both positions of strength in a line or in a hemistich:

> Du palais d'un jeune lapin
> Dame Belette un beau matin
> S'empara. . . .[VII,15]

> Je devais par la royauté
> Avoir commencé mon ouvrage.[III,2]

Fallait-il pour cela, dit-elle, m'appeler.[X,1]

10. FIGURES

The vigour of La Fontaine's style is also due to his use of the whole
arsenal of figures of speech, grammar and rhetoric. In his verse, they lose
the vague classical colouring they still too often retained in contemporary
authors and gain a new strength from the picturesque and concrete
language of the poet; they become the instrument of an original imagin-
ative creation: the mould is that of tradition, the cast La Fontaine's own.
An exhaustive study of these figures would be repetitive and a few
examples will suffice to illustrate the poet's manner.

Enumerations and accumulations are organized to form compelling
gradations of the kind described by Gamaches, when he writes:

'Il est toujours à propos que les dernières idées enchérissent d'une
manière sensible sur celles qui les précèdent comme quand Don
Diègue dit à son fils: Va, cours, vole et nous venge.'[2]

Ils sont pour vous d'airain, d'acier, de diamant.[V,16]

> Voilà mon homme aux pleurs; il gémit, il soupire,
> Il se tourmente, il se déchire.[IV,20]

In the line:

L'attelage suait, soufflait, était rendu,[VII,8]

---

[1] F. Boillot, *Psychologie de la construction dans la phrase française moderne*, pp. 117-8.
[2] E. S. de Gamaches, *Les agréments du langage*, pp. 143-4.

the gradation is not only based on the meaning of the verbs but also on
the transition from active to passive. These enumerations and accumulations may also form neat parallelisms which increase their effect:

> Je n'irai par monts ni par vaux
> M'exposer au vent, à la pluie.[IV,3]

> Avec ses compagnons tout le jour badiner,
> Sauter, courir, se promener,

> Propos, conseil, enseignement,
> Rien ne change un tempérament.
> Le jeune homme inquiet, ardent, plein de courage

> Mit son lit en plein champ, loin des toits, sous les cieux.

> Il dépend d'une conjoncture
> De lieux, de personne, de temps,

> Comment percer des airs la campagne profonde?
> Percer Mars, le soleil et des vides sans fin?[VIII,16]

Repetitions stress a character's features, significant details or important
circumstances:

> Un jour sur ses *longs* pieds allait je ne sais où
> Le héron au *long* bec emmanché d'un *long* cou.[VII,4]

> Vous êtes *maigre* entrée, il faut *maigre* sortir.[III,17]

They may suggest the generalization or the duration of an action:

> Guillot, le vrai Guillot, étendu sur l'herbette,
> *Dormait* profondément,
> Son chien *dormait aussi*, comme *aussi* sa musette.
> La plupart des brebis *dormaient* pareillement.[III,3]

> Il passait les nuits et les jours
> A *compter, calculer, supputer* sans relâche,
> *Calculant, supputant, comptant* comme à la tâche.[XII,3]

> Comme *il sonna* la charge, *il sonne* la victoire.[II,9]

Etymological repetitions produce the same effects:

> Et faisait *sonner* sa *sonnette*.[I,4]

> Creusez, fouillez, bêchez; ne laissez nulle place
> Où la main ne *passe* et *repasse*.[V,9]

Pleonasms, more readily accepted at the time than in modern literature, are not ruled out:

> Le cas parut étrange, et contre l'ordinaire.[XI,4]

> Imprudents et peu circonspects.[XII,1]

Forceful antitheses abound:

> Les petits et les grands sont égaux à leurs yeux.[XII,21]

> Le prince voulut voir ces richesses immenses;
> Il ne trouva partout que médiocrité,
> Louanges du désert et de la pauvreté;
> C'étaient là ses magnificences,[X,9]

as well as striking oxymora:

> Et je sais même sur ce fait
> Bon nombre d'hommes qui sont femmes.[VIII,6]

> On n'en voyait point d'occupés
> A chercher le soutien d'une mourante vie.[VII,1]

Similes are few, but effective and often most original:

> Puis cet homme et son fils le portent comme un lustre.[III,1]

Periphrases, though at the time a traditional ornament of poetry, are seldom purely decorative in the *Fables*; they are usually devised to allow additional effects of a strictly functional nature, such as emphasis on a particularly significant circumstances:

> Pour sûreté de son trésor,
> Notre avare habitait un lieu dont Amphitrite
> Défendait aux voleurs de toutes parts l'abord,[XII,3]

on a comparison, by means of an etymological repetition rendered possible by the periphrasis:

> Elles filaient si bien que les sœurs filandières
> Ne faisaient que brouiller au prix de celles-ci,[V,6]

on a contrast stressed by an antithesis also dependent on the periphrasis:

> Les filles du limon tiraient du roi des astres
> Assistance et protection.[Appendix I, *Le Soleil et les Grenouilles*]

In one instance, a periphrasis creates a deliberate ambiguity, amusingly stressed by a comment of the narrator purporting to correct it:

> A ces mots, l'animal pervers
> (C'est le serpent que je veux dire,
> Et non l'homme: on pourrait aisément s'y tromper). . . .[X,1]

Even when the periphrases appear to be used simply as traditional features of poetic style, La Fontaine often comments on them; thus, they become pretexts for the introduction of the tone of familiarity characteristic of the *Fables*:[1]

> Les reines des étangs, grenouilles, veux-je dire
> (Car que coûte-t-il d'appeler
> Les choses par noms honorables?) [Appendix I, *Le Soleil et les Grenouilles*]

> Ce parasite ailé
> Que nous avons mouche appelé.[XII,13]

Thus, the reader is made to hear the rich, vigorous and free language of the *Fables* spoken by the warm or ironical voice of a genial story-teller.

---

[1] In VII, 12, 'la gent qui porte crête' is not only a mock-epic periphrasis, it is also a parody of Malherbe's 'la gent qui porte le turban'; *Ode, à la Reine, sur sa bienvenue en France*, in Malherbe, *Œuvres*, vol. I, p. 50, *l.* 112. Scarron also uses this appellation in *Remerciement à Monsieur le Cardinal*, 1642, in *Poésies diverses*, Vol. I, p. 99.

CHAPTER III

FAMILIARITY

1. The Presence of the Fabulist

An impression of familiarity in the tone of the author, diffused throughout the work, cannot fail to strike the reader of the *Fables*. This tone suits them admirably since, as popular stories transmitted by oral as well as written tradition, they lend themselves to an informal treatment which suggests the physical presence and the very voice of the narrator. La Fontaine's achievement in this respect is remarkable: the poet combines the confidential tone of Racan's most subjective poems with the playful and often ironical asides found in Voiture's light verse; the result is an air of apparent improvisation, personal confidences, and *badinage* reminiscent of that of the familiar letter, a genre much in favour at the time and successfully practised by La Fontaine. Indeed, there are even some striking similarities between the presentation of some of his fables, not to mention the *Discours à Madame de La Sablière*, and that of the letter in verse.[1] But if the poet's intervention is often less obvious, it is nevertheless recurrent throughout the fables so that it is not paradoxical to say that La Fontaine himself is the chief character of the *Fables*. This is partly due to his short digressions, occasional judgements and confidences through which the charm of his pleasant personality is reflected in his work. In the words of Borgerhoff, 'somewhere, he has learned the value of openness'.[2] Thus, by means of reflexions on his art, on his subject, on the limitations of his talent, he associates the readers closely with the process of composition: the technical problems cease to be the preserve of men of letters and the writer is no longer a complete stranger: 'La Fontaine is exploiting himself . . . In openly revealing himself, he forces his readers to share some of the responsibility for their enjoyment of his art'.[3] A slightly different effect is obtained through cross-references between the fables: here, heedless of the conventions prescribing the distance to be

---

[1] E.g. *Fables*, VIII, 4; VIII, 13; XII, 1; XII, 2; XII, 5; XII, 15; XII, 23; etc. See Haraszti, *En glanant chez La Fontaine*, pp. 50–1. It is to the same tone that the *Contes* owe their originality and most of their merit.
[2] E. B. O. Borgerhoff, *The Freedom of French Classicism*, pp. 140–2.
[3] Ibid.; see *Fables*, II, 1; III, 1; IV, 1; IV, 18; V, 1; VI, 1; etc.

kept between an author and his work, La Fontaine, with much apparent simplicity, plunges the reader still more deeply into the world he has created. The device is reminiscent of Honoré de Balzac's technique of the 'retour des personnages':

> Autrefois Carpillon fretin
> Eut beau prêcher, il eut beau dire. . . .[IX,10]
>
> Jadis l'erreur du souriceau
> Me servit à prouver . . .[XI,7]

A new character is introduced as:

> Un hérisson du voisinage,
> Dans mes vers nouveau personnage. . . .[XII,13]

Sometimes, La Fontaine intervenes to anticipate objections and make the anecdote acceptable however improbable it may be:

> Du temps que les bêtes parlaient,
> Les lions, entr'autres, voulaient
> Etre admis dans notre alliance.
> Pourquoi non? puisque leur engeance
> Valait la nôtre en ce temps-là . . .[IV,1]
>
> Un loup rempli d'humanité
> (S'il en est de tels dans le monde). . . .[X,5]

These signs of complicity between the author and his readers are the extreme form of the familiar tone which pervades the *Fables*, the tone of an informal and good-humoured story-teller, aware of the importance of establishing contact with his audience. He achieves this by apostrophizing the reader and inviting him to reflect on a character's behaviour:

> Qui d'eux aimait le mieux? que t'en semble, lecteur?[VIII,11]
>
> Fit-il pas mieux que de se plaindre?[III,11]

Elsewhere, the poet discreetly threatens those against whom the moral is directed:

> Trompeurs, c'est pour vous que j'écris,[I,18]

or, playing upon the illusion he himself has created, addresses his characters:

> Bergers, bergers, le loup n'a tort
> Que quand il n'est pas le plus fort.[X,5]

Sometimes, he composes an imaginary dialogue between himself and his audience whose reactions he anticipates:

> L'oiseau . . .
> Va tout droit imprimer sa griffe
> Sur le nez de sa Majesté.
> Quoi? sur le nez du roi? Du roi même en personne.
> Il n'avait donc alors ni sceptre ni couronne?
> Quand il en aurait eu, c'aurait été tout un.[XII,12]

In so doing, the poet suggests the actual presence of the public and gives the fables the liveliness and freedom one associates with improvised story-telling and the studied naïvety of Marotic style. In one fable in particular, La Fontaine even refines and perfects this technique; in the opening line of *Le Loup et le Renard*,

> Mais d'où vient qu'au renard Esope accorde un point?

> J'en cherche la raison, et ne la trouve point,[XI,6]

the initial *mais* suggests a whole unrecorded discussion of which the fable is the conclusion. This beginning contrary to all precepts is reminiscent of the way in which the first line of a seventeenth-century play often suggests a conversation in progress:

> Oui, puisque je retrouve un ami si fidèle.[1]

La Fontaine himself uses this device in his dramatic works:

> Hé bien! on vous a dit qu'elle était empêchée:
> Est-ce là le sujet dont votre âme est touchée?

> Nous nous revoyons donc, heureuse Briseis![2]

In fact, La Fontaine accomplishes a stylistic feat since by beginning with the restrictive adverb *mais*, he suggests an imaginary preamble to his fable and, at the same time, emphasizes the conversational tone of his judge-ment on Æsop.

Parentheses also play an important part:

> 'On doit encore éviter les parenthèses dans la poésie. . . . Mais dans les ouvrages enjoués, les parenthèses ne se souffrent d'ordinaire que lorsqu'elles sont courtes, plaisantes, et ingénieuses,'

[1] J. Racine, *Andromaque*, I, 1.
[2] *L'Eunuque*, I, 1, *O.D.*, p. 263; *Achille*, I, 1, *O.D.*, p. 453.

writes Richelet,[1] drawing his examples of permissible parentheses from La Fontaine's *Contes*. In the *Fables* too, they enable the poet to comment on his narrative, his characters and their behaviour, and, in so doing, to appear in person from the wings and wink at the audience. Sometimes, it is an ironical aside:

> Un passager pendant l'orage
> Avait voué cent boeufs au vainqueur des Titans.
> Il n'en avait pas un: vouer cent éléphants
> N'aurait pas coûté davantage.[IX,13]

Sometimes, it is a proverb or even a pseudo-proverb of La Fontaine's invention, to give a statement the authoritative stamp of popular wisdom and tradition:

> Volontiers on fait cas d'une terre étrangère:
> Volontiers gens boiteux haïssent le logis.[X,2]

It may be a remark of general value expressed in impersonal terms:

> Alléguer l'impossible aux rois, c'est un abus,[VIII,3]

or a personal observation made in the first person:

> ... J'ai maints chapitres vus,
> Qui pour néant se sont ainsi tenus.[II,2]

Elsewhere, it is a comment on the characters or on the situation, meant to be understood on an altogether different level from that of the narrative. A parenthesis with or without brackets indicates the change

> ... Pour un pauvre animal,
> Grenouilles, à mon sens, ne raisonnaient pas mal.[VI,12]

> (Car que faire en un gîte, à moins que l'on ne songe?)[II,14]

Leisurely and casual proems:

> L'homme au trésor caché qu'Esope nous propose,
> Servira d'exemple à la chose,[IV,20]

impertinent preteritions:

> Il n'est pas besoin que j'étale
> Tout ce que l'un et l'autre dit,[VIII,26]

---

[1] Richelet, *La Versification française ou l'art de bien faire et de bien tourner les vers*, Paris, 1677, pp. 134-5.

and occasional trivial corrections in the rhetorical sense of the word:

> Mais venons à la fable, ou plutôt à l'histoire
> De celui qui tâche d'unir tous ses enfants.
>
> Mes chers enfants, dit-il, (à ses fils il parlait)....[IV,18]

help to create an impression of ease and informality.

2. STUDIED NEGLIGENCE

However, it would be incorrect to infer from the preceding observations that this apparent casualness reflects that of the poet towards his work: the familiarity of his tone is the result of studied negligence, a particularly perilous technique which he masters with virtuosity. Often devices which, on the surface, lend, for example, a conversational tone to the text, produce additional effects at another level. Thus, remarks of affected indifference to factual precision of sources of information, conceal in fact a desire for authenticity; the references even if omitted are hinted at:

> J'ai lu dans quelque endroit qu'un meunier et son fils,
> L'un vieillard, l'autre enfant, non pas des plus petits,
> Mais garçon de quinze ans, si j'ai bonne mémoire ...[III,1]

In the line,

> Certain renard Gascon, d'autres disent Normand,[III,11]

imprecision, combined with references to two popular phrases, adds a touch of familiarity, but it also suggests the possibility of two different interpretations of the fox's behaviour: as Littré points out, *Gascon* and *Normand* are usually considered as synonyms and mean liar, 'mais avec les différences propres aux provinces qu'ils rappellent'.[1] A *Normand* lies because of his natural astuteness and shrewdness, a *Gascon*, from pride, to boast or to save his face. This list of the various forms taken by parentheses in the *Fables*, though not exhaustive, justifies the judgement of a modern critic on La Fontaine: 'Il est le raisonneur de la pièce'.[2]

---

[1] Littré, *Dictionnaire de la langue française*, item *Gascon*. See also *Fables*, VIII, 10:
> Se tirer en Gascon d'une semblable affaire
> Est le mieux. Il sut donc dissimuler sa peur.

and VII, 6:
> Ne soyez à la cour, si vous voulez y plaire,
> Ni fade adulateur, ni parleur trop sincère;
> Et tâchez quelquefois de répondre en Normand.

[2] G. Michaut, *La Fontaine*, Paris, 1913–14, vol. II, p. 115.

These parentheses give the apologue a new complexity, unknown to La Fontaine's predecessors. Michaut regrets that this technique tends to weaken the dramatic quality of the fable, but gives little evidence to support his assertion. It is true that the reader's attention is occasionally drawn from the puppets to the showman; yet, the parentheses are never irrelevant digressions but, on the contrary, extremely concise means of introducing important additional touches to the fables beside that of familiarity. They remain an integral part of the fable; thus, the style gains in economy, the narrative in ease and directness. Not long after the poet's death, Houdart de La Motte already remarked that

'Les réflexions sont encore un des ornements de la fable; mais elles en doivent prendre le ton dominant, et être aussi naturelles dans leurs expressions qu'amenées naturellement par le sujet. La Fontaine dit:

Certaine fille un peu trop fière
Prétendait avoir un mari
Jeune, bien fait, et beau, d'agréable manière,
Point froid et point jaloux: notez ces deux points-ci.

Cette réflexion, car c'en est une, quoiqu'elle ne soit pas déployée, et que l'auteur ne la fasse qu'en avertissant de la faire, cette réflexion, dis-je, plaît par le naturel même, parce que loin d'être recherchée, toute ingénieuse qu'elle est, elle naît presque nécessairement du fait: et que ces deux conditions que la fille exige, présentent d'elles-mêmes à l'esprit l'opposition qu'elles ont l'une à l'autre. Ajoutez que cette réflexion rapide ... n'apporte aucune gêne à la narration; et l'on dirait qu'au lieu d'être interrompue, elle en devient plus vive et plus légère; ces sortes de traits jettent du sens et de la solidité dans la fable; et sans nuire à la vérité totale et essentielle, ils y répandent d'autres vérités surnuméraires que le lecteur est bien aise de recueillir en passant, acquisition d'autant plus flatteuse, qu'il y avait moins lieu d'y compter.'[1]

Several of La Fontaine's asides, closely related though they are, like Montaigne's, to the main theme, constitute real digressions. These are usually short, reveal the most varied moods and aspects of his personality and range from caustic witticisms of the type:

---

[1] Houdart de La Motte, *Discours sur la fable*, in *Fables nouvelles*, Paris, 1719, pp. xxxiii–xxxix.

Je ne suis pas de ceux qui disent; Ce n'est rien;
  C'est une femme qui se noie.
Je dis que c'est beaucoup; et ce sexe vaut bien
Que nous le regrettions, puisqu'il fait notre joie.[III,16]

to castigating contempt;

Je définis la cour un pays où les gens,
Tristes, gais, prêts à tout, à tout indifférents,
Sont ce qu'il plaît au prince, ou, s'ils ne peuvent l'être,
  Tâchent au moins de le paraître,
Peuple caméléon, peuple singe du maître:
On dirait qu'un esprit anime mille corps;
C'est bien là que les gens sont de simples ressorts.[VIII,14]

or discreet emotion:

Amants, heureux amants. . . .[IX,2]

Solitude ou je trouve une douceur secrète. . . . [XI,4]

Both parenthesis and longer digression retain the simplicity, the directness, the naturalness which give them the tone of a casual remark or that
of a confidence; Rémond de Saint-Mard remarked:

'Un récit que ne va pas tout à fait de suite, qui prend haleine, qui
se donne des repos, pourvu qu'ils soient petits, en a l'air plus
naturel. Frappés plus ou moins d'un fait, il est rare que nous le
rapportions nuement; nous ne manquons guères à rendre compte, par
quelques petits mots, de l'impression qu'il fait sur nous; et quand ce
compte n'est pas trop long, et qu'il n'écarte pas l'esprit du fait, il
l'anime, le soutient et le rend plus aimable. Tel est l'endroit où La
Fontaine dit:

Sur le bord d'un puits très profond
Dormait, étendu de son long,
Un enfant alors dans ses classes;
Tout est aux écoliers couchettes et matelas
Un honnête homme en pareil cas
Eût fait un saut de vingt brasses.

La Fontaine ne va pas droit au fait; mais on le lui pardonne. On est
charmé de lui entendre dire que tout est aux écoliers couchettes et
matelas; l'écart est si naturel qu'on croirait qu'il n'a pas pu se dis-
penser de le faire; et voilà, en tout genre, le caractère du vrai beau: il

vous surprend d'abord, et quand vous êtes revenu de votre étonne-
ment, vous êtes étonné de ce que vous avez été surpris d'une chose si
naturelle, qu'il semble que vous l'eussiez dite vous-même.'[1]

This apparent simplicity and familiarity are due to a relatively limited
number of devices skilfully used by La Fontaine. The vocabulary and
idiom of these parentheses are very simple, exclusively composed of
everyday conversational linguistic elements, and, since their variety is
rather limited, the poet repeats the same phrases, the same conversational
clichés from fable to fable, with little, if any, alteration: *voici comme*,
voici comment, *voici pourtant*[2], *selon moi*, *quant à moi*, *pour moi*[3], *dis-je*[4];
the same may be said of *je laisse à penser*, *à juger*[5], introducing preteritions, of *on dit*, *dit-on*, *ce dit-on*[6], *je ne sais*[7], *à ce que dit la fable*, *l'histoire*[8],
phrases frequently used to give the fables an air of improvised variation
on an old theme for which the author rejects all responsibility; *Il avait
raison*[9] is a comment often made by the poet on his heroes.

A similar effect of simplicity is obtained by the use of intentionally
artless and familiar transitions between the fable proper and the poet's
digressions. These often show La Fontaine's willingness to intervene in
the fable when the subject lends itself to personal development, as well as
his determination to return to the apologue when he becomes conscious
of his prolonged parenthesis. Thus, in *L'Astrologue qui se laisse tomber
dans un puits*[II,13], the poet abandons the anecdote after four lines and
declares rather abruptly:

> Cette aventure en soi, sans aller plus avant,
> Peut servir de leçon à la plupart des hommes.

then follows a long metaphysical meditation of great poetic value which
La Fontaine ends no less abruptly with the pedestrian remark:

> Je m'emporte un peu trop; revenons à l'histoire
> De ce spéculateur, qui fut contraint de boire.

The elementary form of such transitions, of which *bref* is the most
rudimentary, contrasts significantly with the subtlety of those he uses

---

[1] Rémond de Saint-Mard, *Réflexions sur la fable*, in *Œuvres*, The Hague, 1734, vol. III,
pp. 116–17.
[2] IV, 1; IV, 22; XI, 6; XI, 9, etc.
[3] I, 14; V, 3; V, 11; XII, 12, etc.
[4] III, 18; V, 5; V, 6; V, 8, etc.
[5] I, 9; II, 8; VII, 12; IX, 2, etc.
[6] III, 8; V, 3; VI, 6; VII, 7; VIII, 4; VIII, 16; VIII, 20; IX, 5; XII, 12, etc.
[7] III, 16, V, 18; VII, 4; VIII, 17, etc.
[8] V, 13; VIII, 12, etc.
[9] IV, 17; VI, 11; VI, 19; VIII, 1; XII, 10, etc.

when the keynote is not familiarity but wit, elegance or poetry, as is the case within the poetic meditation of the same fable or the first part of the *Discours à Madame de La Sablière*.

The voice of La Fontaine speaking *in propria persona* is not solely heard in his apostrophes and parentheses; it never fades out of the *Fables* and its warm, cheerful, sensitive intonation is also heard in the narrative and descriptive passages. A whole range of stylistic devices gives the fables a pervasive oral tone and evokes the permanent presence of the narrator: bold syneses suggest near solecisms unavoidable in improvisations:

> La caravane enfin rencontre en un passage
> Monseigneur le lion. Cela ne leur plut point.[IV,12]
>
> Dans Athènes autrefois, peuple vain et léger....[VIII,4]
>
> Voilà le verger plein de gens
> Pires que le premier....[IX,5]

So do anacolutha:

> Notre homme eût pû trouver des gens sûrs au besoin;
> Il aima mieux la terre, et prenant son compère,
> Celui-ci l'aide. Ils vont enfouir le trésor.[X,4]
>
> Et pleurés du vieillard, il grava sur leur marbre
> Ce que je viens de raconter.[(XI,8) 1]

Even at the time, such loose agreements and telescopic constructions were rejected by the purists: Bellegarde judged less bold cases with great severity:

> 'L'auteur qui s'est exprimé de la sorte a-t-il parlé régulièrement? L'âme des femmes n'est pas moins fardée que leur visage; on trouve de pareils exemples dans tous les livres; cependant ce rapport est vicieux. Visage qui est un nom substantif masculin ne peut se construire avec fardée adjectif féminin. On a beau dire qu'on sous-entend fardé; il ne suffit pas de le sous-entendre, il fallait l'exprimer ou chercher un autre tour; je le passerai dans la conversation où les manières abrégées sont d'un grand secours; mais il faut être plus correct dans un livre.'[2]

---

[1] Stendhal writes of the latter anacoluthon: 'Divin style qui peint tout; et qui, supprimant les vaines particules, rapproche le Francais de langues anciennes.' Stendhal, *Pensées*, Divan, Paris, 1931, vol. I, p. 103.

[2] J.-B. Morvan de Bellegarde, *Réflexions sur l'élégance et la politesse du style*, p. 231. Cf. Racine, *Phèdre*, *l*, 3, l. 234:
> Songez-vous qu'en naissant mes bras vous ont reçue?

Dangeau wrote of the participle:

'Les dépendances du verbe ... se doivent toujours rapporter au substantif qui fait le sujet de la proposition, ainsi je dirai bien "en entrant chez moi j'ai trouvé mon cousin malade", parce que c'est moi qui suis le sujet de la proposition et qui ai trouvé mon cousin malade, mais si je dis, "en entrant chez moi mon suisse m'a donné un livre", je parlerai mal, parce que le sujet de la proposition est mon suisse, et que je ne veux pas dire que c'est mon suisse qui entrait au logis, mais que c'est moi qui y entrais.'[1]

Historic infinitives and nominal sentences make the narrative sound like the first-hand account of an event taking place under the narrator's very eyes. These devices are often combined with others also characteristic of a familiar style, such as the ethic and affective possessive and dative:

Et mon chat de crier, et le rat d'accourir. . . .[VIII,22]

Voilà mon âne à l'eau. . . .[II,10]

The ethic possessive is often in the first person plural, and thus the reader is somehow associated with the telling of the fable: when La Fontaine writes 'notre baudet[VIII,17], notre laitière[VII,9], nos deux Messieurs'[IX,9], he assumes that our vision of these characters is as precise as his own, that they have become old acquaintances of ours as well as of his. The link which normally exists between an artist, his work and his public is, in the *Fables*, exploited by La Fontaine, and becomes yet another component of his intricate technique. The ethic dative, a pronoun in the second person plural, is a typical feature of oral, familiar style; it emphasizes a statement by means of an apostrophe to the listener. La Fontaine uses it frequently and even combines it with the ethic possessive:

. . . On vous happe notre homme,
On vous l'échine, on vous l'assomme.[XII,22]

It is remarkable that the dative, in the *Fables*, is used almost exclusively with verbs of action implying the sudden use of physical strength, or motivated by a sudden brutal decisions:

Aussitôt fait que dit: le fidèle émoucheur
Vous empoigne un pavé. . . .[VIII,10]

Il vous prend sa cognée, il vous tranche la bête . . .[VI,13]

[1] Dangeau, *Réflexions sur la grammaire française*, in *Opuscules sur la grammaire*, ed. Manne Ekman, Uppsala, 1927, p. 138.

... Les fils vous retournent le champ.[V,9]

Il vous prend un levier, met en pièces l'idole. ... .[IV,8]

Elle en dit tant, que Monsieur, à la fin,
Lassé d'entendre un tel lutin,
Vous la renvoie à la campagne. ... .[VII,2]

Et d'Indou qu'il était on vous le fait Lapon.[VII,5]

La Fontaine also uses more subtle devices: at times, for example, he exploits the ambiguity of certain constructions more or less related to the *style indirect libre*.[1] The absence of an introductory verb of speech or opinion makes it impossible for the reader to decide whether the statement concerned is La Fontaine's own or the reported speech or thought of his characters. Thus, the voice of the poet is heard at least as a possible alternative to that of the character: does the line:

Pauvres gens, idiots, couple ignorant et rustre[III,1]

transcribe La Fontaine's opinion of the miller and his son, or the abuse shouted by 'le premier qui les vit'?

... Et la nuit,
Si quelque chat faisait du bruit,
Le chat prenait l'argent. ... .[VIII,2]

Is this fantastic accusation meant to be taken as a *mot de nature* to measure the cobbler's obsession, or is it merely an ironical comment of the poet? The passage:

Le moine disait son bréviaire:
Il prenait bien son temps! Une femme chantait;
C'était bien de chansons qu'alors il s'agissait![VII,8]

may be read as a description enlivened by the author's sarcastic comments or as a circumstantial record of the fly's grievances. Such ambiguities are not rare in the *Fables*;[2] in each case, the reader may well show a preference for one alternative but cannot reject the other altogether, and the poet's voice will always harmonize with that of his characters. In *Le Pouvoir des fables*[VIII,4], La Fontaine illustrates the intersection of the

---

[1] Free indirect speech, Cf. R. Quirk, *The Use of English*, London, 1962, pp. 248–9.
[2] Cf. XI, 6, 'Car comment remonter. ...'; V, 6, 'De çà, de là, vous en aurez ...', etc. See Marguerite Lips, *Le style indirect libre*, Paris, 1926, pp. 130–48; and Jan Adriaan Verschoor, *Étude de grammaire historique et de style sur le style direct et les styles indirects en Français*, Groningen, 1959, p. 39.

two planes, that of the fable and that of the telling of the fable, in a striking manner. Here, we are privileged to be shown a fable in the making: La Fontaine's fabulist, particularly eager to draw and retain the attention of his frivolous audience, first uses some of La Fontaine's own mannerisms: he chooses a verbal phrase instead of a plain verb, and, when the narrative reaches its climax, the verb tenses change from past to historic present. Then, the fictitious fabulist addresses his public *in propria persona*, but with words which he attributes to Cérès, his heroine. The blending of these various voices is made yet more complex since we are dealing with a fable within a fable, of which La Fontaine is, in fact, sole author.

3. SYMPATHY

La Fontaine's range of moods, feelings and emotions when familiarly speaking *in propria persona* is extremely varied. On each occasion, the poet chooses the means of expression best suited to the nature of the confidence. For practical reasons, we shall limit our study to his technique in the expression of sympathy; this feeling is often present in the *Fables* and, whereas it is always expressed with the utmost discretion and delicacy, it constitutes one of the characteristic and most attractive aspects of our poet's personality. It also qualifies his familiarity and makes it totally different from that of *burlesque* writers. La Fontaine often reveals his sympathy towards some of his characters by means of a single adjective. Adjectives are relatively rare in the *Fables* so that even the seemingly most banal have, when used, a rich significance. The poet's sympathy for the victims, his reprobation of their tormentors are obvious when he writes of 'les deux pauvres servantes[V,6], le pauvre baudet si chargé qu'il succombe[VI,16], la pauvre aragne n'ayant plus que la tête et les pieds[X,6], cette bête cruelle, cet animal plein de rage'[I,10], etc. This sympathy extends to the representatives of the vegetable kingdom: 'la pauvre haie[IV,4], le pauvre potager[ibid.], ces pauvres habitants [i.e. trees]'[XII,20]. A diminutive often produces a similar effect:

> L'oiseleur repartit: ce petit animal
> T'en avait-il fait davantage?[VI,15]

'Le pauvret[IV,16], le pauvre carpillon[V,3], leur chère et fidèle compagne, pauvre chevrette'[XII,15], such are the endearing terms by which La Fontaine refers to trapped animals.

The expression of sympathy towards ill-fated characters was tolerated even on the part of historians. Du Plaisir writes of these adjectives which 'semblent bien moins être une louange qu'une de ces caresses naturelles que les honnêtes gens font aux personnes qui n'ont point mérite d'être malheureuses; et d'ailleurs les lecteurs attendris sont très satisfaits, pour avoir moins de honte de leur faiblesse, de trouver dans l'historien même un compagnon de leur pitié.'[1]

In La Fontaine, his sympathy is not even denied to unworthy characters in their predicament: thus, the wolf, although avowedly determined to devour children at the first opportunity, becomes 'la pauvre bête'[IV,16] when he meets his death. The resemblance of idiom, 'étouffer la pauvre bête'[IV,19], assommer la pauvre bête'[IV,16], in different fables, where different characters of contrasting moral standards come to a just or unjust end, shows that La Fontaine's sympathy is a reaction due to his sensitiveness rather than to a discriminative ethical judgement. The wolf masquerading as a shepherd becomes 'le pauvre loup'[III,3] when unmasked, the redoubtable fox is, in different fables, 'le pauvre écourté'[V,5] and 'le pauvret'[XII,23] when defeated and ridiculed; even a deceived and disappointed thief is referred to as 'le pauvre voleur'[X,4].

The delicacy of the poet's sympathy is often matched by the subtlety of its expression: La Fontaine shows discretion even in such obvious devices as parentheses: after the return of the unfortunate pigeon, he concludes:

Voilà nos gens rejoints; et je laisse à juger
De combien de plaisirs ils payèrent leurs peines.[IX,2]

Here, the plural has an affective value: one pigeon only travelled and faced a series of ordeals. Yet the anxiety and loneliness of the other who awaited his home-coming are equated to the former's tribulations; they shared their sufferings, just as they now share their pleasure. Thus, the preterition proves most evocative, the plural affective and, to a certain extent, poetic. Sometimes, the poet adds affective touches to the picture by means of an antithesis, a gradation, or a correction:

La soeur de Philomèle, attentive à sa proie,
Malgré le bestion happait mouches dans l'air,
Pour ses petits, pour elle, impitoyable joie.[X,6]

Whilst the precision, 'joie pour ses petits, pour elle', insists on the pleasant aspect of the scene, the swallow feeding its young, the adjective *impitoyable* evokes its consequences disastrous for the starved spider. The gradations:

[1] Du Plaisir, *Sentiments sur les Lettres et sur l'Histoire, avec des scrupules sur le style*, Paris, 1683, pp. 133-4.

Ses œufs, ses tendres œufs, sa plus douce espérance. . . .[II,8]

Gâtait jusqu'aux boutons, douce et frêle espérance,
Avant-coureurs des biens que promet l'abondance.[IX,5]

. . . Il s'enfuit par un trou,
Non pas trou, mais trouée, horrible et large plaie
Que l'on fit à la pauvre haie . . .[IV,4]

have the compelling value of incantations to avert fate, and the moving quality of a poetic lament.

The importance of these manifestations of the author's sympathy is great indeed: La Fontaine's interventions in the course of the fables, however discreet, often qualify the traditional moral, attenuate its brutal simplicity and give it the flexibility and the charm of a tolerant and philosophical observation of human nature. It would be difficult indeed to analyse the twist given to the traditional moral interpretation of an apologue by the poet's *bonhomie*, more successfully than Clarac, when he writes of the line from *La Cigale et la Fourmi:*

C'est là son moindre défaut:

'Le tour a disparu de l'usage; il équivaut à: "C'est le défaut qu'elle a le moins"; entendez qu'elle ne l'a à aucun degré. On saisit la malice: pour la fourmi, prêter est un défaut, le plus grand défaut qui soit, celui dont elle se défendrait au besoin avec indignation. Voilà sa ladrerie tournée en ridicule. L'apologue ésopique ne tendait qu'à blâmer l'imprévoyance; il donnait le dernier mot à la dure ménagère. D'un sourire, La Fontaine fait du lecteur son complice et remet les choses au point.'[1]

Pascal had remarked: 'Le cœur a son ordre; l'esprit a le sien, qui est par principe et démonstration';[2] La Fontaine, a rarity among moralists, chose the former. From the aesthetic point of view, the voice of the poet, heard throughout the *Fables*, conversing freely in a friendly familiar tone is the chief element of unity in this collection of 242 distinct poems. 'Le favole non sono scritte ma piuttosto dette', this judgement of Lugli[3] sums up what makes La Fontaine's *Fables* an achievement unique in classical literature.

[1] P. Clarac, *La Fontaine par lui-même*, p. 160. See also Grammont, *Psychologie linguistique: style et poésie*, Paris, 1950, p. 202.
[2] Pascal, *Pensées*, ed. Brunschvicg, item 283, p. 460.
[3] V. Lugli, *Il Prodigio di La Fontaine*, p. 237.

CHAPTER IV

HUMOUR

THE popular origin of the traditional fable accounts for conventions which must be accepted if one is to enjoy it: the improbable assumption that animals can talk, the gratuitous assimilation of our own behaviour to that of animals, incredible behaviour at that. When used solely as an illustration for the purpose of elementary moral teaching, the original fable requires little adaptation: its simplicity enhances its didactic value. However, to turn it into a poetic genre and a work of art was a more difficult undertaking, the refined French readers to which it would be addressed being more sceptical than either the very young or the rustic public of the traditional fable. Yet La Fontaine did not attempt to alter these conventions: in his *Fables*, animals behave as they do only in the world of fables, where foxes feed on grapes, and cows, goats and ewes associate with lions to trap stags.[1]

It is in tone and style, rarely in invention, that La Fontaine shows originality. On the one hand, as we have already remarked,[2] the poet accepts all the conventions of the popular fable and even stresses its naïve and rustic aspects; on the other, he stands apart from the subject and makes his readers perceive a whole texture of far more sophisticated elements beneath the apparent simplicity of the genre: these, to La Fontaine, are the components of *la gaieté*. They are not solely *ornements* but also all manner of *traits*.[3] It is understandable that his declared intention of introducing the former into the fable incurred the disapproval of Patru[4] who, at that early stage, could hardly expect anything more than a rhetorical amplification of the ancient apologue. In fact, the poet, following his natural inclination[5] and the contemporary taste for subtlety, was to include the ingredient of humour in his particular kind of *gaieté*. The naïve apologues, the rich composite language, the popular and familiar tone of the *Fables* did not necessarily imply the addition of a touch of humour; indeed, the didactic connotations of the genre seemed to preclude it. Yet the presence of these elements and the impression of informality which they gave

---

[1] *Fables*, II, 1; III, 11; I, 6; etc.   [2] See ch. I.
[3] See ibid.   [4] *Fables*, Preface, vol. I, p. 7.
[5] *Psyché*, O.D., p. 173; *A Son Altesse Sérénissime Mgr le Prince de Conti*, ibid., pp. 697–8. *Fables*, XII, 28. *l*. 300.

created the most suitable conditions for a humorous treatment. Méré, anticipating Bergson, writes:

> 'Pour ce qui est du rire, il aime à surprendre; et ceux qui promet-tent d'être plaisants ne le sont jamais; ce qu'on peut faire pour y disposer, c'est d'inspirer de la joie et d'éloigner tout ce qui paraît triste et sombre.'[1]

Both this humour due to surprise and 'l'autre qui réjouit l'âme intérieure-ment et fait rire plus efficacement parce qu'il est fondé sur la raison'[2] are to be found combined in the *Fables*. An undercurrent of manifold allusions can be seen running parallel with the moral anecdote to which it constitutes an ironical commentary. This superimposition perceptible to the cultured reader produces a very complex effect; the *Fables* can be understood and enjoyed on distinct levels: that of moral apologues relieved by a tone of light-hearted familiarity and that of a collection of poems distinguished by an ingenious and witty use of all the resources of a complex choice of words, a smooth combination of seemingly irreconcil-able styles and humorous literary allusions. Thus the *Fables*, like most of La Fontaine's other works, do not cause laughter but rather a series of knowing smiles. The lighter aspect of his *gaieté* is akin to modern humour and often to wit; it is, for the most part, of a literary nature and not with-out relationship with Voiture's *enjouement* although it is neither so laboured nor so gratuitous. It appeals to the more refined reader without diminishing the pleasure of the less sophisticated. The anonymous author of *Connaissance des beautés et des défauts de la poésie et de l'éloquence* hinted at this universality of appeal when he remarked:

> 'Je ne connais guère de livre plus rempli de ces traits qui sont faits pour le peuple, et de ceux qui conviennent aux esprits les plus délicats; aussi je crois que de tous les auteurs La Fontaine est celui dont la lecture est d'un usage plus universel.'[3]

We cannot but agree with Haraszti when he says that 'on doit regretter

---

[1] Méré, Letter IV, *A Madame la Duchesse de Lesdiguières*, in *Lettres de Monsieur le Cheva-lier de Méré*, Paris, 1682, vol. I, p. 28. See also Pellisson, *Discours sur les œuvres de M. Sarasin*, in Sarasin, *Œuvres*, p. 18: '... Car comme rien ne fait rire que ce qui surprend, rien ne divertit agréablement que ce qu'on n'attendrait pas', and Marguerite Buffet, *Nouvelles observations sur la langue française*, Paris, 1668, p. 170; '... Comme le plaisir assaisonne toutes choses, le discours ne peut être agréable et éloquent s'il ne brille de tant d'esprit que nous en soyons surpris.'

[2] Monchesnay, *Bolœana*, pp. 86–8.

[3] This book is attributed to Voltaire, elsewhere so often unjust to La Fontaine and imper-vious to his poetic charm. In Voltaire, *Œuvres Complètes*, vol. XLIII, Paris, 1821, pp. 70–1.

qu'il manque encore une étude spéciale du rire chez La Fontaine'.[1] It is true that since this was written, an article of J. Barchilon and Madame de Mourgues's remarkable work have enlightened us on the subject.[2] Their conclusions can be summed up in the words of Bellessort: 'Il faut bien reconnaitre que le naturel de son comique vient encore plus de l'art que de la connaissance de la nature'.[3] To trace and analyse the ingredients of this elevated and discreet form of humour is the aim of this chapter.

Seventeenth-century critics acknowledged and analysed mainly two forms of humour: the *gaulois* and the *burlesque*, both severely censured at the time of the *Fables*; references to a more subtle comic quality particularly suited to poetry are rare[4] and, in any case, such a polished achievement as La Fontaine's is nowhere to be found at the time outside his own work. His name is associated with humour for the first time in the correspondence between Clément and a learned but anonymous, and probably fictitious, Englishman, inserted by Clément in *Les Cinq Années Littéraires ou Nouvelles Littéraires, etc. des années 1748, 1749, 1750, 1751 and 1752*, published at The Hague in 1754. The nature of humour is the subject of Letter XCIV, in which the Englishman writes:

> 'Ce que nous entendons par notre *humor* est une plaisanterie aussi naturelle que singulière, naïve même, et qui n'a rien de particulièrement opposé ni au bon goût, ni aux bienséances. . . . Chez vous, La Fontaine, Molière, Regnard, Dufresny, Lesage, Mr. Piron etc. en sont pleins.'[5]

We owe Montesquieu the first well illustrated definition of humour:

> 'L'humeur des Anglais est quelque chose qui est indépendant de l'esprit et en est distingué comme on le verra par les exemples. Cette humeur est distinguée de la plaisanterie; c'est plutôt le plaisant de la

---

[1] J. Haraszti, *En glanant chez La Fontaine*, p. 32.
[2] J. Barchilon, 'Wit and Humor in La Fontaine's Psyché', in *French Review*, XXXVI, October 1962, pp. 23–31. O. de Mourgues, *O Muse, fuyante proie . . .*, pp. 131–51. See also M. Guiton, *La Fontaine, Poet and Counterpoet*, p. 35.
[3] Bellessort, 'Réflexions sur La Fontaine', in *La Revue des Deux Mondes*, XVIII, 1913, p. 908; reprinted in '*Sur les grands chemins de la poésie classique*, Paris, 1914.
[4] See *Lettre sur le Misanthrope*, in Molière, *Œuvres*, vol. V, p. 440; Monchesnay, *Bolœana*, pp. 86–8; Guez de Balzac, *Socrate chrétien, avant-propos*, in *Œuvres*, vol. II, p. 12; Pellisson, *Discours sur les œuvres de M. Sarasin*, in Sarasin, *Œuvres*, p. 55; Méré, letters LXVIII and CLXXI, quoted by Borgerhoff, in *The Freedom of French Classicism*, pp. 94 and 98–9. See also La Fontaine's own judgement on Plautus and Terence, *O.D.*, pp. 261–2.
[5] See also review of 'Essai sur les différentes espèces du ridicule', London, 1754, in *Journal Etranger*, Avril 1755, pp. 46–65, which considers '. . . cet *humour* dont les Anglais se vantent, et qu'ils ont souvent possédé; mot dont l'explication est aussi difficile en Français, que l'imitation de la chose. Il renferme la triple idée de plaisanterie vive, enjouée et naturelle.' (p. 65)

H

plaisanterie. Ce n'est point la force comique, le [sic] vis comica;
c'est plutôt la manière de la force comique. Je la définirai, dans la
plaisanterie, la manière de rendre plaisamment les choses plaisantes,
et c'est le sublime de l'humeur, et, dans les choses ingénieuses, la
manière de rendre plaisamment les choses ingénieuses. Ce que les
images sont dans la poésie, l'humeur est dans la plaisanterie. . . . Et
la difficulté de l'humeur consiste à vous faire trouver un sentiment
nouveau, dans la chose, qui vient pourtant de la chose. . . . Dans
[l'épigramme de J. B. Rousseau] de ce moine où un pénitent vient
s'accuser d'avoir, par la vertu d'une recette, fait des choses admirables,
et à qui le moine dit:

> "Or baille-moi la joyeuse recette
> Et te promets mon absolution",

l'idée est plaisante, et l'auteur y a ajouté de l'humeur par le mot de
mon. S'il avait dit l'absolution, l'épigramme n'était plus que plaisante. Le moine dit mon absolution pour faire le troc . . . C'est un
plaisant qui est accessoire à la plaisanterie, que l'humeur; mais il faut
qu'il se trouve dans la chose même . . . Enfin l'humeur est le sentiment plaisant ajouté au sentiment plaisant, comme les épithètes sont
l'image particulière ajoutée à l'image générale.'[1]

So humour results from the surprise caused in the reader by his sudden
awareness of an additional amusing though strictly relevant implication
in an explicit statement expressed in an elegant, concise and already
amusing manner.

1. HUMOUR AND THE FABLE

La Fontaine derives many amusing effects from the intersection
of the human and the animal planes. Although accepting the basic conventions of the genre without reservations, the poet often reveals the
fascination which its symbolism has upon him: his references to mirrors,[2]
to the *double image*[3] and his treatment of the same fable on the two
distinct planes,[4] are indicative of this. The juxtaposition of *Le Héron* and
La Fille[VII,4] stresses the amusing resemblance and the contrast between

---

[1] Montesquieu, *Pensées*, in *Œuvres complètes*, ed. Masson, Paris, 1950, vol. II, pp. 437–8.
[2] I, 11.
[3] V, 1.
[4] VII, 4. X, 10 also contains the remarkable parallelism of two identical events involving,
the one animals, and the other human beings; but both actions are knit together.

human behaviour and its stylized image in the animal world of the traditional apologue. Such a clear division between the two is most unusual in La Fontaine and it here takes on the value of a demonstration: in this fable, La Fontaine lays bare one of his favourite devices, the amusing intermingling of the animal and human elements. Although this confusion is chiefly a matter of presentation of the descriptive and narrative parts of the fable, the poet also uses stylistic resources to bring it about.

The simplest device consists of juxtapositions of the type:

Un citoyen du Mans, chapon de son métier . . .,[VIII,21]

On conte qu'un serpent voisin d'un horloger . . .,[V,16]

which equate and assimilate the animal with man. It is worth noting that, in the fables, a juxtaposition is sufficient to make the equation acceptable to the reader whilst, in an altogether different context, the poet has to resort to a more explicit construction:

Les nonnes sont un étrange bétail. . . .

[Je] reviens à mes moutons,
Ces moutons, Madame, c'est Votre Altesse et Madame Mazarin.[1]

Here, the crude humour of incongruity is gratuitous and can hardly compare with the effect produced by the same device used in the *Fables*, where the incongruity of words, though still felt, is tempered and enriched by close associations of ideas obvious to all readers of fables. This anthropomorphism takes many forms and its effects are generally complex, though in one predominant tone of light humour: when Gilles, the monkey, introduces himself as

Cousin et gendre de Bertrand,
Singe du pape en son vivant,[IX,3]

the anthropomorphic elements *cousin* and *gendre* are immediately followed by a line which evokes the animal but as holder of an imaginary official function in the world of man. Commenting on the line

Un chat faisant la chattemite,[VII,15]

---

[1] *Contes*, vol. I, p. 173 (Mazet de Lamporecchio). Cf. Molière: 'Ah! les étranges animaux à conduire que des comédiens . . .' *Impromptu de Versailles*, I, in *Œuvres*, vol. III, p. 389, and *Fables*, IX, 5:
Et ne sais bête au monde pire
Que l'écolier, si ce n'est le pédant.
Also *A Madame la Duchesse de Bouillon, O.D.*, p. 670.

Rudler writes: 'Le vers traduit en langage chat ce que le [vers] précédent disait en langage homme'.[1] The perfect propriety of the word *chattemite*, the alliteration, the etymological figure and the zoological origin of a phrase elsewhere used as a metaphor with reference to human beings and here restored to its original meaning, contribute to make the comic quality of the line subtle and effective.

The activities of the animals are described in terms evoking actions specifically human and yet in keeping with their personality. When the vocabulary is precise or technical, the incongruity between action and agent becomes obvious and the latter is at the same time equated with man though still remembered as an animal:

> Le lion, pour bien gouverner,
> Voulant apprendre la morale,
> Se fit un beau jour, amener
> Le singe, maitre ès arts chez la gent animale.[XI,5]

The last words prevent the reader from being quite taken in by the serious tone of the opening lines. The poet wants us to picture the scene of the lecture on ethics but, although his teaching is perfectly sound and to be taken seriously, he does not let us forget that it is given by a monkey! If the topic is no laughing matter, at least, the contrast between the words and the speaker is amusing and 'maître ès arts chez la gent animale', is here to prevent us from missing it. Thus, the characters are never entirely assimilated to man: they are only *travestis*, a nuance which unfortunately had not been preserved by the authors of some of the numerous branches of the *Roman de Renart*, although it accounts for the charm of its medieval illustrations. A complete list of similar examples would contain most of the fables. However, the effectiveness of this technique can be just as clearly demonstrated by a glance at one of the rare fables in which it is lacking: *La Chauve-souris, le Buisson et le Canard*[XII,7]. Here we have many commercial terms whilst the characters are referred to only in a very general manner: tous trois, notre trio, nos gens, le trio. *Le buisson* is mentioned as such in line 29, *le plongeon* in line 33, *l'oiseau chauve-souris* in line 34 but the interference of the human and animal planes is nowhere perceptible. The fable leaves the reader with the impression of a good but—in spite of a few puns (le buisson accrochait les passants, le plongeon sous les eaux . . .)—humourless poem. Such fables are extremely rare in La Fontaine.

[1] G. Rudler, *L'Explication française, principes et applications*, Paris, 1948, p. 93.

The use of titles of nobility, office or address can be comic. As early as 1718, Houdart de La Motte observed that

> 'Une source du riant dans la fable, c'est de transporter aux animaux des dénominations humaines, maître corbeau, compère Renard, Sa Majesté lionne. Ce badinage dirigé par de fines convenances, a d'ailleurs son étendue et sa fécondité: comme je donne aux animaux des dénominations humaines, j'en donne de même à tout ce qui leur appartient. Leur espèce est une République; l'assemblée de plusieurs, une Diète, un Sénat; leurs instincts différents seront des Règlements et des Lois. Mascarade ingénieuse qui ne va pas à les faire méconnaître, mais seulement à nous mieux représenter en eux, et qui offre tout à la fois à l'imagination, et l'animal et l'homme joué en son nom.'[1]

This device was not entirely limited to the fable and occurred in light and *burlesque* poetry such as Tristan's *Sujet de la comédie des fleurs*:

> D'autre côté Madame Ortie,
> Qui veut être de la partie
> Avec son cousin le Chardon . . .,

and Scarron's *Requête au Roi*:

> Grand Monarque, chez qui Mesdames les Vertus
> Ont choisi leur demeure. . . .[2]

The use of such titles in the *Fables*, is not systematic but, wherever it occurs, it is always appropriate and often rich in additional implications of a humorous kind: for example, the title *Maître* 'donné aux avocats, aux docteurs, aux magistrats, aux prêtres',[3] is particularly well-suited to the black-frocked crow; the character's situation:

> Sur un arbre perché[1,2]

is, on the one hand, convincing when one thinks of the crow as a bird and, on the other, incongruous when one thinks of it as *maître*; in the same manner, the bird is fond of cheese, the learned fool of *langage fleuri*. In

[1] Houdart de La Motte, *Discours sur les fables*, in *Fables nouvelles*, Paris, 1719, p. xxxvi.
[2] Scarron, *Requête au roi*, 1643, in *Poésies diverses*, vol. I, p. 102; Tristan L'Hermite, *Les Amours et autres poésies choisies*, Paris, 1925, p. 274. See also Sarasin, *Galanterie à une dame à qui on avait donné le nom de Souris* (pre-1648), in *Œuvres*, Paris, 1926, vol I, p. 380:

> 'Aussi Mesdames les souris
> Vont chantant tout haut dans Paris. . . .'

[3] Furetière, *Dictionnaire universel*, item *Maître*.

spite of the parallelism of the first four lines which might suggest the contrary, 'Maître Renard' conjures up quite a different picture. Here, *Maître* is 'celui qui a fait son apprentissage en quelque métier'[1] and the word recalls that the traditional character attributed to the fox in the fables is that of a rogue 'passé maître en fait de tromperie'[III,5]. It also suggests that the fox is master of the situation. Finally, the word *maître* has in both cases pejorative connotations: 'se dit aussi odieusement à l'égard de ceux qui se signalent par quelque mauvaise qualité. ... Un maître sot, un maître maraud'.[2] To call a pig 'Dom Pourceau'[VIII,12] and a monkey 'Dom Bertrand'[XII,3] is to add irreverence to anthropomorphism since 'on se sert de ce mot en parlant de quelques religieux comme des Chartreux, des Célestins, des Bernardins et des Feuillants'.[3] 'Dom Coursier' suggests a horse endowed with the stature and haughtiness of a Spanish grandee. This is emphasized by the respectful manner in which, in the same fable, the wolf refers to 'Nosseigneurs les Chevaux': 'Voilà que se décline!' Philaminte would say.[4] In *La Besace*[I,7], La Fontaine uses the same term of appellation to refer to two very different animals: the elephant calls the whale which he finds too large 'Dame Baleine', this title suggesting in itself an important, and by association of ideas, a portly lady. The very next line reads:

Dame Fourmi trouva le ciron trop petit.

Here, the suggestion is identical, the ant considering itself enormous compared with a mite; yet the similarity in terms and associations contrasts amusingly with the disparity in the size of the two *Dames* concerned.[5] The most surprising:

Vous voulez de l'argent, ô Mesdames les Eaux[IV,2]

is, in the mouth of the shepherd who once fancied himself as Coridon and Tircis and has been since reduced to the state of plain Pierrot, the transposition of the 'Amphitrite' allegory in the opening lines of the fable. It implies a satirical reference to popular clichés concerning women's rapacity and could also be a sarcastic parody of extreme forms of compliments which Guez de Balzac mocks in these words:

---

[1] Richelet, *Dictionnaire français*, item *Maître*.
[2] Furetière, *Dictionnaire universel*, item *Maître*.
[3] La Touche, *L'Art de bien parler français*, Amsterdam, 1696, vol. II, p. 108.
[4] Molière, *Les Femmes savantes*, III, 3, *l.* 838. See also, *Fables*, VIII, 10, 'Nosseigneurs les ours'.
[5] See also VII, 8, 'Dame mouche'.

'Un de ces curieux lui commença il y a quelques jours sa harangue
par "le respect et la vénération qu'il avait toujours eus pour lui et
pour Messieurs ses livres". Il n'y a rien de plus historique que ceci, et
vous pouvez voir par là jusqu'où peut aller le style des compliments.'[1]

On the whole, La Fontaine's use of titles is most varied and in no way
systematic. It is true that certain animals constitute an aristocracy and
others the *bourgeoisie* and a colourful *tiers-état*; yet, within the range of
appellations pertaining to each class of society, the choice of terms, in
each case, depends on their suitability to the context and on their aesthetic
value rather than on the personality of the character. Thus, in spite of
their completely different personalities, the fox and the wolf are both in
turn 'compère, Sire, Maître', etc.[2] 'Sa Majesté lionne' becomes 'ce Monseigneur du Lion là'[VII,6] when majesty gives place to unbridled tyranny;
'Dame Belette'[VII,15] appropriates the rabbit's burrow but

> Damoiselle Belette, au corps long et fluet
> Entra dans un grenier par un trou fort étroit.[III,17]

La Fontaine's use of proper nouns often produces humorous effects:
sometimes the poet, by means of a capital letter and elision of the article,
changes a generic name into a proper noun; the effect is rather subtle. The
animal is thus individualized as a specific character and yet retains all the
features of the species:

> Capitaine Renard allait de compagnie
> Avec son ami Bouc des plus haut encornés . . .[III,5]

The effect of surprise is greater when the device is applied to an inanimate
object:

> Pot de fer son camarade
> Se met droit à ses côtés.[V,2]

But, again, La Fontaine's practice is not systematic; it varies sometimes
within the same fable and, of 242 fables, 117 have heroes referred to only
by a common noun.

La Fontaine sometimes invents amusing and appropriate names for

[1] Guez de Balzac, *Entretien VII*, 1657, in *Œuvres*, vol. II, p. 350. See also: 'J'ai laissé
Mesdemoiselles les règles à la porte, j'ai vu la comédie . . .' in Montfaucon de Villars, *La
critique de Bérénice*, Paris, 1671, Vol. I, p. 7, which called forth the comment from Racine:
'Croit-il réjouir beaucoup les honnêtes gens par ces . . . Mesdemoiselles mes règles, et quantité
d'autres basses affectations qu'il trouvera condamnées dans tous les bons auteurs, s'il se mêle
jamais de les lire.' *Bérénice*, Preface, in *Œuvres*, vol. II, p. 370.
[2] I, 18 and XI, 6; XI, 6 and VIII, 13; I, 2 and I, 5.

his characters, showing his skill in the substantivization of all parts of speech:

> Elle [la Discorde] et Que-si que-non, son frère,
> Avec Tien-et-mien son père. . . .[VI,20]

> Le médecin Tant-pis allait voir son malade
> Que visitait aussi son confrère Tant-mieux,[V,12]

grotesque figures which recall the characters of mediaeval morality plays,

> . . . Le chat Grippe-fromage,
> Triste-oiseau le hibou, Ronge-maille le rat,
> Dame Belette au long corsage . . .,[VIII,22]

where the proper nouns have also the value of Homeric epithets introducing a *burlesque* touch into the fable.

2. VARIETY OF DEVICES

La Fontaine does not hesitate to use the cruder forms of literary humour: even puns and paronomasiae are not excluded:

> *Point* froid et *point* jaloux: notez ces *deux points-ci.*[VII,4]

> Ce malheureux. . . .
> Ne possédait pas l'or, mais l'or le possédait.[IV,20]

> Belle nécessité d'interrompre *mon somme*!
> Le sort de sa plainte touché
> Lui donne un autre maître, et *l'animal de somme*
> Passe du jardinier aux mains d'un corroyeur.[VI,11]

> *Croquant* mainte volaille, *escroquant* maint fromage. . . .[IX,14]

These puns are not gratuitous but closely related to the fables; admittedly, they are not indispensable but neither do they constitute a digression and, on the contrary, they enable the poet to emphasize points which are strictly relevant, by means of a smile. In this respect, they differ from the *fantaisie verbale* which, according to Garapon, 'est essentiellement gaspillage'.[1] There is nothing approaching this in La Fontaine where the festival of puns and the seemingly futile verbosity of *La Mouche et la Fourmi*:[IV,3]

---

[1] R. Garapon, *La Fantaisie verbale et le comique dans le théâtre français du Moyen Age à la fin du XVIIème siècle*, Paris, 1957, p. 10.

Certain ajustement, dites-vous, rend jolie.
J'en conviens: il est noir ainsi que vous [the fly] et moi [the ant]
Je veux qu'il ait nom mouche; est-ce un sujet pourquoi
    Vous fassiez sonner vos mérites?
Nomme-t-on pas aussi mouches les parasites?

    Les mouches de cour sont chassées,
Les mouchards sont pendus . . .,

constitute the very point of the fable,

    Adieu: je perds le temps: laissez-moi travailler.
    Ni mon grenier ni mon armoire
    Ne se remplit à babiller.

Most appropriate to the fable is the pun based on the name of an animal first taken in its concrete meaning and immediately repeated for its metaphorical implication:

    Un vieux renard, mais des plus fins

    Sentant son renard d'une lieue. . . . [V,5]

    Il est un singe dans Paris
    À qui l'on avait donné femme.
    Singe en effet d'aucuns maris,
    Il la battait. . . .[XII,19]

    Certain ours montagnard, ours à demi léché

    Si bien que tout ours qu'il était,
    Il vint à s'ennuyer de cette triste vie.[VIII,10]

But, however ingenious, a pun or a paronomasia is more explicit than ambiguity and represents a lower form of humour. Ambiguity is more subtle since it expresses different meanings equally relevant to the given context, by means of one single word or set of words. Bouhours, who condemns puns, accepts ambiguities:

'Toutes ces raisons discréditent fort les pures équivoques parmi les personnes de bon sens. Je dis les pures équivoques, car toutes les figures qui renferment un double sens ont chacune en leur espèce

des beautés et des grâces qui les font valoir quoiqu'elles tiennent
quelque chose de l'équivoque.'[1]

Boileau, denouncing the abuse of conceits,

> Chaque mot eut toujours deux visages divers:
> La prose la reçut [la pointe] aussi bien que les vers,

tolerates it in the light genres,

> Pourvu que sa finesse, éclatant à propos,
> Roulât sur la pensée, et non pas sur les mots.[2]

Such was Voiture's *badinage* according to Callières:

> 'Je crois . . . ne pouvoir citer un meilleur modèle de cet agréable
> badinage que celui qui se trouve dans plusieurs des lettres de Voiture,
> outre le tour ingénieux qu'il y donne à ses pensées, il badine souvent
> sur les mots en se servant bien à propos de leurs différentes signi-
> fications pour s'exprimer avec plus d'agrément; il y emploie même
> quelquefois les proverbes qui ont rapport aux choses dont il parle et
> aux termes dont il s'est servi, mais il le fait d'une manière si fine et si
> naturelle qu'on peut dire qu'en cela l'adresse de l'ouvrier donne
> tout le prix à la matière qu'il met en œuvre.'[3]

Naturalness, relevance and good taste are the criteria by which ambiguities
are to be judged. Guéret attacks those who 'ramassent comme trésors
précieux, toutes les allusions et les équivoques'; Nicole agrees that 'c'est
avec beaucoup de raison qu'on traite de ridicules ceux qui les recherchent
et qui prétendent nous les faire passer pour traits d'esprit'.[4] The anonymous author of the *Préface du Recueil de poésies chrétiennes et diverses* shows
common sense in his moderation:

> 'Il y en a qui blâment généralement les équivoques et ils ont
> généralement raison; mais parmi ces sortes de figures il s'en trouve
> néanmoins qui plaisent, qui surprennent et qui éveillent l'esprit. Et
> je ne vois pas pourquoi l'on serait obligé d'être de mauvaise humeur
> pour s'accorder avec la règle qui les condamne.[5]

---

[1] D. Bouhours, *La Manière de bien penser dans les ouvrages d'esprit*, Paris, 1687, p. 22. Cf.
Vaugelas, *Remarques sur la langue française*, pp. 163-4; 'Certainement quand cette figure se
présente, et que les paroles qu'il faut nécessairement employer pour expliquer ce que l'on
veut dire font l'allusion, alors il faut la recevoir à bras ouverts et ce serait être ingrat à la
fortune et ne pas savoir prendre ses avantages que la rejeter.'
[2] Boileau, *Art poétique*, II, in *Œuvres*, vol. II, pp. 323-4.
[3] F. de Callières, *Des Bons mots et des bons contes, de leur usage, de la raillerie des Anciens,
de la raillerie et des railleurs de notre temps*, Paris, 1692, pp. 187-8.
[4] Guéret, *L'Orateur*, Paris, 1672, pp. 64-5; Nicole, *Traité de la beauté des ouvrages d'esprit
et particulièrement de l'épigramme*, Paris, 1689, pp. 33-4.
[5] *O.D.*, p. 775.

Incidentally, this statement is remarkably like those of Poliphile and Gélaste in *Psyché*, published only one year before.[1] Bouhours's analysis of equivocations which met with his approval help to understand the qualities which La Fontaine's contemporaries looked for in the device:

> 'Martial dit à Domitien: "Les peuples de votre empire parlent divers langages; ils n'ont pourtant qu'un langage lorsqu'ils disent que vous êtes le véritable père de la patrie." Voilà deux sens, comme vous voyez et deux sens qui font antithèse: parlent divers langages, n'ont qu'un langage. Ils sont tous deux vrais selon leurs divers rapports, et l'un ne détruit point l'autre. Ils s'accordent au contraire au contraire ensemble, et de l'union de ces deux sens opposés il résulte je ne sais quoi d'ingénieux qui est fondé sur le mot équivoque de *vox* en latin et de langage en français.'

> 'Une épigramme, répliqua Eudoxe, tire souvent toute sa grâce du figuré et du propre joints ensemble; et celle qui fut faite quand le Maréchal de Bassompierre sortit de la Bastille après la mort du Cardinal de Richelieu, en est un exemple:

> > Enfin dans l'arrière saison
> > La fortune d'Armand s'accorde avec la mienne.
> > France, je sors de ma prison
> > Quand son âme sort de la sienne.

> Le mot de "prison" est pris au troisième vers dans le sens propre et au dernier dans le figuré; et ce qui rend l'épigramme plus heureuse, c'est que

> > France, je sors de ma prison,

> est l'anagramme de François de Bassompierre à une lettre près.'[2]

La Fontaine certainly seems to revel in all forms of ambiguity and these are to be found in all his works, particularly in the *Fables*. He is an expert at writing statements which, behind the appearance of a straight-forward meaning, hide intricate implications or meaningful allusions. The contrast between these various levels of meaning, between the innocuous appearance of the statement and its less obvious suggestions produces a humorous effect involving surprise, hesitation as to which of the possible interpretations was meant by the author, and aesthetic

---

[1] *Psyché*, O.D., p. 173.
[2] D. Bouhours, *La Manière de bien penser . . .*, pp. 22–3 and 135.

satisfaction at the strict relevance and extreme conciseness of the device. The whole fable of *Le Satyre et le Passant*[V,7] turns on double meaning, literal and metaphorical, of the phrase 'souffler le chaud et le froid'. The phrases 'jeux de prince' in *Le Jardinier et son Seigneur*[IV,4], chair et poisson' in *La Grenouille et le Rat*[IV,11], 'traîner son lien'[1] in *Le Cheval s'étant voulu venger du Cerf*[IV,13] provide similar word-play. It is remarkable that the old proverbs provide the poet with material for many an amusing equivocation. Most of them are popular and colourful metaphors which gain new life through being given back their concrete meaning. The perfect congruence of the accepted metaphorical meaning and its new concrete application emphasizes the vivid expressive quality of what might have been, in the reader's eyes, a purely figurative cliché. Here again, surprise causes amusement:

> N'étant pas de ces rats qui les livres rongeants
> Se font savants jusque aux dents.[VIII,9]

The warning:

> Ne tombez jamais sous ma patte[III,9]

has a particularly compelling quality when uttered by a wolf. Similarly, the lines

> . . . .Le boeuf vient à pas lents.
> Quand il eût ruminé tout le cas dans sa tête. . . .,[X,1]

contain a most appropriate metaphor.

La Fontaine also gives a humorous flavour to the most ordinary language, by means of the same devices:

> . . . .Le chat qui n'en démord pas [Appendix II, *La Ligue des Rats*]

shows his stubbornness in refusing to free the mouse which he already holds between his teeth;

> Le buisson accrochait les passants. . . . [XII,7]

as a shrub but also as an unfortunate tradesman eager to increase his practice. In the following line:

> Le nouveau saint ferma sa porte[VII,3]

'le nouveau saint' may be taken as the recent enthusiastic convert or as this unheard of kind of saint, this saint of a new kind. Here, there is an

---

[1] Cf. *Fables*, ed. Radouant, Paris, 1929, p. 143, n. 1.

additional touch of impertinence since the saint is a rat. 'Ma mignonne' is
a term of endearment but, when used by the fly to address the ant[IV,3], it
also becomes, with reference to the ant's size, a term of ironical disparage-
ment. The elephant infatuated with the idea of its own importance becomes 'Sa Grandeur'[XII,21]. In *Les Grenouilles qui demandent un Roi*[III,4],
we read:

> Il leur tomba du ciel un roi tout pacifique
>
> Or c'était un soliveau
> De qui la gravité fit peur à la première,

where *gravité* implies both weight and seriousness. The ambiguity about
the chicken which

> Devait, le lendemain, être d'un grand souper

is, transposed into a humorous key, that of Agamemnon's reply in
Racine's *Iphigénie*: 'Vous y serez, ma fille'.[1] In *Le Rat qui s'est retiré du
monde*, a fable which offered much scope to La Fontaine's playfulness, we
find rich ambiguities:

> La solitude était profonde,
> S'étendant partout à la ronde[VII,3]

suggests *complete* solitude found *deep* in the core of the Dutch cheese,
whilst 'à la ronde' evokes the *spherical* aspect of the rat's retreat. Here,
these ambiguities reflect the intersection of two very distinct planes: the
poetic and the mundane. La Fontaine has found words suitable for rat
and cheese and to suggest the poetic potentiality of the theme of solitude
dear to his heart. The contrast is perceptible, humorous, but the device
of ambiguity, by virtue of its conciseness, preserves the artistic unity of
what is fundamentally a fable told in familiar style. In the words of
Margaret Guiton, 'La Fontaine . . . deliberately cultivated the ambiguities
of language'.[2]

La Fontaine also cultivated meaningful suggestions. These consist in
words and phrases chosen for the associations of ideas which they suggest
in the reader's mind. Their quality depends on the relevance of these ideas
to the fable concerned, and their study pertains to stylistic investigation
in so far as they involve a certain choice of particularly effective linguistic
elements to convey their implications. Thus, the bumptious frog which

> Envieuse, s'étend, et s'enfle, et se travaille[I,3]

[1] Racine, *Iphigénie*, II, 2, *l.* 578.
[2] M. Guiton, *La Fontaine, Poet and Counterpoet*, p. 35.

evokes a diminutive figure literally and metaphorically swelling and
bursting with pride. When the majestic oak points out to the reed that

> Le moindre vent. . . .
> Vous oblige à baisser la tête,[I,22]

it alludes to what is, to it, the state of inferiority and humble subjection
to which the reed is reduced. It also, unwittingly, anticipates the *dénouement* and its derision of the reed is, to the reader, also ironical on a different
plane. Replace the second line by

> Vous force à *remuer* la tête

and all these implications are gone. 'Sa Majesté fourrée'[VII,15] evokes the
image of a powerful, well-fed cat as well as the ermine-trimmed robes of
the judge he impersonates, and also Rabelais's *chats-fourrés* who were,
like our cat, cats, judges and rogues.[1] Numerous are the literary allusions
of this kind in the *Fables*. Others are linguistic, akin to the etymological
figure: thus, in the lines

> Dès que les chèvres ont brouté
>
> Un rocher, quelque mont pendant en précipices,
> C'est où ces dames vont promener leurs caprices,[XII,4]

the word *caprices* is particularly suitable since it derives, like *chèvre*, from
the Latin *capra*. In extreme cases, the allusion verges on impropriety of
terms and metonymy: Perette's spilled milk becomes 'sa fortune ainsi
répandue'[(VII,9)2], Jean Chouart watches the corpse

> Comme si l'on eût dû lui ravir ce trésor.[VII,10]

In fact, in adopting his characters' point of view, La Fontaine ironically
stresses the foolishness of their expectations.

Impropriety of terms is also a frequent device in the *Fables*. These
improprieties are, of course, intentional on the part of the poet and in no
way reflect unfavourably on his use of the language. On the contrary,
such is the precision and correctness of this language that a particular
effect, usually a comic one, is derived from the least of these improprieties: animals are referred to as human beings and we have seen how
La Fontaine succeeds in mingling the vocabulary pertaining to both,
whether he speaks of cockerels as 'ces gens'[X,7], makes the fly proclaim:
'Je m'assieds à la table'[IV,3], or comments on one of his characters:

> Ce loup ne savait pas encor bien son métier.[IX,10]

---

[1] Rabelais, *Pantagruel*, V, ch. XI, ed. Moland, pp. 504 sqq.
[2] Cf. also 'la dame de ces biens' (ibid.), where these *biens* are only imaginary ones.

There are also many improprieties beside those which are, in any case, indispensable in a fable. Some are simple but effective: the hollowed out Dutch cheese is called 'l'hermitage'[VII,3], an attempted suicide is the subject of unsympathetic treatment:

> Il y porte une corde, et veut avec un clou
> Au haut d'un certain mur attacher le licou [i.e. the noose][IX,16]

no worse than that suffered by a patient at the hands of his doctors:

> Ce dernier [doctor] espérait quoique son camarade
> Soutînt que le gisant irait voir ses aïeux.[V,12]

Since Richelet thus defines *gisant*: 'Vieux mot qui signifiait autrefois être couché. Maintenant il ne se dit plus que des morts qui sont dans le sépulcre',[1] it might be argued, of course, that La Fontaine meant the word to be understood in its archaic sense. It would seem more in accordance with his usual practice, that he was fully aware of the ambiguity and chose to let it stand. Indeed, often impropriety is combined with other devices to achieve greater complexity: 'Le pendu ressuscite'[III,18] is the more striking since the cat neither really hanged nor died. When the donkey 'se plaint en son patois', the impropriety stresses the assimilation of the yokel to his ass:

> Le plus âne des trois n'est pas celui qu'on pense.[III,1]

In all these cases, far from constituting a riddle, the impropriety contributes to draw our attention to some important point of the anecdote. The only unmistakable riddle due to this device is required by the subject of *Le Cochet, le Chat et le Souriceau*[VI,5] in which the improprieties and approximations found in the description of the cock, 'une sorte de bras' etc., give the most precise idea of the young mouse's ignorance. This passage is probably a parody of Saint-Amant's portrait of Neptune:

> Il a le corps fait comme nous
> Sa tête à la nôtre pareille
>
> Sa voix a frappé mon oreille
> Son bras d'écailles est couvert
>
> Bref à nous si fort il ressemble
> Que j'ai pensé parler à lui
>
> Il porte un pennache superbe . . .[2]

---

[1] Richelet, *Dictionnaire français*, item *gisant*.
[2] Saint-Amant, *Le Contemplateur*, in *Œuvres poétiques*, Paris, 1930, pp. 14–15.

In his use of impropriety, La Fontaine succeeds, as usual, in expressing complex notions by means of extreme conciseness. For example, in the lines:

> Le loup quelques jours écoulés
> Revient voir si son chien n'est point meilleur à prendre[IX,10]

and:

> Mon galant ne songeait qu'à bien prendre son temps
> Afin de happer son malade,[V,8]

the possessive betrays wishful thinking on the part of the wolf who sees himself as already having secured his prey. In the latter case, the effect is rendered more subtle as the wolf is not a doctor and the horse is not suffering from any ailment, and, in this accumulation of tricks, the confidence of the main trickster is going to be cruelly disappointed. Elsewhere, a demonstrative produces a similar effect:

> Il obtint qu'on rendrait à ces Grecs leur figure.[XII,1]

The demonstrative points to a motley collection of animals into which Ulysses's companions have been metamorphosed and stresses the comic discrepancy between their appearance and their human nature.

Antiphrasis, also used by La Fontaine, is but an extreme form of impropriety: the ironical judgement which it implies is usually fairly obvious, as when the poet calls the donkey's braying 'chant gracieux'[IV,5] or the frog 'notre bonne commère' whilst it tries to drown its host

> Contre le droit des gens, contre la foi jurée.[IV,11]

Antiphrasis often conveys implications of pseudo-naïvety which, handled with skill, may be devastating. Thus, the courteous reply of the reed is rich in innuendoes:

> Votre compassion, . . .
> Part d'un bon naturel. . . . [I,22]

When La Fontaine apologizes for his precision

> A ces mots, l'animal pervers
> (C'est le serpent que je veux dire,
> Et non l'homme . . .),[X,1]

arguing that 'on pourrait aisément s'y tromper', he adds insult to injury
since he stresses even more strongly the assimilation of man to a dangerous animal. Bouhours observed that

> 'On peut tout dire en riant, et même si vous y prenez garde, le
> faux devient vrai à la faveur de l'ironie: c'est elle qui a introduit ce
> que nous appelons contre-vérités.'[1]

La Fontaine's taste for subtle ambiguities sometimes makes his ironical
antiphrases difficult to perceive. Haraszti shows how debatable are the
interpretations given of the poet's ideas and ethics:

> 'L'humour s'inspire, chez notre poète, d'une ironie pessimiste qui
> d'une part condamne nos faiblesses et nos vices, d'autre part les fait
> comprendre sinon pardonner. ... La condamnation, chez lui, comme
> en général chez les humoristes, prend souvent la forme ironique d'un
> prétendu applaudissement, l'auteur faisant semblant d'applaudir
> comme une sagesse ce qu'il veut mettre au pilori. C'est ainsi qu'il
> faut entendre les vers célébres sur la tergiversation politique qu'on
> a avec Régnier souvent expliqués au préjudice du caractère moral du
> poète:
>
> > Le sage dit, selon les gens:
> > Vive le roi, vive la ligue.'[II,5]

and the critic adds, quoting the lines

> > ... Et, lui sage, il leur dit:
> > Point de courroux, Messieurs, mon lopin me suffit:
> > Faites vôtre profit du reste,

of the fable VIII,7 in which the 'wise' dog squanders his master's lunch,
'malgré la protestation du commentaire de Régnier, on doit bien voir de
l'ironie, de l'humour dans cette épithète.'[2]

A form of eulogistic writing is closely related to antiphrasis: it is that
which extols qualities which, real though they may be, are completely
irrelevant to the subject or the situation and form with it a comic contrast: in the following examples, it suggests the sarcastic tone of the
threatened chicken:

> Et ce beau cuisinier armé d'un long couteau ...,[VIII,21]

and of the spiteful wolf:

---

[1] D. Bouhours, *La Manière de bien penser dans les ouvrages d'esprit*, p. 29.
[2] Haraszti, *En glanant chez La Fontaine*, pp. 104–5.

I

Que quelque jour ce beau marmot
Vienne au bois cueillir la noisette . . .[IV,16]

The adjective, on the whole rare in La Fontaine, has in such cases a particular importance and sets the tone of the sentence.

Periphrases are, technically speaking, an elaborate form of impropriety and, as such, may cause an effect of amused surprise; the elements which constitute them lend themselves to comic or humorous treatment and allow the poet to contrive additional effects of impertinence: 'De ces gens nommés médecins'[III,8], or incongruity: 'La femme du lion mourut'[VIII,14]. If a similar periphrasis may be tolerated in the elevated style of *La Captivité de saint Malc*,

La cruelle moitié du monstre de Lybie,

it is only because all its terms have been transposed in the same style thereby avoiding any incongruity of words.[1] The comic and aesthetic value of a periphrasis may be easily assessed by restoring the *mot propre*, *la lionne, ces médecins*, in the sentence and then comparing it with the original text. In the examples, the suppression of the periphrasis results in the loss of the contrast *femme-lion* and of the doubt concerning the genuineness of the doctors. The chief quality of La Fontaine's humorous periphrases is their strict relevance to the characters, the circumstances, the implications of the fable: 'des bêtes à laine' insists on the nature of the shepherd's fortune and, in different words, repeats the opening line:

Du rapport d'un troupeau dont il vivait sans soins . . .[IV,2]

The religious reference

Et qui ne connaissait l'Avent ni le Carême,[IV,11]

applied to the fat rat together with the title of *Messire*, given to clerics, evokes the rotund monkish figure of the *gaulois* tradition. 'L'habitant des forêts'[IV,21] contrasts significantly with 'cette étable' where the stag believes that he has found shelter and where he is in fact trapped.

. . . Ce parasite ailé
Que nous avons mouche appelé[VIII,10]

is a more complex creation: the length of the periphrasis contrasts with the size of the insect; the fly is also introduced as it is seen by the bear: to him, it is first a nuisance to be driven off and then, a winged nuisance, omnipresent, swift, difficult to catch. Rudler would say that the fly is first mentioned 'en langage ours' and then 'en langage homme'.

---

[1] *Poème de la captivité de saint Malc*, O.D., p. 58.

Litotes or understatement is very common in the *Fables*; La Fontaine exploits the contrast between the nature of the real fact and the restrained manner in which he describes it. This device gives an impression of complete control, on the part of the poet, over his material and means of expression; thus, it draws the reader's attention to the presence of the writer behind his text and, in the *Fables*, litotes are often found in La Fontaine's familiar parentheses to which they add a touch of humorous *bonhomie*:

> Éconduire un lion rarement se pratique[IV,12]
>
> Grenouilles à mon sens ne raisonnaient pas mal[VI,12]
>
> Les jardins parlent peu. . . .[VIII,10]

A cruder kind of humour results from the contrast between a litotes and the repetition of the idea in a brutal and impertinent manner:

> -Si tôt? Etes-vous sage?
> Repartit l'animal léger.
> Ma commère, il vous faut purger
> Avec quatre grains d'ellébore.[VI,10]

Euphemism is a kind of litotes aiming at attenuating the statement of an unpleasant fact. La Fontaine excels at such transpositions which enable him to draw humorous effects from the contrast between the meaning implied and the additional suggestions due to the means chosen for its expression. To take only one example, here are some oblique references to death; each time, the tone of the euphemistic periphrasis is well-suited to the circumstances, the character or the whole fable: with the equanimity of one not personally concerned, the doctor

> Soutint que le gisant irait voir ses aïeux.[V,12]

The drunkard, fearing that he may be dead, is far more cautious in his conclusion:

> Oh, dit-il, qu'est ceci? Ma femme est-elle veuve?[III,7]

Death himself alludes to an old man's protest and ironically quotes the centenarian's evasive phraseology:

> Je devrais, ce dis-tu, te donner quelque avis
> Qui te disposât à la chose . . .[VIII,1]

In *Le Bassa et le Marchand*[VIII,18], a euphemism contributes to evoking the eastern background:

Et le bassa du tout est averti.
Même on lui dit qu'il jouera, s'il est sage,
    A ces gens quelque méchant parti,
Les prévenant, les chargeant d'un message
Pour Mahomet, droit en son paradis.

When the thieves drown in 'l'onde noire', we are told that

Tous deux au Styx allèrent boire.[VIII,23]

Vultures and pigeons fight a deadly battle in mid-air:

. . . Les deux troupes éprises
D'ardent courroux n'épargnaient nuls moyens
De peupler l'air que respirent les ombres.[VII,7]

Elsewhere, the humour often is due to the discrepancy between the pain
of death and its figurative representation which implies a light-hearted
and mocking comment:

Sa grimace déplut. Le monarque irrité
L'envoya chez Pluton faire le dégoûté.[VII,6]

Un citoyen du Mans, chapon de son métier,
    Etait sommé de comparaître
    Par devant les lares du maître,
Au pied d'un tribunal que nous nommons foyer.[VIII,21]

Here, the contrast between the reassuring homely ideas associated by man
with the word *foyer* and the culinary connotations which the very same
word has for the chicken is very entertaining. So is the shrewd old cat's
promise to the mice:

. . . Vos cavernes creuses
Ne vous sauveront pas, je vous en avertis;
Vous viendrez toutes au logis.[III,18]

As for the definition of a prey by the wolf 'rempli d'humanité' and about
to become vegetarian,

Et bien, ne mangeons plus de chose ayant eu vie,[X,5]

ironically, it reflects both the cruelty ('ayant eu vie') and the guilelessness
('chose') of the law of nature.

Simpler devices are often used with the maximum of effect. Surprise

also causes amusement when it results from the sharp anticlimax of a
sentence ending on a short word set 'en rejet';

> L'homme au trésor arrive et trouve son argent
> Absent.[IX,16]

Here, the anticlimax is also stressed by the combination of incompatible
terms *trouve, absent*, which expresses the disappointment of the man's
expectation admirably. The lines:

> C'est promettre beaucoup; mais qu'en sort-il souvent?
> Du vent[V,10]

produce a similar effect by the same device. Sometimes, the effect is
slightly different: in the following example, the irony comes from the
contrast between the serious and learned tone of the first line and the
ludicrous restriction implied in the second:

> Et le gouvernement de la chose publique
> Aquatique.[IV,11]

The range of possibilities offered by this device is well illustrated by the
contradictory comments made by perceptive critics on the lines

> Même il m'est arrivé quelquefois de manger
> Le berger.[VII,1]

Some see in the *rejet* an attempt to indicate a change in the lion's voice in
order to pass quickly and discreetly over the shocking admission; others
argue that the change of tone indicated here stresses the deed of which
the lion is most proud.[1]

Sometimes, La Fontaine even draws amusing effects from his handling
of grammatical forms, as when, like Scarron, Racan and Cotin, he treats
an impersonal verb as a personal one:

> . . . Notre homme
> Tranche du roi des airs, pleut, vente, et fait en somme
> Un climat pour lui seul . . .,[VI,4]

or when he uses alternative constructions in one and the same line to
suggest a quarrel more vividly:

> L'un voulait le garder; l'autre le voulait vendre.[I,13]

A simple plural may sometimes be rich in implications:

> Quand la marierons-nous? Quand aurons-nous *des gendres?*[IV,4]

---

[1] Chamfort, quoted by Régnier, la Fontaine, *Œuvres*, vol. II, p. 96, n. 19; Clarac, *La
Fontaine par lui-même*, pp. 165–6.

A full treatment of the sources of humour in the *Fables* would entail
many repetitions of points already dealt with incidentally in the preceding
chapters. It should be sufficient to recall that archaic or popular vocabulary provides the poet with an inexhaustible supply of material for playful
expression. In the words of Le Hir, 'au dix-septième siècle, utiliser un
mot archaïque, sans l'accompagner d'un sourire, est une faute de style.'[1]
This is a fault to which La Fontaine is not prone:

> La galande fit chère lie,
> Mangea, rongea, Dieu sait la vie,
> Et le lard qui périt en cette occasion.[III,17]

> Un chat nommé Rodilardus
> Faisait de rats telle déconfiture
> Que l'on n'en voyait presque plus,
> Tant il en avait mis dedans la sépulture.[II,2]

Set phrases and proverbs are recast in an amusing manner:

> Nos galants y voyaient double profit à faire,
> Leur bien premièrement, et puis le mal d'autrui.[IX,17]

> ... Tous les enfants
> Qui sont passés entre vos dents
> N'avaient-ils ni père ni mère?[X,12]

> Il mangeait plus que trois. ...[VIII,18]

Here, the reader cannot fail to enjoy the appropriate variations on *le bien
d'autrui*, *passer entre les mains de q.qn.*, and *manger comme quatre*.

Often, the devices which introduce familiarity and informality into the
Fables also give a humorous or an ironic undertone: parentheses often
produce this double effect:

> Dindenaut prisait moins ses moutons qu'eux leur ours:
> Leur, à leur compte, et non à celui de la bête.[V,20]

> Deux vrais amis vivaient au Monomotapa:
> L'un ne possédait rien qui n'appartînt à l'autre.
> Les amis de ce pays-là
> Valent bien, dit-on, ceux du nôtre.[VIII,11]

---

[1] Le Hir, *Rhétorique et stylistique de la Pléiade au Parnasse*, p. 74.

Une souris tomba du bec d'un chat-huant:
Je ne l'eusse pas ramassée;
Mais un Bramin le fit, je le crois aisément:
Chaque pays a sa pensée.
La souris était fort froissée:
De cette sorte de prochain
Nous nous soucions peu . . .,[IX,7]

so does this impertinent conclusion to the moral of *Les Vautours et les Pigeons*[VII,7]:

Ceci soit dit en passant. Je me tais.

Preterition, restrictions and corrections may serve a similar purpose:

Il est assez de geais à deux pieds comme lui,
Qui se parent souvent des dépouilles d'autrui,
Et que l'on nomme plagiaires.
Je m'en tais; et ne veux leur causer nul ennui;
Ce ne sont pas là mes affaires.[IV,9]

Un point sans plus tenait le galant empêché:
Il nageait quelque peu; mais il fallait de l'aide.[IV,11]

Un mari fort amoureux,
Fort amoureux de sa femme . . .[IX,15]

In fact, La Fontaine resorts to practically all the figures of thought, speech and style to diffuse his humour through the *Fables*; repetition:

J'ouvrirais pour si peu le bec! Aux dieux ne plaise!
Il l'ouvrit pour bien moins . . .,[VII,4]

parallelism:

Un mort s'en allait tristement
S'emparer de son dernier gîte;
Un curé s'en allait gaîment
Enterrer ce mort au plus vite.[VII,10]

Entre la veuve d'une année
Et la veuve d'une journée
La différence est grande . . .,[VI,21]

gradations:

> Le rat devait aussi renvoyer, pour bien faire,
> La belle au chat, le chat au chien,
> Le chien au loup . . .,[IX,7]

anticlimax:

> Il fit parler les morts, tonna, dit ce qu'il put.
> Le vent emporta tout; personne ne s'émut,[VIII,4]

antithesis:

> Et mon chat de crier, et le rat d'accourir,
> L'un plein de désespoir, et l'autre plein de joie,[VIII,22]

comparison:

> Les sages quelquefois, ainsi que l'écrevisse,
> Marchent à reculons . . .,[XII,10]

metaphor:

> Le réveille-matin eut la gorge coupée,[V,6]

metonymy:

> Trafiqua de l'argent, le mit entier sur l'eau;
> Cet argent périt par naufrage,[IV,2]

zeugma:

> Voilà mes chiens à boire; ils perdirent l'haleine,
> Et puis la vie . . ., [VIII,25]

and syllepsis:

> . . . Dieu sait la vie,
> Et le lard qui périt en cette occasion.[III,17]

It is very rarely that these figures constitute the only source of humour in any given instance; nor is humour the only effect which derives from them: La Fontaine's art is not one of simplification but rather of pervasion. This constant use of the resources of rhetoric is never obtrusive but, on the contrary, gives the impression of a neat stylization well in keeping with that of naturalness and the ease which one expects from an amusing tale told by a witty and friendly narrator. This is the tone which delighted Stendhal when he wrote:

> 'Rien d'agréable, au fond, à mes yeux que l'esprit naturel, celui qui est inventé à chaque instant par un caractère aimable sur toutes les circonstances de la conversation. La raison en est simple: il donne une comédie de caractère dont le protagoniste est aimable . . . Voilà le véritable esprit . . . celui de La Fontaine.'[1]

[1] Stendhal, *Journal*, March 7th 1805, ed. Divan, Paris, 1937, vol. II, p. 119

3. LITERARY WIT

This 'esprit' is often of a literary kind and occasional pastiches of the most varied genres and styles are found in the *Fables*.[1] Self-imposed and much enjoyed exercises akin to pastiche had been La Fontaine's method of acquiring and of perfecting his literary skill. This was in his day the traditional method of humanistic education and La Fontaine's originality lies in the obvious pleasure and profit he derives from these exercises continued into middle age. Not only the heroic, the *précieux* and the *burlesque* styles, in which Lanson saw 'trois états du même goût, trois styles du même art',[2] but also the *galant*, the pastoral and others mingle freely in his work. An exhaustive enumeration of the devices particular to these distinct styles most often met with in the *Fables*, would contribute but little to the appreciation of La Fontaine's skill. More rewarding is the study of the extent to which he used them and of the effect produced. For example, the poet's treatment of the epic style shows him perfectly at ease in the elaborate language which he thus succeeds in introducing into the fable: La Fontaine writes pastiches rather than parodies and, unlike *burlesque* writers, too often content with accumulations of rather crude devices such as anachronisms and ludicrous transpositions, he reproduces the stylistic qualities as well as the mannerisms of the epic; his aim is to ridicule neither the epic genre nor his characters but rather to amuse his reader by the interplay of form and subject-matter. Thus, genuine epic devices, such as sustained comparisons and Homeric epithets,

> Tel, et d'un spectacle pareil,
> Apollon irrité contre le fier Atride
> Joncha son camp de morts . . .

> Tel encore autour de sa tente
> Ajax, à l'âme impatiente,
> De moutons et de boucs fit un vaste débris . . .,[XI,3]

or hyperbolical periphrases,

> Peu s'en fallut que le soleil
> Ne rebroussât d'horreur vers le manoir liquide,[ibid.]

---

[1] From Ciceronian oratory, 'O temps, ô moeurs!'[XII,6], to Biblical phraseology, 'chat exterminateur',[III,18,] and:

> Tu mérites, dit-il, d'être pasteur de gens;
> Laisse là tes moutons, viens conduire des hommes[X,9]

See also X, 10.

[2] 'Etudes sur les rapports de la Littérature française et de la Littérature espagnole au XVIIème siècle', in *Revue d'Histoire Littéraire de la France*, III, 1896, p. 331.

give the fable *Le Fermier, le Chien et le Renard* a convincing Homeric flavour, which the low subject and the familiar setting cannot dispel.

Le Berger et son Troupeau[IX,19] contains a perfect example of pastoral poetry with a touch of elegiac inspiration:

> Robin Mouton, qui par la ville
> Me suivait pour un peu de pain,
> Et qui m'aurait suivi jusques au bout du monde.
> Hélas! De ma musette il entendait le son!
> Il me sentait venir de cent pas à la ronde.
> Ah le pauvre Robin Mouton!

The gentle but ill-fated lamb, the *musette*, the sentimental qualifications, 'un peu de pain, le pauvre Robin', and interjections 'hélas!, ah!', the vague hyperboles 'jusques au bout du monde, cent pas à la ronde', and above all the song-like quality of the rhythm and of the return, at the end of the passage, of the name which opened it (*redditio* or προσαπόδοσις), all the mannerisms of the idyll are represented. Yet, it is the context and not the text itself which betrays the intention of parody.

The charm and the dignity of the delicate and elevated styles remain perfectly perceptible in these imitations in spite of the ironical touch given by the author. The quality of this form of humour is indeed very remote from the *burlesque*. In the eighteenth century, Gaillard already saw in 'cet enjouement si fin, si vrai, si soutenu, si sûrement communiqué la plus forte critique de l'ignoble burlesque dont les grimaces révoltent lors même qu'elles font rire.'[1] This judgement is, however, rather harsh for a style which La Fontaine did not reject altogether and from which he borrowed many elements well-suited to the familiar and light-hearted tone of the *Fables*: archaisms and proverbs, realistic vocabulary and colourful popular language, the familiar treatment of noble subjects

> Au nez de Jupiter la fumée en monta . . .,[IX,13]

and the elevated treatment of low subjects

> Les reines des étangs, grenouilles veux-je dire . . . ^{Appendix I, *Le Soleil et les Grenouilles*}

This latter form of *burlesque* is that of *Le Lutrin*, which Boileau, ignoring La Fontaine's remark

---

[1] G. H. Gaillard, *Eloge de La Fontaine*, 1774, in P. L. Solvet, *Etudes sur La Fontaine*, Paris, 1812, p. xxi.

...Que coûte-t-il d'appeler
Les choses par noms honorables?,[ibid.]

claimed to have invented: 'c'est un burlesque nouveau, dont je me suis
avisé en notre langue; car, au lieu que dans l'autre burlesque Didon et
Enée parlaient comme des harangères et des crocheteurs, dans celui-ci
une horlogère et un horloger parlent comme Didon et Enée.'[1]

Impertinent allusions to mythology and history are the subject of many
comparisons, periphrases, antonomasiae: two goats meeting on a narrow
bridge call forth the comment:

Je m'imagine voir avec Louis le Grand
Philippe Quatre qui s'avance
Dans l'île de la Conférence.[XII,4]

'L'Empédocle de cire' refers to a candle consumed in a fire[IX,12], the fox
becomes another Ajax[XI,3]; a clairvoyante is introduced by the line:

Une femme à Paris faisait la Pythonisse ...,[VII,14]

and Jupiter is addressed in the following terms:

O Jupiter, qui sus de ton cerveau,
Par un secret d'accouchement nouveau,
Tirer Pallas....[X,6]

These few examples should suffice to show that the *burlesque* found its way
into the *Fables* although these could in no way be called a *burlesque* work.
The attitude of the true *burlesque* writer is clear-cut: indeed, consistency
within the conventions of its particular style is a condition of its success.
Since nothing is so systematic or so simple in La Fontaine's use of this
language and these devices, the discussion of this aspect of his work is
difficult. At times, he resorts to a *burlesque* term for metrical convenience
or the sake of variety, as when, in the same fable[X,6], he uses both *Jupiter*
and *Jupin* without deriving any particular effect from either. It is extremely difficult to determine which elements are properly *burlesque* and
which come from Marot and Rabelais; some even seem to be borrowings
from or allusions to La Fontaine's contemporaries, the *galant* poets, used
with an intention of parody. To quote but a few examples, the jackdaw
which

... se vit bafoué,
Berné, sifflé, moqué, joué,[IV,9]

---

[1] Boileau, *Le Lutrin*, *Au lecteur*, in *Œuvres*, vol. 2, p. 405.

recalls Boisrobert's reference to Mazarin,

> . . . cet homme bafoué,
> Sifflé, vendu, moqué, joué.[1]

The Latin phrase 'exemplum ut talpa', a joke on a standard example of Latin grammar books then in use, inserted in the text of *Les Compagnons d'Ulysse*[XII,1], was already in Voiture:

> Par moi vous en voyez exemplum ut talpa
> Qui, pour être sans yeux, n'évite pas ses charmes.[2]

Our analysis of humorous devices might lead the reader to the erroneous conclusion that the playful tone of the *Fables* is mainly due to an even distribution of ingenious conceits. However impressive their variety and their frequency these devices are in no way obtrusive; they are smoothly woven into the texture of the *style enjoué* peculiar to La Fontaine: humour is the congenial complement of poetic wit. For La Fontaine's style is based, as we have seen, on an appreciative and, at the same time, critical use of all the resources offered to him by the poetic styles of his day, which he had practised with varying success but remarkable thoroughness. The time had come for him to give a synthesis of all his experiments, which would amount to a humorous blending of all styles. The *Fables* in 1668 and *Psyché* in 1669 are the outcome of this combination of learning, critical judgement, invention, talent and taste: styles of all kinds are admirably blended, aesthetically integrated into the fable and yet remain distinct to the eyes of the perceptive reader whilst the poet plays on the illusions created by the multi-coloured rays of this shifting spectrum. Sometimes La Fontaine himself, by pointing out the change of style, acknowledges his satisfaction at treating one theme in various manners. The interest of these exercises resides in the light which they throw on the skill of the poet and on a technique which is elsewhere not so obvious: *Contre ceux qui ont le goût difficile*[II,1] and *Le Cierge*[IX,12] contain samples of stylistic variations accompanied by comments stressing

---

[1] Boisrobert, *A Mr. Scarron*, 1652, in *Epîtres en vers*, Paris, 1921, vol. II, p. 126.

[2] Voiture, *Pour la taupe*, (pre-1659), in *Œuvres*, Vol. II, p. 422. Such allusions are frequent in the literature of the time. Who could say with certainty whether La Fontaine's contemporaries did not see in D'Assoucy's prandial lyricism:

> Et toi, cher et friand morceau
> Gigot, que tu me sembles beau. . . .

Aventures burlesques, Paris, 1858 (1st publ. 1670), p. 55, a jocular and pointed allusion to the fox's eulogy:

> Que vous me semblez beau!

(*Fables*, I, 2)?

their limitations and their artificiality. More often, the changes in style are neither announced nor commented upon and only the perceptive reader is aware of the shift: thus, in *La Tortue et les deux Canards*[X,2], the incidental remark expressed in a general and rather abstract manner

> Volontiers on fait cas d'une terre étrangère

is immediately followed by its translation into popular and proverbial speech:

> Volontiers gens boiteux haïssent le logis,

where the contrast of vocabulary is emphasized by a parallelism, a repetition and antitheses ('faire cas, haïr; terre étrangère, logis'). The plebeian proverb confirms and particularizes the moralist's general remark. Yet the difference in their quality, in their methods of observation and in their expression is implied by the change in style from the first to the second line. This is an example of the *naïveté* which all contemporary critics praise as a supreme quality in the *Fables*. But this perfect congruence of style and subject-matter is in no way comic; if the lines quoted here are faintly amusing, this is due to the juxtaposition of contrasting styles. Very different is the effect of a shift in style warranted by some aspect of the subject-matter and yet totally incongruous in the context. Thus, in *La Vieille et les deux Servantes*[V,6], a fable where the familiar and the realistic tone predominates, some circumstances which, elsewhere, would lend themselves to a poetic treatment, are expressed, here, in the heroic style. The incongruity is obvious but the elevated style is not sustained and is adulterated by the intrusion of familiar language:

> Dès que Thétis chassait Phébus aux crins dorés,
> Tourets entraient en jeu, fuseaux étaient tirés
>
> Dès que l'Aurore, dis-je, en son char remontait,
> Un misérable coq à point nommé chantait.

On the one hand, these poetic flashes contrast with the sordid environment, stress its squalor and, to a certain extent, suggest the existence of another finer world, that of nature. On the other, the realistic elements stress, by contrast, the fallacy inherent in poetic conventions. To the juxtaposition of contrasting styles, La Fontaine prefers the contamination of one style by another; thus, in the lines

> Du palais d'un jeune lapin,
>
> Jeannot Lapin retourne aux souterrains séjours,[VII,15]
>
> Le phaéton d'une voiture à foin,[VI,18]

the poet, with a smile, associates languages and ideas reputed irreconcilable, and leaves the reader unable to decide whether it is the naïve world of the fable which acquires new poetic prestige or the poetic idiom which is rendered naïve. Both effects are probably intended as well as the mixed feeling they produce in the reader; to his many ambiguities, La Fontaine adds that of the aesthetic feeling and this is where he departs from the *burlesque* writers of his time. They aimed at ridiculing, at depreciating one style by means of another. In La Fontaine, both styles are given an equal chance to provoke the reader's imagination: his frequent use of heroic and epic styles is not due to any disparaging intention. These references and allusions constitute rather a counterpoint to his humble anecdotes and imply an identity of circumstances, of human relations and reactions behind the disparity of styles. 'I write of animals, the poet might say, and of course I have to use low style, thereby depriving the reader and myself of the pleasure of a finer language. However, I also, by implication, write of man whose actions, although little different from those of my animals, are deemed worthy of the elevated style.' And, by means of a few epic devices, he evokes the charm of this 'langue des dieux'. This process is apparent in *Les deux Coqs*[VII,12]: the fable opens in a pedestrian way:

> Deux coqs vivaient en paix; une poule survint,
> Et voilà la guerre allumée.

A comment from the moralist raises the subject to the level of classical literature:

> Amour, tu perdis Troie. . . .

With this evocation of the *Iliad*, whose subject differs little from that of the fable, La Fontaine proceeds to give his treatment of the quarrel an Homeric touch:

> La gent qui porte crête au spectacle accourut.
> Plus d'une Hélène au beau plumage
> Fut le prix du vainqueur. . . .

The cultured reader cannot but reflect on the correctness of the implied comparison between the Trojan War and this poultry yard quarrel and, at the same time, smile at the discrepancy of words which betrays an irreducible discrepancy of ideas inherent in the disparity of genres.[1] The result

---

[1] The same remark has been made on Pope's handling of the mock-epic:'He very nearly turns mock-epic tension back into epic tension. He does not maintain the genre tension between low and high style in a simple one-to-one fashion: he brings in a third dimension . . . The two-way tension inherent in mock-heroic is transformed by Pope into a three-way tension pointing back towards epic seriousness.' R. Price Parkin, *The Workmanship of Alexander Pope*, University of Minnesota, USA, 1955, p. 126.

is an amusing new style which profits from the qualities of the elevated without losing the realistic flavour of the fable. Thus, the rule of *bienséance* is both proved right and successfully transgressed.

Elsewhere, La Fontaine makes a similar use of the idyllic style: *Le Loup devenu Berger*[III,3] acquires with his disguise all the artistic finery which centuries of poetic tradition have attached to it. The distance between reality and the world of the Pastoral is first implied in:

> Fait sa houlette d'un bâton,
> Sans oublier la cornemuse.

Further on, in the narrative, the deceptive transposition of reality

> ... Ses pieds de devant posés sur sa houlette

(for 'ses pattes posées sur son bâton'), associates the wolf masquerading as a shepherd with the *beaux-esprits* masquerading as shepherds, in an amusing manner. The brutal ending of this 'idyll' is full of irony:

> Il voulut ajouter la parole aux habits ...

> Il ne put du pasteur contrefaire la voix. . . .

And the wolf perishes a victim of poetic illusion, for imitating a mythical overdressed and loquacious 'pasteur', whilst an impersonation of a real 'berger' would, no doubt, have succeeded. Thus, the artificiality of the Pastoral genre and its dangers have incidentally and implicitly been discussed in the fable. In *Le Mal Marié*[VII,2], the long-suffering husband sends his wife back to her parents, 'a la campagne'. So far, the action has been no more than a purely domestic drama treated in low style. The sudden mention of the country conjures up literary associations of rural activities and pastoral scenes in the manner of the idyll. The heroine has just as little in common with the sweet shepherdess of poetry as real farm animals have with the beribboned flock tended by the shepherdess, so that when the poet writes:

> ... La voilà donc compagne
> De certaines Philis qui gardent les dindons
> Avec les gardeurs de cochons,

the association of the wife with Philis reflects amusingly her well-deserved fate whilst the incongruity of the association 'Philis-dindons-gardeurs de cochons' underlines the artificiality of the pastoral convention. Yet this rapid allusion momentarily introduces into the fable the fleeting charm of pastoral grace.

William Empson's definition of ambiguity constitutes a good sum-
mary of the specific nature of La Fontaine's humour and wit:

> '. . . A word may have several distinct meanings; several mean-
> ings connected with one another; several meanings which need one
> another to complete their meaning; or several meanings which unite
> together so that the word means one relation or one process . . .
> Ambiguity itself can mean an indecision as to what you mean, an
> intention to mean several things, a probability that one or other or
> both of two things has been meant, and the fact that a statement has
> several meanings. It is useful to be able to separate these if you wish,
> but it is not obvious that in separating them at any particular point
> you will not be raising more problems than you solve.'[1]

To provoke aesthetic, moral and philosophical reflexions by means of
pleasantly stimulating and unassuming fables is one of our poet's greatest
achievements and his avowed aim: 'Je n'appelle pas gaité ce qui excite
le rire, mais un certain charme, un air agréable qu'on peut donner à
toutes sortes de sujets, même les plus sérieux'.[2] We cannot but agree with
Clarac when, after quoting these very words of our poet, he concludes:
'Il ne définirait pas autrement la poésie'.[3]

[1] W. E. Empson, *Seven Types of Ambiguity*, Penguin Books, London, 1961, pp. 5–6.
[2] *Fables*, Preface, vol. I, p. 10.
[3] P. Clarac, *La Fontaine, l'homme et l'œuvre*, p. 75.

CHAPTER V

ELEGANCE

'THE perfect balance between realism, humour and a certain stylised but easy elegance appears so simple to achieve. . . .' Thus Geoffrey Brereton sums up the impression formed on reading the *Fables* and we cannot but agree with him that, for this reason, 'the product is unique'.[1] This elegance is extremely elusive and has much in common with the *je ne sais quoi* of the seventeenth-century critics. It is a combination of a thorough knowledge of the language, an exact appreciation of the effect that will be produced, innate taste and the most careful obliteration of any trace of effort. The general impression left by an elegant style is one of neatness and supreme ease, concealing stylistic ingenuity, sometimes even virtuosity, perceptible only to the critic's trained eyes. Gamaches writes that 'la netteté du style naît de l'ordre et de la précision',[2] providing us with two elements to be considered in our study: the quality of the expression and the arrangement of its components.

Precision is achieved by a rigorous choice of words and phrases as well as by a drastic rejection of any less effective alternative and irrelevant phraseology. La Bruyère remarks that:

'Entre toutes les différentes expressions qui peuvent rendre une seule de nos pensées, il n'y en a qu'une qui soit la bonne. On ne la rencontre pas toujours en parlant ou en écrivant; il est vrai néanmoins qu'elle existe, que tout ce qui ne l'est point est faible, et ne satisfait point un homme d'esprit qui veut se faire entendre.'[3]

Such is the principle which guides La Fontaine and to which the critic must refer when attempting to define the specific elegance of his style. Thus Stendhal comments on the lines:

A quoi bon charger votre vie
Des soins d'un avenir qui n'est pas fait pour vous?[XI,8]

'Un rimeur du dix-huitième siècle aurait substitué à ce *charger* qui fait une image si juste quelque expression bien métaphysique et

---

[1] G. Brereton, *An Introduction to the French Poets*, p. 82.
[2] E. S. de Gamaches, *Les Agréments du langage*, p. 3.
[3] La Bruyère, *Les Caractères*, in *Œuvres*, vol. II, p. 30.

bien froide; et la tournure encore! la forme dramatique, et dans cette forme, ce qu'il y a de plus vif: l'interrogation.'[1]

In the language of modern criticism, Jean Boudout has formulated a judgement which sums up most of the features which constitute La Fontaine's elegance of style:

> 'Les qualités que nos contemporains, Valéry, Gide, apprécient au premier rang chez La Fontaine, c'est la maîtrise dans l'imitation, l'économie des moyens d'expression à l'effet que l'on veut obtenir, l'art de toujours rester en deçà.'[2]

It is this moderation which makes him content, in *La Besace*[1,7], to progress gradually from the monkey to the bear, from the bear to the elephant, from the elephant to the whale and then makes him break off the gradation just as it becomes monotonous, to bring in the ant. Yet the appellation of *Dame* used both for the whale and the ant, as well as the contrast in size of both animals make the humorous transposition easy and perfectly natural.[3] La Harpe once wrote:

> 'Il me semble que si La Fontaine dans ses *Fables* n'est pas remarquable par la brièveté, il l'est par la précision. J'appelle un style précis celui dont on ne peut rien ôter sans que l'ouvrage perde une grâce ou un ornement, et sans que le lecteur perde un plaisir. Tel est le style de La Fontaine dans l'apologue. On n'y sent jamais ce qu'on appelle langueur. On n'y trouve jamais de vide. Ce qu'il dit ne peut être dit en moins de mots, ou vous ne le diriez pas si bien. Il faut qu'on me pardonne de citer:

> > Un octogénaire plantait.
> > Passe encor de bâtir; mais planter à cet âge! . . .

> > Deux coqs vivaient en paix; une poule survint,
> > Et voilà la guerre allumée.
> > Amour, tu perdis Troie. . . .

> > Un lièvre en son gîte songeait,
> > (Car que faire en un gîte, à moins que l'on ne songe?)

> . . . Je crois qu'il est impossible de mêler plus rapidement le récit et la réflexion, et c'est ainsi qu'écrit toujours La Fontaine.'[4]

---

[1] Stendhal, *Pensées*, ed. Divan, vol. I, pp. 102–4.
[2] In J. Bédier and P. Hazard, *Littérature française*, Paris, 1948, vol. I, pp. 445–6.
[3] See Grammont, *Psychologie linguistique*, p. 168.
[4] La Harpe, *Éloge de La Fontaine*, in *Recueil de l'Académie de Marseille*, pp. 24–5.

1. CONCISENESS AND PRECISION

It is true that La Fontaine does not try to imitate Phaedrus's brevity and that he sometimes indulges in personal remarks and short digressions in which resides part of the charm of the *Fables*. Even so, as La Harpe points out, his style remains precise and concise. The poet, in his search for the neatest and most exact turn of phrase, does not hesitate to draw terms from popular, technical and even archaic language and thus the effect of his precision is often combined with that of vividness which we have examined already.

The economy of words is remarkable in the *Fables: La Cigale et la Fourmi*[1,1] is a neat little anecdote told in 109 words; *Le Corbeau et le Renard*[1,2] is told in 132 words, and yet, as Brereton says;

> 'The whole scene is drawn with picturesqueness, humour and some suggestion of character. There is no trace of compression or haste. Nothing needs adding. Intellectually the story and its moral are complete.[1]

It is true that the Æsopic originals are approximately of the same length but in them terseness alternates with prolixity without ever producing an effect as evocative as La Fontaine's neatness. Besides, throughout the fables of Phaedrus and Æsop, the pattern as well as the wording of the apologue is repetitive and monotonous whilst La Fontaine's linguistic and stylistic resources are infinitely varied and ingenious.

His choice of words and idioms is exemplary; not only would any rewriting necessarily increase the number of words, but the rich implications and visions suggested by the poet's phrasing would disappear in the process; one would thus achieve the paradoxical feat of using more words for a lesser effect, which is the very condition of verbosity. For example, in the lines:

Il vous prend sa cognée, il vous tranche la bête,
Il fait trois serpents de deux coups. . . .[VI,13]

Une femme à Paris faisait la Pythonisse. . . .[VII,14]

Deux vrais amis vivaient au Monomotapa:
L'un ne possédait rien qui n'appartînt à l'autre,[VIII,11]

all the relevant information concerning an action, an occupation, and a situation is given in the neatest possible manner and yet, in each case,

---

[1] G. Brereton, *An Introduction to the French Poets*, pp. 82-3.

the sentence amounts to more than a simple statement of facts. The first suggests a compelling vision of the result of the action, the second a sarcastic judgement, and the third contains an ingenious use of reciprocal pronouns and synonymous expressions which stresses the interdependence of the friends described. Elsewhere, a bold syntactical construction adds pungency to a zeugma

> Il avait dans la terre une somme enfouie,
> Son coeur avec. . . .[IV,20]

which, even by itself, would be striking as in the lines:

> Il retourne chez lui; dans sa cave il enserre
> L'argent et sa joie à la fois.[VIII,2]

Whilst an exhaustive study of the means used by La Fontaine to achieve this neatness and conciseness of style—vivid vocabulary, frequency of verbal forms, etc.—would entail many repetitions of points dealt with in the previous chapters, an examination of his use of adjectives might provide some indication of his reaction when confronted with a wide choice of words. In the seventeenth century, of all genres, the epistle in verse fostered the multiplication of gratuitous adjectives. Thus, Boisrobert begins an epistle to Monsieur Bignon in these terms:

> Savant Bignon, dont l'esprit adorable
> Accompagné d'une humeur admirable,
> Fait de Paris le plus riche ornement
> Et tout l'honneur de ce grand Parlement,
> Quiconque a dit que ta bonté propice . . . etc.[1]

La Fontaine's Fables include five epistles, among them one to Madame de Montespan and one to the Duc de Bourgogne; yet all are almost devoid of stock laudatory epithets,[2] whilst giving an impression of humour, warm-heartedness, and sincerity rarely associated with that genre. The poet's praise even when resorting to traditional clichés, gives them a renewed charm; the lines

> Sévigné, de qui les attraits
> Servent aux grâces de modèle,
> Et qui naquîtes toute belle,
> A votre indifférence près. . . .[IV,1]

[1] Boisrobert, Épîtres en vers, vol. II, p. 141.
[2] Fables, IV, 1; VII, A Madame de Montespan; VIII, 4; IX, Discours à Madame de La Sablière; XII, A Monseigneur le Duc de Bourgogne.

suggest the perennial quality of his correspondent's beauty and, paradoxically, imply its perfection by means of a restriction; the eulogy achieves the dual aim of flattering and teasing. One cannot fail to notice that in most fables, the adjectives are rare. Yet it would not be difficult to find and quote passages which contain an accumulation of adjectives, as in *Le Singe et le Léopard*[IX,3]. It seems that in his use of adjectives, the poet is guided solely by his concern for strict relevance; thus, whether numerous or few, the adjectives which he retains are indispensable and never give the impression of gratuitous ornamentation. In the fable concerned, they help to suggest, in a few lines, the irrepressible showman's prattle. In *Les Oreilles du Lièvre*[V,4], one of the rare adjectives of the fable is to be found in a periphrasis, in the very first line:

> Un animal *cornu* blessa de quelques coups
> Le lion ...

The strength and importance of this adjective could not be overlooked; it explains the daring crime of *lèse-majesté*, the collective banishment of goats, rams, bulls, stags, etc. decreed by the lion and, to a certain extent, it justifies the hare's fear. When, in *Le Loup et le Chien*[I,5], the dog is described as

> ... Aussi puissant que beau,
> Gras, poli ...,

these adjectives are most relevant to the anecdote and indispensable for our understanding of it: it is because the dog is strong that the wolf enters into conversation with him instead of attacking him; the fact that the dog is fat illustrates his praise of his way of life and explains its appeal to the famished wolf; as for *poli*, it refers to the excellent quality of the dog's fur and, by implication, accounts for the wolf's astonishment when discovering the only imperfection in the dog's fur and in his argument. These examples illustrate La Fontaine's favourite means of achieving elegance: the expression of a complex notion by extremely concise phrasing. Thus, the poet's discretion in the use of adjectives is compensated for by the intensity of their effect, since, as La Motte Le Vayer remarks:

> 'Les épithètes relèvent merveilleusement une période, mais il en faut user, selon la comparaison de ce même philosophe [Aristote], comme l'on fait des assaisonnements dont on ne se sert que pour aiguiser l'appétit et qui ne passent jamais pour viandes solides.

Autrement son opinion est qu'il n'y a rien de plus froid et de plus mauvaise grâce.'[1]

Throughout the *Fables*, the adjectives are almost always associated with precise stylistic effects or integrated into figures of rhetoric. Virolle has remarked that in *Les Deux Amis*[VIII,11], there are thirty-six verbs and only five adjectives, three of which—*véritable, vrai, véritable*—imply the notion of genuineness which is the very subject of the fable.[2] In *La Mouche et la Fourmi*[IV,3], 'terrible manière' and 'vil et rampant animal' form a contrast stressed by the presence of the adjective 'égal' at the end of the next line. Besides, the hyperbolic use of 'terrible' is also a feature of the *précieux* jargon and seems particularly appropriate in the speech of the snobbish fly. 'Chétive et misérable' (*l.* 9) insists on the ant's helplessness revealing, as does 'hautes pensées' (*l.* 36) the fly's contempt for it. 'Noir' (*l.* 31) emphasizes the resemblance of the fly to a beauty spot implied in the homonymous terms *mouche*. 'Fausse ou véritable gloire' form another antithesis remarkable for its conciseness. As for 'blancheur naturelle' and 'prompt trépas', these are set phrases and yet, in the fly's speech, the former implies a claim to perfect the work of nature whilst the latter amounts to a hypallage:

> Et je sais que d'un prompt trépas
> Cette importunité bien souvent est punie

(for 'est souvent punie promptement du trépas') which, together with the inversion, stresses the rapidity of the sequence of events.

This relevance of the wording to characters and circumstances, recommended by Bellegarde:

> 'Quelle grâce donnent aux discours les épithètes bien choisies. . . . Mais il faut qu'elles tiennent du caractère des choses qu'elles représentent, et qu'elles soient faites pour le lieu où on les place'[3]

is very probably the quality which contemporaries appreciated in the *Fables* under the name of *naïveté*, a notion which also included psychological verisimilitude in the speech of the characters. Thus, in 1718, La Motte writes:

---

[1] La Motte Le Vayer, *Considérations sur l'éloquence française de ce temps*, p. 98.
[2] R. Virolle, 'Explication de texte, l'amitié selon La Fontaine', in *L'Ecole*, XLVII, January 7th 1956, p. 252.
[3] J.-B. Morvan de Bellegarde, *Réflexions sur l'élégance et la politesse du style*, p. 82. See also Desmarets de Saint-Sorlin, *La Comparaison de la langue et de la poésie française avec la grecque et la latine*, Paris, 1670, pp. 71–2: 'Ce n'est pas que les épithètes doivent être pointues, mais elles doivent ajouter de la force au mot; et ce n'est pas grande chose que d'appeler le lait doux et la neige blanche.'

'Les occasions du naïf sont peut-être plus fréquentes dans la fable, et l'éloge de La Fontaine est de n'en avoir guère manquées. Dans la fable du Pot au Lait, le discours qu'il prête à sa laitière est un chef-d'œuvre de naïveté, d'autant plus singulier que sous l'apparence du raisonnement le plus suivi, le sentiment se montre dans toute sa force, ou pour mieux dire, dans toute son ivresse.'[1]

Two centuries later, Ernest Hello developed and illustrated this judgement:

'Et comme il [La Fontaine] est de bonne foi, il n'exagère jamais. Si Perrette n'était pas de bonne foi, elle exagérerait le porc dont elle prévoit la naissance. . . . Mais La Fontaine et Perrette sont de bonne foi:
Il était, quand je l'eus, de grosseur raisonnable. Raisonnable est merveilleux! Perrette a évidemment la vue nette et actuelle de ce porc; mais elle se réveillerait elle-même de son sommeil si elle le poussait trop loin. Elle introduit la sagesse dans son rêve pour y introduire la vraisemblance.'[2]

Thus, La Fontaine's moderation in the use of adjectives, his accurate evaluation of their effect—and this is also true of his use of other parts of speech—to a certain extent account for the restraint and the elegance of his style.

The contrast between the discretion of some stylistic devices and the richness of their effects always give the careful reader new subjects of wonder and admiration: a singular isolated amidst plural nouns introduces variety in an enumeration and more precision in the assessment of the sociological composition of a coachload of travellers:

Femmes, *moine*, vieillards, tout était descendu.[VII,8]

The majestic plural in the mouth of a plebeian character reveals his patronizing attitude:

Nous vous mettrons à couvert,
Repartit le Pot de fer.[V,2]

One single noun of an incriminating nature is sufficient to provide the explanation of a mystery:

Un pâtre à ses brebis trouvant quelque mécompte,
Voulut à toute force attraper le *larron*.[VI,1]

---

[1] Houdart de La Motte, *Discours sur la fable*, in *Fables nouvelles*, p. xli.
[2] Ernest Hello, *L'Homme*, pp. 410–11.

One single verb indicates the distance still separating the competitors after the arrival of the tortoise at the winning post:

Hé bien! lui *cria*-t-elle, avais-je pas raison?[VI,10]

The same observations could be made with regard to figures of thought and speech. Bretteville stresses the challenge which these offer to the orator and the writer when he points out their dual aspect:

> 'Ce qu'on appelle figures d'éloquence, n'est autre chose que certains tours d'expression et de pensées dont on ne se sert point communément, qui surprennent, qui plaisent, qui remuent le coeur, et qui excitent les passions. . . . Il est étrange qu'il n'y ait rien dans l'éloquence dont on se serve si mal que des figures puisqu'il n'y a rien de si aisé et de si naturel; car la nature les a si fort gravées dans nos cœurs, et même sur nos langues, que si on ne se gâtait pas l'esprit par trop d'art, on trouverait dans son propre fonds, et suivant simplement les mouvements de la nature, tous ces tours sublimes, véhéments et agréables, auxquels on a donné le nom de figures. J'ai souvent pris plaisir à entendre des paysans s'entretenir avec des figures de discours si différents, si vives, si éloignées du vulgaire, que j'avais honte d'avoir si longtemps étudié l'éloquence, voyant en eux une certaine rhétorique de nature beaucoup plus persuasive et plus éloquente que toutes nos rhétoriques artificielles.'[1]

Gamaches draws practical conclusions in these terms:

> 'Tout ornement qui ne sert que pour la montre dégénère en une affectation vicieuse. . . . Les tours brillants ne peuvent contenter l'esprit que lorsqu'ils servent à réveiller son attention sur ce qu'il lui importe de remarquer; il ne veut point qu'on l'amuse. Il s'indigne, pour ainsi dire, quand on l'oblige de se rendre attentif à ce qui peut impunément lui échapper. . . . Il faut souvent savoir manquer d'esprit pour paraître en avoir.'[2]

Such seem to be the principles guiding La Fontaine: thus, the contrast between Borée's frantic useless agitation and the traveller's composure is emphasized by the stylistic contrast between the *style orné* of the lines devoted to the former and the matter-of-fact quality of those devoted to the latter:

---

[1] Bretteville, *L'Eloquence de la chaire et du barreau selon les principes les plus solides de l'éloquence sacrée et profane*, Paris, 1689, pp. 204-5.
[2] E. S. de Gamaches, *Les Agréments du langage*, Paris, 1718, pp. 35 and 307.

> ... Notre souffleur à gage
> Se gorge de vapeurs, s'enfle comme un ballon,
>   Fait un vacarme de démon,
> Siffle, souffle, tempête, et brise en son passage
> Maint toit qui n'en peut mais, fait périr maint bateau.
>   Le tout au sujet du manteau.
> Le cavalier eut soin d'empêcher que l'orage
>   Ne se pût engouffrer dedans.[VI,3]

Whilst the *Fables* display a remarkable range of rhetorical devices, one notices the poet's partiality towards those which lend the style a greater conciseness and ingeniously suggest a flexible interpretation rather than impose one single limited image. Thus—and this is without precedent in seventeenth-century poetry—comparisons which, by their nature, would introduce additional and often irrelevant elements, are very scarce indeed in the *Fables*, whilst metaphors and catachreses which amount to implied comparisons and can be integrated into the text abound:

> Le souper du croquant avec elle s'envole....[II,12]

> ... Il vendit son troupeau,
> Trafiqua de l'argent, le mit entier sur l'eau;
> Cet argent périt par naufrage[IV,2]

Among all the figures found in the *Fables*, ellipses, litotes and euphemisms occur far more frequently than they do in any other poetical work of the time. These contribute to enhance the conciseness, the discretion, the moderation of the expression and lend themselves admirably to the complex combinations of effects and implications which the poet relishes. We have already analysed the sarcastic flavour of the lines:

> La fourmi n'est pas prêteuse;
> C'est là son moindre défaut[I,1]

due to the epigrammatic quality of the euphemism. When the oak pities the reed:

> La nature envers vous me semble bien injuste,[I,22]

'envers vous' implies 'mais pas envers moi.'[1]

Elliptic devices are considered as elegant by most theorists, who would agree with Boileau's comment to Brossette:

---

[1] See C. W. Rosen, *Style and Morality in La Fontaine*, p. 185.

'Où en serait un poète si on ne lui passait je ne dis pas une fois mais vingt fois dans un ouvrage ces *subaudi?* Où en serait M. Racine si on allait lui chicaner ce beau vers. . . .

Je t'aimais inconstant, qu'aurais-je fait fidèle?

Ces sortes de petites licences de construction non seulement ne sont plus des fautes, mais même sont assez souvent un des plus grands charmes de la poésie principalement dans la narration où il n'y a point de temps à perdre. Ce sont des espèces de latinismes dans la poésie française qui n'ont pas moins d'agrément que les hellénismes dans la poésie latine.'[1]

In the *Fables*, such devices are not rare:

. . . Et, lui sage, il leur dit.[VIII,7]

. . . Mon voyage dépeint
Vous sera d'un plaisir extrême.[IX,2]

Indeed, many elliptic devices used by La Fontaine are modelled on Greek and Latin patterns, a fact which, at the time, enhanced their charm in the eyes of the cultured readers accustomed to look for and to collect elegant and ingenious turns of phrase in their reading of classical writers. For example, the substantivization of verbs, adjectives and other parts of speech—frequently found in the *Fables*—is a hellenism which, curiously, also suggests popular speech:

Et le financier se plaignait
Que les soins de la Providence
N'eussent pas au marché fait vendre le dormir
Comme le manger et le boire.[VIII,2]

Avec son marcher lent, quand arriverait-elle?[XII,15]

Le trop d'expédients peut gâter une affaire.[IX,14]

The absolute clause is also a favourite construction with La Fontaine:

. . . L'arbre étant pris pour juge,
Ce fut bien pis encore.[X,1]

Le coffre étant ouvert, on y vit des lambeaux. . . .[X,9]

La tanche rebutée, il trouva du goujeon.[VII,4]

[1] Boileau, Letter of August 2nd 1703 in *Lettres à Brossette*, ed. Boudhors, Paris, 1942, p. 67.

Le père mort, les fils vous retournent le champ.^{V,9}

Socrate un jour faisant bâtir,
Chacun censurait son ouvrage.^{IV,17}

However, the last example shows a flexible adaptation of the original Latin device, the ablative absolute, since, here, the absolute clause is, in fact, related to the main clause.

The hendiadys is an elegant hellenism which gives conciseness and distinction to the following lines:

Je vous raconterai Térée et son envie . . .^{IX,18}

Chat et vieux, pardonner? Cela n'arrive guère . . .^{XII,5}

In this latter example, the hendiadys is combined with an exclamative ellipsis similar to that found in the following lines of the abbé de Villiers:

On s'en plaignit, comment tant de filles se taire?

on which Bellegarde comments:

'Il y a quelque chose de sous-entendu dans le dernier vers, et c'est peut-être ce qui en fait l'agrément; car si 'au lieu de dire on s'en plaignit, comment tant de filles se taire, l'auteur eut mis, comment tant de filles auraient-elles eu la force de se taire ou quelque terme semblable, la construction serait à la vérité plus unie et plus régulière, mais moins belle et moins piquante.'[1]

The ellipsis of the article in verbal phrases and enumerations, that of the subject in front of seriated verbs are recommended as elegant by most theorists of style and La Fontaine as we have seen in earlier chapters, conforms with their advice.[2] Gamaches recommends the ellipsis of the conjunctions and particularly those expressing causality:

'Il est souvent à propos de supprimer dans le discours les liaisons qu'on y peut aisément suppléer. Quelque fois on supprime ce qui marque la liaison d'un effet avec la cause; . . . [Sans cela] l'expression languirait. . . . On ne doit point mettre de liaison entre les propositions qui sont unies par le sens . . . c'est à ceux à qui nous parlons à sentir les rapports que pareilles propositions ont entre elles.'[3]

---

[1] J.-B. Morvan de Bellegarde, *Réflexions sur l'élégance*, p. 229.
[2] See Andry de Boisregard, *Réflexions critiques sur l'usage présent de la langue française*, pp. 601–5; D. Bouhours, *Remarques nouvelles sur la langue française*, pp. 301–4; Vaugelas, *Remarques sur la langue française*, p. 420; E. S. de Gamaches, *Les Agréments du langage*, pp. 73 sqq., etc.
[3] E. S. de Gamaches, op. cit., pp. 81–2.

Juxtapositions expressing implicit causality or consequence are very
frequent in the *Fables*:

> Leur compliment fut court, ainsi qu'on peut penser.
> Le sage est ménager du temps et des paroles.[VIII,26]

> Toutes deux de même sang,
> Traitez-nous de même sorte.[VII,16]

> Le roi n'éclata point: les cris sont indécents
> A la Majesté Souveraine.[XII,12]

The elegance of the latter example can be explained in Gamaches's words:

> 'Entre les propositions incidentes, il y en a qui servent à marquer
> la raison de ce que renferme la proposition principale; celles-là
> doivent toujours être énoncées à part; c'est qu'elles font toujours
> partie d'un raisonnement abrégé; et qu'il faut que tout raisonnement
> soit exprimé de manière qu'il se développe comme de lui-même.
> Au lieu de dire, "Dieu qui est toujours juste dans ses jugements, ne
> souffrira pas que l'impie jouisse d'une longue prospérité" je dirais,
> "Dieu ne souffrira pas que l'impie jouisse d'une longue prospérité;
> il est toujours juste dans ses jugements.'[1]

The poet often uses the gnomic style that befits fables; its devices are
little different from those which we have just analysed and its general
effect combines the authoritative force of the statement with the conciseness of its form;

> ... Corsaires à corsaires,
> L'un l'autre s'attaquant ne font pas leurs affaires.[IV,12]

> Il n'est meilleur ami ni parent que soi-même.[IV,22]

These remarks provide a comment on the particularized anecdote in
general terms and their conciseness, relevance and stylized form make
them comparable to the devices of emblematic literature, the fable itself
replacing the graphic illustration.

2. INGENUITY. THE FABLE AND THE EMBLEM

The fable as a genre, and that of La Fontaine in particular, has many
features in common with the emblem and the device (or motto), two

---

[1] E. S. de Gamaches, *Les Agréments du langage*, pp. 44–5.

genres then flourishing both in literature and in the decorative arts. They proceed from a symbolical, didactic and aesthetic intention. The emblematic genres required an ingenuity of form and invention similar to that which La Fontaine introduced into the fable. Menestrier, in *L'Art des Emblèmes*, indicates the close link relating the fable to the emblem:

> 'Les apologues d'Esope sont aussi d'eux-mêmes des emblèmes, parce que ces apologues où les auteurs font parler les plantes, les animaux, et les autres choses naturelles ou artificielles ont toujours leur instruction morale jointe aux discours et aux actions de ces animaux. En voici un exemple tiré des *Fables choisies* de Monsieur de La Fontaine.'

Here follow the illustration and the text of *Les Deux Mulets*[1,4] with Menestrier's comment:

> 'Pour faire de cet apologue un emblème régulier, il ne faut que peindre ces deux mulets, l'un couché par terre et blessé, après que les voleurs lui ont enlevé sa charge; et l'autre chargé de son sac d'avoine, et ajouter ce vers à la peinture:

> Il n'est pas toujours bon d'avoir un haut emploi.[1]

Many are the fables which could be summed up in one single line used as a legend to a relevant engraving: *Les Membres et l'Estomac*[III,2]:

> S'il a quelque besoin, tout le corps s'en ressent,

Le Loup devenu Berger[III,3]:

> Quiconque est loup agisse en loup,

Le Renard et les Raisins[III,11]:

> Fit-il pas mieux que de se plaindre?,

Le Rat et l'Huître[VIII,9]:

> Tel est pris qui croyait prendre.

Emblems, like fables, are illustrated proverbs. Menestrier also draws attention to fables which, in their conciseness, qualify as emblems as they stand:

---

[1] C. F. Menestrier, *L'Art des Emblèmes*, Paris, 1684, pp. 27–8. Early editions (e.g. Lyon, 1662) had been published before the first collection of La Fontaine's *Fables*. Later, Menestrier revised his book devoting many pages to the poet. The close relationship between the fable, proverbs and emblems can also be observed in J. A. de Baïf, *Les Mimes, enseignements et proverbes*, Paris, 1880.

'L'Astrologue qui se laisse tomber dans un puits en voulant con-
templer les astres, est un autre apologue dont on peut aisément faire
un emblème. Monsieur de La Fontaine fait en quatre vers la peinture
et le mot de cet emblème:

> Un Astrologue un jour se laissa choir
> Au fond d'un puits. On lui dit: Pauvre bête,
> Tandis qu'à peine à tes pieds tu peux voir,
> Penses-tu lire au-dessus de ta tête?

Les deux premiers vers font la peinture, et les deux autres le mot
et l'application des figures à la morale, qui nous apprend de ne pas
négliger ce qui est nécessaire pour notre conduite, pour nous
attacher à des choses qui sont au dessus de nous.'[1]

L'Oiseau blessé d'une Flèche[II,6] also constitutes a perfect emblem:

> Mortellement atteint d'une flèche empennée,
> Un oiseau déplorait sa triste destinée,
> Et disait, en souffrant un surcroît de douleur:
> Faut-il contribuer à son propre malheur?

So does a single line such as:

> Fortune aveugle suit aveugle hardiesse.[X,13]

These examples show La Fontaine's skill at achieving the conciseness indispensable to an elegant emblem. However, his preoccupation with variety
made him often indulge in a more leisurely style which retains conciseness without ever showing the monotonous terseness of Benserade's
quatrains for the fable motifs decorating the fountains of the labyrinth at
Versailles. These, and even his 226 rondeaux on Ovid's *Metamorphoses*,
were nevertheless highly appreciated by his contemporaries. Menestrier
writes:

> 'Les trente-neuf fables qui sont autant de fontaines dans le
> Labyrinthe de Versailles, sont presque autant d'emblèmes par les
> tours ingénieux que leur a donnés Monsieur de Benserade en les
> expliquant en vers avec de courtes moralités.'[2]

---

[1] C. F. Menestrier, *L'Art des Emblèmes*, p. 29.

[2] C. F. Menestrier, op. cit., pp. 29–30. Benserade's quatrains can be found in Piganiol
de La Force, *Nouvelle description des châteaux et parcs de Versailles et de Marly*, Paris, 1724,
vol. II, pp. 95–135. Perrault, too, wrote short poems on these fountains but, unlike Benserade's,
these were not intended to form an integral part of the decoration and remained a purely
literary exercise. Whilst Benserade's quatrains developed the fables themselves, Perrault's
short pieces of unequal length expound, in verse, the moral of Æsop's fables given in prose
translation. See G. Couton, *La Poétique de La Fontaine*, p. 21 and Perrault, *Recueil de divers
ouvrages en prose et en vers*, Paris, 1676, pp. 234 ff.

The ingenuity required in the emblem and the device, whether French or Latin,[1] combined conciseness of form and richness of meaning, culminating in intended ambiguities similar to those which we have already pointed out in the *Fables*. Thus, Montfaucon de Villars comments on a device composed by Bouhours:

> 'La devise pour le roi est un soleil éclairant le globe de la terre, avec ce mot: Mihi sufficit unus. Ce mot se peut entendre et du monde et du soleil, et dans toutes les deux significations il renferme un sens admirable et exprime une vertu particulière; en sorte que tous les deux sens font l'assemblage des deux vertus qui composent le caractère du roi et qui le distinguent heureusement des plus grands rois qui furent jamais. Si c'est le globe de la terre qui dit que ce soleil lui suffit, ce mot présente d'abord à notre esprit cette sagesse si consommée et cette prudence étonnante dont le roi gouverne lui seul son grand empire: et si c'est le soleil qui dit qu'un monde lui suffit, il nous met devant les yeux cette modestie plus qu'héroïque, qui fait qu'un conquérant si heureux se contente de son royaume et laisse à ses voisins et ce qu'il a conquis et ce qu'il lui serait si facile de conquérir.'[2]

3. ELEGANCE AND *Copia*

Elegance is not confined to the use of elliptical and telescopic devices. In the *Fables*, elegance and *copia* are not incompatible. Ease and naturalness enhance the rich synonymy of the poet's vocabulary; emphasis is never constrained:

> Tout travaille pour elle [la grandeur royale] et réciproquement
> Tout tire d'elle l'aliment.
> Elle fait subsister l'artisan de ses peines,
> Enrichit le marchand, gage le magistrat,
> Maintient le laboureur, donne paie au soldat,
> Distribue en cent lieux ses grâces souveraines,
> Entretient seule tout l'Etat.[III,2]

---

[1] The foundation, in 1663, of *L'Académie des Inscriptions et Médailles*, which was to become *des Inscriptions et Belles Lettres* in 1716, illustrates the importance given to the composition of emblematic devices and mottoes. See J. Jacquiot, 'Devises pour les médailles et jetons de Louis XIV, composées par J. Racine', in *Actes du 1er Congrès International Racinien*, Uzès, 1962, pp. 77–94.

[2] Montfaucon de Villars, *De la Délicatesse*, Paris, 1671, pp. 258–61.

Here, in terms of seventeenth-century appreciation, the achievement consists in expressing in an elegant manner an elevated but nevertheless prosaic idea. The merit of La Fontaine is to succeed in developing this idea without transposing it onto the plane of abstractions and by means of a rich concrete vocabulary, in suggesting precise contemporary types whilst still emphasizing the nature and extension of the economic process which is the subject of these lines. A comparison of them with two lines of Boileau which La Fontaine is said to have admired most is illuminating. In 1695, Boileau wrote to Maucroix:

> 'Plus les choses sont sèches et malaisées à dire en vers, plus elles frappent quand elles sont dites noblement et avec cette élégance qui fait proprement la poésie. Je me souviens que M. de La Fontaine m'a dit plus d'une fois, que les deux vers de mes ouvrages qu'il estimait davantage, c'était ceux où je loue le roi d'avoir établi la manufacture des Points de France, à la place des Points de Venise. Les voici. C'est dans la première *Epître à Sa Majesté*:
>
>> Et nos voisins frustrés de ces tributs serviles
>> Que payait à leur art le luxe de nos villes.'[1]

The subject of both passages is prosaic; both poets see an added merit in the poetic treatment of such a subject and, in this respect, share their contemporaries' opinion that ingenuity is an ingredient of art. Both are obviously satisfied with Boileau's rendering and yet, even if we make an allowance for the lesser difficulty of La Fontaine's undertaking, we cannot but acknowledge the superiority of his lines over Boileau's: the simplicity, the naturalness of La Fontaine's wording conceal the aridity of the subject whilst Boileau's abstract vocabulary, metaphors and inversion betray it. To conceal itself in the guise of ease and naturalness is the supreme achievement of ingenuity and the unmistakable mark of elegance.

Many are the instances of elegant *copia*. In enumerations, for example, La Fontaine conforms with the principle formulated by Bellegarde:

> 'Le discours . . . est bien plus vif, et plus élégant, quand plusieurs substantifs, qui demandent naturellement le verbe au pluriel, sont liés par un terme qui change le nombre du verbe, et qui veut qu'on le mette au singulier:
>
>> L'intérêt, la raison, l'amitié, tout vous lie.

---

[1] *Œuvres de Mr. Boileau Despréaux avec des éclaircissements historiques données par lui-même*, vol. II, p. 319 (4° ed.); vol. IV, pp. 142–3 (12° ed.).

L'expression serait plus languissante, si l'on disait

> L'intérêt, l'amitié, et la raison vous lient.'[1]

Collective pronouns summing up an enumeration and followed by a verb in the singular abound in the *Fables*:

> La bagatelle, la science,
> Les chimères, le rien, *tout* est bon ...[IX, *Discours à Mme de la Sablière*]

> Valeur, adresse, et ruses, et surprises,
> *Tout* s'employa....[VII,7]

The device is even more striking when the collective represents human beings:

> Femmes, moine, vieillards, *tout*[2] était descendu.[VII,8]

> Petits et grands, *tout* approuva...[II,20]

> Facteurs, associés, *chacun* lui fut fidèle.[VII,13]

The effect of neatness resulting from this device is particularly obvious in the case of enumerations framed between two collectives:

> Il avait vu sortir *gibier* de toute sorte:
> Veaux de lait, agneaux et brebis,
> Régiments de dindons, enfin bonne *provende*.[IV,16]

> Une nouvelle hôtesse, à qui *toute la ville*,
> Femmes, filles, valets, gros Messieurs, *tout enfin*
> Allait comme autrefois demander son destin.[VII,14]

This impression of neatness is still more vividly emphasized when contrasted with 'untidy' enumerations, not infrequent when the poet wishes to insist on the thoroughness of an action. In these, an item left-over trails behind the collective:

> Il vendit son tabac, son sucre, sa canelle
> Ce qu'il voulut, sa porcelaine encor.[VII,13]

Here, the poet sacrifices elegance to expressiveness.

Repetition too, like ellipsis, can contribute to elegance, for clarity is more important than conciseness; only unnecessary repetitions are to be avoided according to Bouhours:

---

[1] J.-B. Morvan de Bellegarde, *Réflexions sur l'élégance*, p. 309.
[2] 'Tout se prend quelque fois élégamment pour les personnes'. D. Bouhours, *Remarques nouvelles sur la langue française*, p. 23.

'Ce savant auteur [Vaugelas] des *Remarques sur la langue française* dit que la principale de ces négligences est quand on répète deux fois dans une même page une même phrase sans qu'il soit nécessaire. Il ajoute que si la phrase est plus noble, la faute est encore plus grande parce qu'étant plus éclatante, elle se fait mieux remarquer. Comme il y a des répétitions nécessaires qui regardent la construction et la pureté, il y en a d'élégantes, qui ne contribuent qu'à la politesse et à l'ornement. Ce sont des redites qui plaisent; et on pourrait dire que ces sortes de répétitions sont dans le discours ce que sont dans la peinture les seconds coups de pinceau, qui en rendent les couleurs plus vives et plus fortes.'[1]

Such repetitions which Guez de Balzac called *recharges*[2] are frequent in the *Fables* where, far from betraying any lack of imagination or any clumsiness, they contribute to the vividness of the evocation:

Un jour sur ses *longs* pieds allait je ne sais où
Le héron au *long* bec emmanché d'un *long* cou.[VII,4]

Celui-ci parmi chaque espèce
Manda des *médecins*; il en est de tous arts.
Médecins au lion *viennent de toutes parts*;
De tous côtés lui *vient* des donneurs de recettes.[VIII,3]

In the latter example, the repetition of *venir* does not preclude variety since both the personal and the impersonal use of the verb are to be found, whilst the device provides the poet with an elegant chiasmus. Even emotional repetitions can be made elegant; Gamaches writes:

'Quand un mot ne peut être rendu par un autre, pour le corriger on l'ajoute à lui-même, mais accompagné de quelque terme propre à rendre sa signification plus énergique.'

And the example which the theorist quotes:

Là, mon fils, mon cher fils, a terminé ses jours[3]

is similar to La Fontaine's moving and fluid lines:

Amants, heureux amants, voulez-vous voyager? . . .[IX,2]

Ses oeufs, ses tendres oeufs, sa plus douce espérance.[II,8]

---

[1] D. Bouhours, *Remarques nouvelles sur la langue française*, p. 180.
[2] J. L. Guez de Balzac, *Socrate chrétien*, in *Œuvres*, vol. II, p. 15, and B. Gibert, *Jugement des savants sur les auteurs qui ont traité de la rhétorique*, Paris, 1712–19, vol. II, p. 393.
[3] E. S. de Gamaches, *Les Agréments du langage*, pp. 144–5.

In each case, an adjective relieves the monotonous repetition which, by becoming a *gradatio*, gains in force.

4. THE *Tours*

More than the choice of a specific word or a specific figure, the arrangement of linguistic elements within the sentence, the *tours*, account for the impression of extreme elegance given by the *Fables*. Vaugelas remarks:

> 'L'arrangement des mots est un des plus grands secrets du style: qui n'a cela, ne peut dire qu'il sache écrire. Il a beau employer de belles phrases et de beaux mots, étant mal placés, ils ne sauraient avoir ni beauté ni grâce, outre qu'ils embarrassent l'expression et lui ôtent la clarté, qui est le principal . . . Si l'on sait bien placer et entre-lacer le verbe au milieu des autres parties de l'oraison on saura un des plus grands secrets et la principale règle de l'arrangement des paroles. L'autre règle est de suivre le même ordre en écrivant que l'on tient en parlant.'[1]

Such a statement, in order to be correctly interpreted, requires some qualification such as that provided later by Ortigue de Vaumorière:

> 'L'Histoire et la Fable, qui sont plus faciles à comprendre q'un raisonnement subtil, sont aussi plus propres à gagner l'attention du peuple. Pour lui plaire, le style se doit relâcher, les expressions doivent être claires et familières. Je ne voudrais pourtant pas qu'elles fussent trop basses, et qu'elles sentissent la halle. Le peuple n'aurait pas trop de déférence pour les sentiments d'un homme qui ne parlerait pas mieux que lui. Il pourrait, au contraire, admirer ce qui serait au dessus de sa portée, et même en être touché sans savoir pourquoi. . . . Le peuple veut entendre ce qu'on lui dit aussi bien que les honnêtes gens, il est bien aise de voir qu'un habile homme n'emploie que des mots dont il pourrait se servir lui-même; mais il a encore plus de plaisir de remarquer que ces mots sont dans un meilleur ordre qu'il ne leur pourrait donner, et de tirer une espèce d'instruction de cette remarque.'[2]

For Gamaches, conciseness and relevance are deemed to be essential requirements to achieve this stylistic quality:

[1] Vaugelas, *Remarques sur la langue française*, p. 483.
[2] P. d'Ortigue de Vaumorière, *Harangues sur toutes sortes de sujets avec l'art de les composer*, Paris, 1693, p. 64.

'Lorsqu'une phrase manque d'harmonie, n'en cherchez la raison
que dans le mauvais arrangement des parties qui la composent: mettez
entre toutes ses parties l'ordre le plus convenable, à coup sûr vous
la rendrez harmonieuse. C'est à quoi ne prennent pas garde ceux qui
pour donner plus de cadence à leurs phrases, et pour les rendre plus
nombreuses les chargent de mots oisifs qui ne font qu'étendre la
diction, sans rien ajouter au sens. La mesure de nos périodes doit
être remplie par les termes mêmes dont nous sommes indispensable-
ment obligés de nous servir pour nous faire entendre.'[1]

Word-order within the sentence is of primary importance. On the one
hand, it must sound perfectly natural and suggest that of the spoken
language. The naturalness and simplicity of a narration such as *Le Rieur
et les Poissons*[VIII,8] is remarkable: this account of a somewhat peculiar
behaviour is given in brief and most precise terms which leave us with the
clear and factual impression of a complex action. *Les Deux Perroquets, le
Roi et son Fils*[X,11] also contains an exemplary exposition of an intricate situation and relationship, set in only twelve lines. On the other hand, the
expression must be stylized as befits light poetry which allows and even
requires certain transpositions of words and clauses. The art consists in
using transpositions to increase the suggestive and compelling value of
the sentence. In Richelet's words, 'les transpositions [de mots] bien faites
donnent de la force aux vers'[2] and such are La Fontaine's. The poet, for
example, suggests duration, the chronological sequence of events or of
sensations through ingenious arrangements of words:

Un an se passe et deux avec inquiétude. . . .[VII,4]

Un ruisseau se rencontre, et pour pont une planche.[XII,4]

Inversion, in which poets see a simple means of overcoming difficulties
of rhythm or rime, enables La Fontaine to give a fine image an added
distinction:

Voyez-vous cette main qui par les airs chemine?[I,8]

. . . Tous les noms des chercheurs de mondes inconnus
         Qui n'en étaient pas revenus,
Et que depuis cent ans sous l'abîme avaient vus
         Les anciens du vaste empire.[VIII,8]

[1] E. S. de Gamaches, *Les Agréments du langage*, p. 35.
[2] P. Richelet, *La Versification française*, p. 98.

Bernard Lamy, analysing the effect of such transpositions, writes:

'Lorsqu'on rejette un mot à la fin de la proposition, sans lequel
elle n'a aucun sens, ce retardement que souffre le lecteur le rend plus
attentif, l'ardeur qu'il a de concevoir les choses devient plus grande,
ainsi cette attention fait qu'il conçoit plus clairement. Outre cela,
ce petit renversement lie une proposition et la ramasse, en quelque
manière; car le lecteur est obligé pour l'entendre d'envisager toutes
ses parties ensemble ce qui fait que cette proposition le frappe plus
vivement.[1]

Elsewhere, an inversion attracts the reader's attention to a meaningful
yet discreet qualification or restriction:

Ce sera le meilleur lion
Pour ses amis qui soit sur terre.[XI,1]

Sometimes, not only does the inversion enable the poet to enhance an
image, it also allows him to stress its graphic quality as in the lines:

Celui de qui la tête au ciel était voisine,
Et dont les pieds touchaient à l'Empire des Morts,[I,22]

in which La Fontaine, by means of an elegant and poetic transposition,
brings the words *tête* and *ciel* close to each other just as the actual vision
which he evokes suggests. Gamaches, writing on the traditional word-
order, refers to this use of the inversion when he comments:

'Il faut qu'on le renverse quand on ne peut autrement rapprocher
les idées dont il s'agit de faire voir les rapports.[2]

Chiasmus is an ingenious device which enables the poet to introduce
an elegant variety into a sentence whilst preserving the force of a repetition; in the words of Gamaches:

'Quand les mêmes mots se trouvent répétés dans les parties
correspondantes d'une phrase, ce n'est pas dans le même ordre qu'on
les y doit placer, c'est dans un ordre symétrique ou renversé.'[3]

Thus,

[les moutons] gâtèrent tout et tout broutèrent.[IX,11]

Ils [les animaux] ne mouraient pas tous, mais tous étaient
frappés.[VII,1]

[1] B. Lamy, *L'Art de parler*, Paris, 1676, p. 28.
[2] E. S. de Gamaches, *Les Agréments du langage*, pp. 13–5.
[3] Ibid. pp. 92–3.

L'un [un docteur] disait: il est mort, je l'avais bien prévu.
-S'il m'eût cru, disait l'autre, il serait plein de vie.[V,12]

On a larger scale, a chiasmus may form the neat framework of the moral:

A. Jamais auprès des fous ne te mets à portée.
B. Je ne puis te donner un plus sage conseil.
B.   Il n'est enseignement pareil
A. A celui-là de fuir une tête éventée,[IX,8]

or of the whole anecdote:

Un passager pendant l'orage
A. Avait voué *cent* boeufs au vainqueur des Titans.
B. Il n'en avait pas *un* . . .

Il trouva des voleurs, et n'ayant dans sa bourse
B.   Qu'*un* écu pour toute ressource,
A.   Il leur promit *cent* talents d'or.[IX,13]

5. Structural Patterns

La Fontaine's preoccupation with clarity and elegant neatness appears in the composition of most of his fables. A close examination of sentence-structure often reveals the strict organization of the various elements composing his descriptions, narratives, speeches and morals. Repetitions, parallelisms, antitheses, chiasmus, anaphorae abound and give many passages the symmetrical arrangement and the clarity recommended by all the manuals of rhetorical composition. Discussions, as found in the *Fables*, differ little, at least in their structure if not in their language, from text-book examples of argumentation. Thus, in the prologue of *Le Meunier, son Fils et l'Âne*[III,1], Racan's speech is a model of formal reasoning:

1. Vous qui devez savoir les choses de la vie,
2. Qui par tous ses degrés avez déjà passé,
3. Et que rien ne doit fuir en cet âge avancé,

   1. Vous connaissez mon bien,
   2.   mon talent,
   3.   ma naissance . . .

1. Dois-je dans la province établir mon séjour,
2.   prendre emploi dans l'armée,
3.   ou bien charge à la cour?

    1. Tout au monde est mêlé d'amertume
    2.   et de charmes

      1. La guerre a ses douceurs,
      2. L'hymen a ses alarmes . . .

  1. Si je suivais mon goût, je saurais où buter,
  2. Mais j'ai (a) les miens,
            (b) la Cour,
            (c) le peuple
                      à contenter.

The discussion between *Les Deux Pigeons*[IX,2] is made up of symmetrical *pro* and *con* arguments which recall the pattern of discussions found in tragedy:

. . . Qu' allez-vous faire?	. . . Ne pleurez point.
Voulez-vous quitter votre frère?	Je reviendrai dans peu conter de point en point
. . . Au moins, que les travaux,	. . . Mes aventures à mon frère.
Les dangers, les soins du voyage, Changent un peu votre courage.	
L'absence est le plus grand des maux.	. . . . . . Quiconque ne voit guère N'a guère à dire aussi.
Non pas pour vous, cruel . . .	. . . . . . Mon voyage dépeint Vous sera d'un plaisir extrême.
	Vous y croirez être vous-même.

Speeches lend themselves to this rhetorical treatment but it is not rare to find similar developments in descriptive and narrative passages. In these, La Fontaine often combines neatness of structure with additional effects suited to the subject-matter of the passage. For example, he stresses a strong enmity between characters by symmetrical devices:

Il atteste les dieux; la perfide s'en moque.
Il résiste; elle tire. . . .[IV,11]

Car, si les loups mangeaient mainte bête égarée,
Les bergers de leur peau se faisaient maints habits.
Jamais de liberté, ni pour les pâturages,
Ni d'autre part pour les carnages.[III,13]

In *Le Pouvoir des Fables*[VIII,4], a concise ironical statement of fact following a rhetorical development provides an effective anticlimax which reflects the situation confronting the orator, whilst the repetition of this device shows his renewed efforts and subsequent failure:

Un orateur, voyant sa patrie en danger,
Courut à la tribune, et d'un art tyrannique,
Voulant forcer les coeurs dans une république,
Il parla fortement sur le commun salut.
On ne l'écoutait pas . . .

Il fit parler les morts, tonna, dit ce qu'il put.
Le vent emporta tout, personne ne s'émut.

In many fables, symmetry in sentence structure forms regular patterns which account for the general impression of neatness:

. . . Hippocrate arriva dans le temps

Que celui qu'on disait {n'avoir raison / ni sens}
Cherchait {dans l'homme / et dans la bête}
Quel siège a la raison {soit le coeur, / soit l'esprit.} [VIII,26]

Hercule veut. . .	puis	il aide les gens.
Regarde. . . l'achoppement	qui	te retient.
ôte . . . cette boue	qui	les enduit.
Prends . . . ce caillou	qui	te nuit.[VI,18]

La Fontaine, in his usual manner, relates the effects of such patterns to those required by the circumstances of the narrative. For example, in *Le Berger et la Mer*[IV,2], a complex but neat parallelism stresses the irony of changing fortune:

A   Si sa fortune était petite,

Elle était sûre *tout au moins.*

B   Les trésors le tentèrent si bien qu'il {vendit / trafiqua / mit sur l'eau}

Cet argent périt par naufrage.

A   Son maître fut réduit à garder les brebis,

Non plus berger en chef. . . .

B   Celui qui s'était vu Coridon
     ou Tircis

Fut Pierrot, et rien davantage.

In *Le Fermier, le Chien et le Renard*[XI,3], a similar device emphasizes an implicit comparison:

Si vous maître et fermier
       a qui touche le fait dormez *sans* avoir soin . . .

Voulez-vous que moi chien
                    qui n'ai rien *sans* aucun intérêt, je perde . . .

In *Le Jardinier et son Seigneur*[IV,4], the picture of the garden before and after the coming of the hunt is evoked by means of identical sentence patterns which relate and contrast the present with the past:

Là croissait . . . l'oseille
                  et la laitue
                  de quoi faire . . . un bouquet

Adieu chicorée
      et porreaux
      Adieu de quoi mettre au potage

Thus the anecdote gains in vividness, the fable in elegance. Elsewhere, the pattern spreads throughout the fable, as in *Le Villageois et le Serpent*[VI,13].

Un manant sur la neige étendu,
aperçut un transi,
serpent gelé,
          perclus,
          immobile,
          rendu,
          n'ayant pas à vivre un quart d'heure

Le villageois le prend,
            l'emporte,
            il l'étend,
            le réchauffe,
            le ressuscite

Le serpent lève un peu la tête,
           puis siffle,
           puis fait un long repli,
           son bienfaiteur,
           puis . . . un saut contre son sauveur,
                                son père

[Le manant]

il vous prend sa cognée,
il vous tranche la bête,

il fait trois serpents...

un tronçon,
la queue,
et la tête.

Here, besides giving neatness to the fable, symmetry emphasizes and relates to each other the plight of the snake, the peasant's charitable gesture, the ingratitude of the snake and the peasant's wrath; the structural pattern gives unity to the whole fable.

Sometimes, the whole fable is framed between two identical aphorisms:

Il se faut entraider; c'est la loi de nature.

Je conclus qu'*il faut qu'on s'entraide.*[VIII,17]

or the anecdote itself is set between two parallel statements:

Un mort *s'en allait* tristement
S'emparer de son dernier gîte;
Un curé *s'en allait* gaiement
Enterrer ce mort au plus vite
Notre défunt était en carrosse porté...

Le pasteur était à coté...

Notre curé suit son seigneur;
Tous deux *s'en vont* de compagnie.[VII,10]

When, as in this example, the repetition is made more complex by humorous ambiguities, admiration for the poet's ingenuity increases the satisfaction of the eye and the ear.

Sometimes, the similarity of sentence structure, together with repetitions, links moral and fable closely:[1]

Et, *nouvel Empédocle aux flammes* condamné,
Par sa propre et pure *folie*,
Il se lança dedans...

L'*Empédocle* de cire *au brasier* se fondit:
Il n'était pas plus *fou* que l'*autre*.[IX,12]

---

[1] Sometimes, the link between moral and fable is established by the juxtaposition—in the moral—of an abstract or general term and a concrete word recalling the circumstances of the anecdote with precision:

Aux conseils *de la mer et de l'ambition*
Nous devons fermer nos oreilles.[IV,2]

Il ne les [les princes] faut jamais engager *dans vos guerres*,
Ni les faire entrer *sur vos terres.*[IV,4]

Jamais auprès des *fous* ne te mets à portée.
Je ne puis te donner un plus sage conseil.
Il n'est enseignement pareil
A celui-là de fuir *une tête éventée.*

La raison est-elle garant
De ce que fait un *fou?* Le hasard est la cause
De tout ce qui se passe en *un cerveau blessé.*[IX,8]

These similarities between anecdote and moral give the reader the aesthetic satisfaction of neatly rounded-off arguments. These are frequent in the *Fables*:

... Je revois les *lapins*
Plus gais qu'auparavant revenir *sous mes mains.*
Ne reconnaît-on pas en cela les humains?

Vrais *lapins* on les revoit
Sous les mains de la fortune.[X,14]

6. TRANSITIONS AND UNITY

Leo Spitzer[1] has given a detailed study of transitions in the *Fables* which reveals La Fontaine's secret art and constitutes one of the most illuminating contributions to the analysis of his style. Although it is not our intention to duplicate Spitzer's work here, it would be profitable to consider a few examples of our poet's most frequent types of transitions. Rémond de Saint-Mard, commenting on the prologue to *Les Compagnons d'Ulysse* writes:

'Prenez-vous garde ... à l'air naturel dont ce prologue s'unit avec la fable? On ne voit point la couture tant elle est bien faîte. ... C'est ... avec ce grand art de nuer que La Fontaine, après avoir parlé de la guerre et des dieux, revient avec grâce à des idées plus douces:

Je m'en tais; aussi bien les Ris et les Amours
Ne sont pas soupçonnés d'aimer les longs discours.
De ces sortes de dieux votre Cour se compose.
Ils ne vous quittent point. Ce n'est pas qu'après tout
D'autres divinités n'y tiennent le haut-bout:
Le sens et la raison y règlent toute chose.

[1] L. Spitzer, 'Die Kunst des Übergangs bei La Fontaine', in *P.M.L.A.*, LIII, 1938, pp. 393–433, also in L. Spitzer, *Critica stilistica e storia del linguaggio*, Bari, 1954, pp. 161–226.

Ce haut-bout me charme par sa naïveté. Il vous fait là tout à coup rentrer dans le ton de la fable dont il me semblait que La Fontaine s'était un peu écarté par les idées qu'il y maniait.'[1]

Rosen has pointed out the contrast existing between the transitions of La Fontaine and those of Boileau:

'Boileau is not, in general, interested in this sort of transition [i.e. the subtle transitions of La Fontaine]. In the original version of the *First Epistle*, the fable is introduced with the words: "Muse baisse la voix". Boileau makes no attempt to disguise the change of manner.'[2]

La Fontaine often progresses from the general to the particular or vice-versa by means of series of carefully graded words which mark the stages of the progression and, at the same time, by an ingenious system of cross-reference make this progression perfectly natural: in *Le Paysan du Danube*[XI,7], the poet, starting from a generally accepted aphorism, recalls earlier developments of the theme and, by reference to them, introduces his own character:

Il ne faut point juger *des gens* sur l'apparence.
Le conseil en est bon; mais *il n'est pas nouveau*:
Jadis l'erreur du *souriceau*
Me servit à prouver le discours que j'avance.
J'ai pour le fonder *à présent*
Le bon *Socrate*, *Esope*, et *certain paysan*
Des rives du Danube, homme dont *Marc-Aurèle*
Nous fait un portrait fort fidèle.
On connaît *les premiers*; quant à *l'autre*, voici
Le personnage en raccourci.

Thus, by means of proper nouns, the anecdote is placed in the context of a humanistic tradition, and the evocation of ancient writers is well suited to a fable relating an episode situated in classical antiquity. The passage is both elegant and ingenious in its conciseness and breadth of scope, in the variety of the references it allows (the *souriceau*, Marcus-Aurelius ...), and in its relevance to the fable which it introduces.

In *Le Renard, le Singe et les Animaux*[VI,6], we find a simpler type of transition often used in the *Fables*:

De son étui la couronne est tirée.

<hr/>

[1] Rémond de Saint-Mard, *Réflexions sur la fable*, in *Œuvres*, pp. 110–4.
[2] C. W. Rosen, *Style and Morality in La Fontaine*, p. 76.

Il se trouva que sur tous essayée
A pas un d'eux elle ne convenait.
Plusieurs avaient le tête trop menue,
Aucuns trop grosse, *aucuns* même cornue.
Le singe aussi fit l'épreuve en riant. . . .

Here, a choice of indefinite pronouns provides a satisfactory transition between a description of the reactions of the animal kingdom at the death of the lion and the introduction of one of the main characters of the fable. The process is reversed in *Parole de Socrate*[IV,17], in which the range of indefinite pronouns allows the poet to proceed from Socrates' action to the reactions of the crowd:

Socrate un jour faisant bâtir,
Chacun censurait son ouvrage.
L'un trouvait les dedans, pour ne lui point mentir,
Indignes d'un tel personnage;
L'autre blâmait la face, et *tous* étaient d'avis
Que les appartements en étaient trop petits.

These devices make the change of subject gradual and more natural, they preserve the smooth quality of the narrative style and allow the poet to add successive touches to the scenes which he depicts, 'de les égayer'. Technically speaking, they are not very different from the enumeration and the *gradatio* types of transition identified by Spitzer.

The repetition of a word constitutes the simplest form of transition:

On voit courir après l'ombre,
Tant de fous, qu'on n'en sait pas
La plupart du temps le nombre.
Au chien dont parle Esope il faut les renvoyer.
Ce chien voyant . . .[VI,17]

Yet La Fontaine's use of repetition deserves attention: often repetitions of words and phrases facilitate transitions between the various parts of a fable but also give unity to the whole poem. *Le Fou qui vend la Sagesse*[IX,8] relates the antics of a man who claims to sell wisdom and draws many would-be buyers:

Puis on avait pour son argent

Avec un bon *soufflet* un *fil* long de deux brasses.

The victims' reactions are then described: most are annoyed but to some,

le mieux était de rire,
Ou de s'en aller sans rien dire,
Avec son *soufflet* et son *fil.*

One buyer however comes more precisely into focus:

Du *fil* et du *soufflet* pourtant embarrassé,
Un des dupes un jour alla trouver un sage . . .

The wise man explains:

Les gens bien conseillés, et qui voudront bien faire,
Entre eux et les gens fous mettront pour l'ordinaire
La longueur de ce *fil*; sinon je les tiens sûrs
De quelque semblable *caresse,*

thus revealing the importance and relevance of *le fil* and *le soufflet* which recurred throughout the fable as a leit-motiv linking together every episode of the narrative, and formed a cryptic transposition of the moral.

In *L'Homme et la Couleuvre*[X,1], the reader is constantly reminded of the two major themes of the fable—ingratitude and the abject nature of man—by the repetitions of *ingrat, ingratitude* and the recurrent association of man and snake which amounts to an implicit comparison and finally rounds off the fable:

. . . Ils se mettent en tête
Que tout est né pour eux, quadrupèdes, et gens,
Et serpents.

The repetition of the verb *gâter,* recurring at each of the three stages of the narrative development of *L'Ecolier, le Pédant et le Maître d'un jardin*[IX,5] is also an ingenious means of giving the fable unity: teachers spoil children's minds, the child spoils the garden, the teacher followed by his class comes to put things right and they spoil the garden too. The parallelism of these actions, stressed by the repetition of the verbal element, bring the final comment very naturally:

Et ne sais bête au monde pire
Que l'écolier, si ce n'est le pédant.

The structure of *L'Aigle et la Pie*[XII,11] is even more complex; in the opening lines, parallelisms emphasize the differences in the birds' temperament and their latent enmity, whilst the single verb, having both birds as subject, stresses the similarity of the action which is to cause their encounter:

L'aigle, reine des airs   avec Margot la pie,

Différentes   d'humeur, de langage, d'esprit et d'habit   traversaient. . . .

Le hasard les assemble en un coin détourné.

L'agasse eut peur   mais l'aigle . . . la rassure.

Further on, repetitions of words (*Caquet-bon-bec, babil, babillarde, espion, Margot, habit*) relate the eagle's reply and the moral to the magpie's offer and the first part of the narrative.

Elaborate patterns and the most fluid transitions are to be found in the fables which take the form of epistles and *discours: Le Lion amoureux*[IV,1], *Le Bûcheron et Mercure*[V,1], *Discours à Madame de La Sablière*[IX], *Le Renard anglais*[XII,23], as if the poet wished to capture the ear of his distinguished correspondents by the persuasive grace and charm of his style, and thus compensate for the relative aridity of the subject-matter. To introduce Madame de La Sablière to Cartesian theories with such lightness of touch is no mean achievement. It is this same ease and continuity in the intellectual and poetic development which has led Gutmann to compare the second *Discours à Madame de La Sablière* to Bossuet's *envolées poétiques*.[1] The speech of *Le Paysan du Danube*[XI,7] provides further evidence of La Fontaine's rhetorical skill which, in this fable, is concealed in masterly fashion to leave the reader with the impression that he is hearing an impassioned appeal made by an uncouth orator.[2] The general effect corresponds to the picture of spontaneous eloquence given by Bellegarde:

> 'Il n'en va pas des pièces d'éloquence comme des autres discours, qui demandent un sens rassis et un esprit tranquille; les personnes qui s'écoutent et qui parlent sans passion, observent de l'ordre et de la méthode dans ce qu'elles disent; au contraire, une espèce de désordre ne sied pas mal dans un discours animé, parce que c'est une marque de la passion, qui n'est en effet elle-même qu'un trouble et une émotion de l'âme: voilà pourquoi un orateur retranche quelque fois les liaisons qui applatissant le discours lui ôtent une partie de sa véhémence.'[3]

Yet, the brutality of the expression ('témoin nous que . . ., retirez-les: on ne veut plus . . ., je finis . . .', etc.) gives the impression of a purely impulsive composition, of chaotic arguments. In fact, the whole speech is

---

[1] R. A. Gutmann, *Introduction à la lecture des poètes français*, Paris, 1946, p. 82.
[2] Doucet, 'La Fontaine orateur', in *Les Etudes Classiques*, XXIII, 1955, pp. 427–39.
[3] J.-B. Morvan de Bellegarde, *Réflexions sur l'élégance* . . ., pp. 423–4.

a model of regular composition, rich in effective transitions which give it movement and unity. The ending is meant to be abrupt but the argumentation is rounded off in an exemplary manner and the speaker reverts to the themes with which he opened his speech: rapacity (*ll.* 30 and 76), Rome (*ll.* 31 and 77), the laws (*ll.* 29 and 80), the nature of the speech (*ll.* 25–6 and 81–2). Thus, the impassioned quality of the peasant's speech is the result of a skilfully contrived technique, its apparent artlessness, the result of elegant stylization. The speech retains an impressive unity and conforms closely to the rules formulated by Bernard Lamy in *L'Art de Parler*:

> 'La voix ne se repose à la fin de chaque membre, que pour continuer plus loin sa course: elle ne s'arrête entièrement qu'à la fin de toute la sentence. On peut dire que la voix roule en prononçant une période, qu'elle fait comme un cercle qui renferme tout le sens de la période: ainsi les oreilles sentent facilement la distinction et l'union des membres.'[1]

The *style indirect libre* often provides an effective transition between the main narrative and direct speech. Gohin remarks that:

> 'La transition est alors si habilement ménagée que, par endroits, on ne distingue plus si le fabuliste parle encore ou s'il a cédé la parole à son personnage.'[2]

Thus, the change of voice is made gradually, the speaker is gently brought into focus and the fable gains in variety:

> Rien ne la contentait, rien n'était comme il faut:
> On se levait trop tard, on se couchait trop tôt;
> Puis du blanc, puis du noir, puis encore autre chose.
> Les valets enrageaient, l'époux était à bout:
> Monsieur ne songe à rien, Monsieur dépense tout,
> Monsieur court, Monsieur se repose.[VII,2]

> Il pria le cheval de l'aider quelque peu:
> Autrement il mourrait devant qu'être à la ville.
> La prière, dit-il, n'en est pas incivile:
> Moitié de ce fardeau ne vous sera que jeu.[(VI,16)3]

The fable *Le Pot de Terre et le Pot de Fer*[V,2] opens in narrative style and, through the intermediate stages of indirect speech and *style indirect libre* develops into a dialogue in direct speech.

---

[1] B. Lamy, *L'Art de parler*, p. 131.
[2] F. Gohin, *L'Art de La Fontaine dans ses Fables*, p. 98.
[3] See also VIII, 8; VIII, 19; XII, 15; XII, 20; etc.

The variety of styles which La Fontaine often displays in the same fable requires subtle transitions to preserve the unity of the fable. Not only are the different styles juxtaposed, they also—without losing their individuality—overlap and intermingle to blend into what the poet calls 'un juste tempérament.'[1] The *Discours à M. le Duc de La Rochefoucauld*[X,14] provides an excellent illustration of La Fontaine's care for tonal transitions. The fable proper begins with a poetic evocation of the setting of the action, inspired by obvious classical sources:

> A l'heure de l'affût, soit lorsque la lumière
> Précipite ses traits dans l'humide séjour,
> Soit lorsque le soleil rentre dans sa carrière,
> Et que n'étant plus nuit, il n'est pas encore jour,
> Au bord de quelque bois. . . .

The anecdote follows, precise, realistic, in a minor key, forming an amusing contrast with the poetic preamble. Yet a mythological reference, classical in inspiration like the preamble and light in tone like the anecdote itself, links both passages closely:

> . . . sur un arbre je grimpe,
> Et *nouveau Jupiter du haut de cet Olympe,*
> Je foudroie à discrétion
> Un lapin qui n'y pensait guère.

Similar transitions can be observed, for example, in *Le Fermier, le Chien et le Renard*[XI,3]. Here, the fox's remark in mock-epic style:

> Pourquoi sire Jupin m'a-t-il donc appelé
> Au métier de renard? Je jure les puissances
> De l'Olympe et du Styx, il en sera parlé,

constitutes a suitable transition between the pedestrian style of the first phase of the anecdote and the higher poetic style—with its Virgilian echoes—which follows:

> Roulant en son coeur ces vengeances,
> Il choisit une nuit libérale en pavots. . . .

The gradation then progresses to reach full epic splendour:

> Peu s'en fallut que le soleil
> Ne rebroussât d'horreur vers le manoir liquide. . . .

[1] *Psyché*, Preface, *O.D.*, p. 121.

M

The return to the anecdote is operated through another ingenious transition: the epic evocation of Ajax's wrath

> Tel encore autour de sa tente
> Ajax, à l'âme impatiente. . . .

is followed by its mock-epic application to the animal character of the apologue:

> Le renard autre Ajax aux volailles funeste. . . .

C. W. Rosen in his thesis *Style and Morality in La Fontaine* has given many examples of similar transitions which led him to remark:

> 'Variety is disguised by elegance, the inconsistency veiled by moderation. The various styles are not used for contrast, but for a series of movements which parallel the movements of thought.'[1]

We cannot but agree with this judgement which reveals yet another component of the poet's stylistic elegance whilst insisting at the same time on its discretion. One should however recall that La Fontaine's contemporaries had not been less sensitive than modern criticism to the poet's secret art. In 1715 Boivin, who makes serious reservations on the prosody and versification of the *Fables*,—'Il y a des vers faibles, il y en a de durs, de mal rimés, de superflus'—admires their elegance, deceptive ease and studied negligence which he compares to Homer's and prefers to Vergil's more obvious perfection:

> 'Pour une vingtaine de fables, qu'on peut regarder comme parfaites, peut-être en trouverait-on autant qui paraîtraient peu exactes. Cependant il n'y en a presque pas une, dont la lecture ne fasse un extrême plaisir aux personnes d'esprit et de bon goût; pourquoi? Parce qu'il n'y en a presque pas une où l'on ne remarque quelque beauté neuve et originale, quelque trait de maître, quelque tour heureux, naïf, élégant, quelque terme propre et expressif, dont l'agrément paie le lecteur et le dédommage suffisamment de ce qu'il perd du côté du reste.'[2]

The qualities which Boivin admires, here, in La Fontaine, constitute what our poet himself calls

> cet heureux art
> Qui cache ce qu'il est et ressemble au hasard.[3]

---

[1] C. W. Rosen, *Style and Morality in La Fontaine*, pp. 73–4.
[2] J. Boivin, *Apologie d'Homère et bouclier d'Achille*, Paris, 1715, pp. 250–1.
[3] *Le Songe de Vaux*, II, *O.D.*, p. 82.

CHAPTER VI

POETRY

In his appreciation of the *Fables*, Chamfort, reviewing most of the features so far mentioned in this study, reserved his main admiration for their poetic quality:

'Je suppose en effet que mes rivaux relèvent, l'un l'heureuse alliance de ses expressions [celles de La Fontaine], la hardiesse et la nouveauté de ses figures, d'autant plus étonnantes qu'elles paraissent plus simples; l'autre, ce charme continu de style, qui réveille une foule de sentiments, embellit de couleurs si vives ou si douces tous les contrastes que lui présente son sujet, m'intéresse à des bourgeons gâtés par écolier, m'attendrit sur le sort de l'aigle qui vient de perdre ses œufs. .... Qu'un troisième vous vante l'agrément et le sel de la plaisanterie qui rapproche si heureusement les grands et les petits objets, voit tour à tour dans un renard, Patrocle, Ajax, Annibal, Alexandre dans un chat, ... met de niveau Pyrrhus et la laitière, ... que prouveront-ils ceux qui offriront tous ces traits, sinon, que des remarques devenues communes peuvent être plus ou moins heureusement rajeunies par le mérite de l'expression? Et d'ailleurs, comment peindre un poète, qui souvent semble s'adonner comme dans une conversation facile, qui citant Ulysse à propos des voyages d'une tortue s'étonne lui-même de le trouver là; dont les beautés paraissent quelquefois une heureuse rencontre, et possèdent ainsi, pour me servir d'un mot qu'il aimait, la grâce de la soudaineté; qui s'est fait une langue et une poésie particulière; dont le tour est naïf quand la pensée est ingénieuse; l'expression simple, quand son idée est forte; relevant ses grâces naturelles par cet attrait piquant que leur prête ce que la physionomie ajoute à la beauté; qui se joue sans cesse de son art; qui, à propos de la tardive maternité d'une alouette, me peint les délices du printemps, les plaisirs, les amours de tous les êtres, et met l'enchantement de la nature en contraste avec le veuvage d'un oiseau?'[1]

[1] Chamfort, *Eloge de La Fontaine*, in *Recueil de l'Académie de Marseille*, Paris, 1774, pp. 21–3.

This judgement seems more perceptive than the following assertion of Gutmann:

'Le plus souvent, les fables ne sont pas des poèmes. Elles sont *poétiques* au sens le plus banal et le plus sentimental du mot, dans la mesure exacte où leur sujet l'est. S'il s'agit de petits lapins qui dansent dans la rosée, elles sont poétiques; s'il s'agit des "enfants du hibou" ou d'un noyé, elles ne le sont pas.'[1]

But, to remain on that level and limit ourselves to the examples given by the critic, the loving mother-owl's flattering description of her offspring[V,18] is a faithful illustration of one of the most touching human foibles on which the reader is induced to reflect. The poetic dignity of the reference to maternity:

Il advint qu'au hibou Dieu donna géniture

tempers the irony of the situation; the final remark is hardly sarcastic and constitutes a general observation on human nature—'la commune loi'—rather than a castigation of maternal delusion. The poet's sympathy for the victim pervades the whole fable and gives it a humane warmth which predisposes the reader's mind to entertain emotions and reflections which prolong the inconclusive apologue. Even 'un noyé' may, in *Le Rieur et les Poissons*[VIII,8], become the pretext for a splendid poetic vision.

It is true that La Fontaine sometimes treats subjects which are in them-selves poetic 'au sens le plus banal et le plus sentimental du mot', but the poetry which pervades his work has much deeper roots: in composing his fables, he conjures up and animates a complex and infinitely varied world, a vast poetic myth. In the words of Faguet:

'Il semble que l'essence de la poésie de La Fontaine, c'est le sens de la vie universelle. Pour lui tout vit dans le monde. Le monde est une sorte de concert et de concours d'une foule de vies individuelles. "Tout est plein d'âmes", dira plus tard Victor Hugo. Cela pourrait être la devise de La Fontaine.'[2]

This poetic world is, at the same time, coherent and fantastic, and corresponds closely with Bouhours's definition:

'A la vérité le monde fabuleux, qui est le monde des poètes n'a rien en soi de réel: c'est l'ouvrage tout pur de l'imagination; et le Parnasse,

---

[1] R. A. Gutmann, *Introduction à la lecture des poètes français*, Paris, 1964, p. 78.
[2] E. Faguet, *Histoire de la Poésie française de la Renaissance au Romantisme*, Paris, 1930, vol. IV, p. 184.

Apollon, les Muses avec le cheval Pégase ne sont que d'agréables
chimères. Mais ce système étant une fois supposé, tout ce qu'on
feint dans l'étendue du même système ne passe point pour faux parmi
les savants, surtout quand la fiction est vraisemblable, et qu'elle
cache quelque vérité.'[1]

Gutmann's contention that:

'Tout ce monde "imaginaire" étant devenu pour La Fontaine le
monde "réel", il nous le montre avec ces détails précis et cette netteté
de contour, ce manque de "halo" qui s'oppose au poème ... Les
fables de La Fontaine peuvent s'orner de considérations philoso-
phiques, ironiques, pratiques; elles font réfléchir, sourire, admirer;
jamais rêver.'[2]

contrasts curiously with Baudin's judgement:

'Les vers de La Fontaine, vrai poète, suggèrent toujours plus
qu'ils ne disent, parlent constamment à l'imagination et à la sensibilité, rayonnent naturellement un halo et une aura poétiques qui les
mettent en branle et font rêver.'[3]

This confrontation of opinions gives some idea of the complexity of the
question. Madame de Mourgues has shown that La Fontaine's attitude towards his own poetry is one of amused and knowing detachment. Even in
the most poetic passages, he perceives and expresses the distance between
the language used and the reality evoked. His poetry is enhanced by
poetic wit: the author is fully aware of both the effectiveness and the
limitation of his poetry: the reader himself is induced to perceive them
and to enjoy poetry for what it is, namely a literary achievement. 'La
poésie de La Fontaine est littérature pure; elle commence et elle finit avec
les mots du poème.'[4] In this respect, the *Fables* do not make one dream,
they make one think.

However, it would seem difficult to deny the *Fables* their power of
suggestion. The fable as a genre, with its animals and plants for characters,
lends itself to poetic treatment. Even on the level of the language, 'le
monde des animaux est un ... grand foyer de rayonnement métaphor-
ique',[5] and the fable, taken as an extended metaphor, offers a rich scope for
poetic development. Precision in expression is not incompatible with a
certain form of aesthetic and poetic stylization. The reader's imagination,

[1] D. Bouhours, *La Manière de bien penser*, pp. 10–11.
[2] R. A. Gutmann, *Introduction à la lecture des poètes français*, p. 78–9.
[3] E. Baudin, *La Philosophie morale des Fables de La Fontaine*, Neuchâtel, 1950, p. 96.
[4] O. de Mourgues, *O Muse, fuyante proie ...*, p. 165.
[5] S. Ullmann, *Précis de sémantique française*, Bern, 1952, p. 279.

awakened by the striking precision of a few details retained by the poet to evoke a character, the setting of the action or an incidental reflection, is thus set into motion and led to complete the suggested vision. In the words of Grammont:

> 'C'est ce travail de l'imagination qui constitue à proprement parler la poésie; car la poésie, sauf dans le genre lyrique, n'est que préparée par le poète, et c'est le lecteur qui la réalise.'[1]

1. LANGUAGE AND POETRY

This preparation, in the case of La Fontaine, is almost always effected by a skilful and yet discreet use of linguistic and stylistic resources. One might justifiably fear that the poet's care for the exact term, his fondness for realistic words and phrases, his love of the older language would be detrimental to poetry; yet La Fontaine succeeds in avoiding the cramping effect of these elements without depriving his verse of their qualities. In the *Fables*, the *mot propre* becomes poetic by refraction; as Faguet remarks:

> 'Le goût du mot propre est le penchant dominant de La Fontaine. Son art consiste à appeler les choses par leur vrai nom, en donnant au terme propre une valeur inattendue par le reflet sur lui des mots qui l'entourent.'[2]

Thus, the adjectives 'légère et court vêtue'[VII,9] prepare the reader's mind to see in all the subsequent *mots propres* ('cotillon simple', 'souliers plats', 'ainsi troussée') elements of a pretty and pleasant picture. The rabbit who owns a *palais*[VII,15] cannot be visualized as a mere *lapin*. Periphrases and qualifications such as:

> Un mal qui répand la terreur,
> Mal que le ciel en sa fureur
> Inventa pour punir les crimes de la terre,
>
> Capable d'enrichir en un jour l'Achéron,[VII,1]

contrast with the *mot propre*

> La peste (puisqu'il faut l'appeler par son nom),

---

[1] Grammont, *Psychologie linguistique: style et poésie*, Paris, 1950, p. 156.
[2] E. Faguet, *Dix-septième siècle*, Paris, n.d., p. 181.

and colour it with the gloomy shade of dread, whilst the line:

<blockquote>Faisait aux animaux la guerre</blockquote>

turns it into an allegory.

Sometimes, it is the position of the *mot propre* which accounts for its poetic value. One of the notes from various commentators gathered by J. B. Gail points to the effect of the inversion in the following lines from Philémon et Baucis:

<blockquote>Quelques restes de feu sous la cendre épandus
D'un souffle haletant par Baucis s'allumèrent.[XII,25]</blockquote>

'La grammaire peut être tentée de condamner cette phrase, la poésie doit l'aimer . . . Le vers jusqu'à ce dernier mot [s'allumèrent] marque la lenteur de l'opération; l'hiatus souffle-ha montre et fait sentir la peine de la vieille . . . S'allumèrent, qui s'offre le dernier, peint la subtile apparition et l'éclat de la flamme: que l'on détruise l'inversion, il n'y a plus d'image.'[1]

Poetic effects may be derived even from realistic terms. Many of these have a rustic flavour traditionally associated with poetic celebrations of lowly and humble rural life. Thus, Clarac writes:

'On s'est étonné de rencontrer dans une fable toute réaliste comme *La Mort et le Bûcheron*, une citation empruntée à l'épisode rabelaisien de la Sibylle de Panzoust. La Fontaine ne voit-il donc la vie qu'à travers les livres? Il me paraît, au contraire, que voulant nous rendre aussi présente qu'à lui-même une de ces huttes forestières . . . il a senti que les mots "chaumine enfumée" lui étaient indispensables moins encore à cause de leur justesse que de leur pouvoir d'évocation.'[2]

Archaisms, too, help to diffuse a certain poetic quality throughout the *Fables*. They spread a patina over the text and gave it, even in its first edition, the quaint aspect and the charm of a seasoned antique, evoking earlier, less polished, versions of these ageless apologues:

<blockquote>Il avait dans la terre une somme enfouie,
Son coeur avec, n'ayant d'autre *déduit*
Que d'y ruminer jour et nuit,
Et rendre sa *chevance* à lui-même sacrée.[IV,20]</blockquote>

---

[1] J. B. Gail, *Observations sur les quatre dernières fables de La Fontaine restées jusqu'ici sans commentaire, par Sélis, Delille et La Harpe, recueillies par J. B. Gail*, Paris, 1821, pp. 34–5.

[2] Clarac, *La Fontaine, l'homme et l'œuvre*, p. 77; *Fables*, I, 16.

The modern, more explicit equivalents, *plaisir* and *bien*, would make the narrative altogether more prosaic and would impose the picture of a miser contemporary with the author or the reader. It is remarkable that, whilst most archaisms were frowned upon by the seventeenth-century theorists of style and language, they were still tolerated in poetry. Archaisms, as well as intentional anachronisms, help to evoke a tradition spreading over many centuries and, at the same time, to blend the various elements borrowed from it into a timeless lore of learning, natural wisdom and fantasy. All these aspects of the language of the *Fables* have already been commented upon in an earlier chapter and here, only La Fontaine's poetic use of this language needs to retain our attention.

2. The Poetic Language

In an age when a strict hierarchy of tones and genres corresponded to clear-cut distinctions between languages and styles, La Fontaine used all the poetic languages of his time concurrently. The result is a language of unprecedented richness which, in spite of its smoothness, implies, on the part of the poet, a confrontation of the specific merits of each of its components. This attitude reveals an unquestionable artistic maturity and a certain detachment from all the techniques involved; hence the difficulty of defining his poetry: it is not *précieux*, nor baroque, nor realistic poetry, it is—as Madame de Mourgues has shown[1]—the sum, the harmonious combination of a century's experiments, with one single aim in view, that of poetic expressiveness. It has proved therefore more rewarding to study the poetic style of La Fontaine as a whole; a detailed analysis of each style which constitutes it would necessarily entail many repetitions of points already made earlier in this study.

La Fontaine uses the lyrical language of the time in a manner which reveals a deep awareness, on his part, of the aesthetic qualities of what was often pure mannerism in his predecessors. Many of his words and idioms are clichés of seventeenth-century poetry—'onde', 'bords', 'cavernes creuses', 'liquide manoir', 'Thétis', 'Amphitrite', 'les Filles de Mémoire', 'le Fils de Cythère', etc—yet these terms and figures, however hackneyed, are part of the poetic liturgy and constitute *la langue des dieux* now heard for the first time in unexpected quarters:

[1] O. de Mourgues, *La Fontaine, Fables*, p. 9.

Le Loup en langue des dieux
Parle au Chien dans mes ouvrages. . . .[(IX,1)][1]

It is no longer the irrepressible mannerism of a lyrical poet,[2] nor the systematic device of a *burlesque* writer; it is an altogether new venture: the unprecedented use of a well-established language in a new context, in a new genre, to express, in traditional idiom and imagery, traditional poetic themes considered from a new viewpoint. The *Fables*, by their language, still retain some of the prestige of formal poetry whilst their author, through discriminative selection, and a free handling of poetic speech, invites a new appraisement of the most trite clichés. The novelty of this poetry is not startling, it is simply further-reaching in its effects than that of La Fontaine's predecessors in so far as it contains an element of literary consciousness which reveals the maturity of the artist. Without being exclusively *précieux*, this poetry corresponds with Giraudoux's definition of preciosity:

'. . . .qui consiste à traiter les objets comme s'ils étaient des humains, les humains comme s'ils étaient dieux et vierges, les dieux comme des chats et des belettes, mal que provoquent, non pas la vie dans les bibliothèques, mais les relations personnelles avec les saisons, les petits animaux, un excessif panthéisme et de la politesse envers la création.'[3]

A general appearance of perfect naturalness and disarming simplicity conditions the reader[4] to take part in the poetic ceremony without any self-consciousness and yield to the charm of rapid evocations conjured up, often in one single line, by the combination of traditional poetic vocabulary, elementary sentence-structure, an occasional inversion, and the fluid quality of sounds:

L'onde était transparente *ainsi qu'aux plus beaux jours*[VII,4]

[1] See Pellisson et D'Olivet, *Histoire de l'Académie Française*, ed. Livet, Paris, 1858, vol. II, p. 325: 'Après Marot et Rabelais, La Fontaine n'estimait rien tant que *L'Astrée* de M. d'Urfé. C'est d'où il tirait ces images champêtres, qui lui sont familières, et qui font toujours un si bel effet dans la poésie.' See also J. Arthos, *The Language of Natural Description in Eighteenth-Century Poetry*, Ann Arbor, Michigan, USA, 1949.
[2] See Boileau, *Satire II*, in *Œuvres*, vol. I, pp. 70–5, and Le Verrier's account of Boileau's reaction when Arnauld d'Andilly reproached him with imitating Malherbe unconsciously, Le Verrier, *Commentaire des Satires de Boileau corrigé par lui-même*, in *Les Satires de Boileau commentées par lui-même*, p. 27.
[3] Jean Giraudoux, *Juliette au pays des hommes*, Paris, 1924, pp. 229–30.
[4] This conditioning of the reader's disposition to enjoy the poet's vision of a pleasurable world is, to a certain exent, akin to that achieved by Stendhal in *La Chartreuse de Parme*, e.g. the meeting of Fabrice and Clelia Conti on the road to Milan, ed. Martineau, Paris, 1946, pp. 106–11.

Morphée avait touché *le seuil de ce palais*[VIII,11]

Le long d'*un clair ruisseau* buvait une colombe[II,12]

[Tircis] chantait un jour le long *des bords*
D'une onde arrosant *des prairies*,
Dont *Zéphire* habitait *les campagnes fleuries*.[X,10]

Un vivier vous attend *plus clair que fin cristal*.[ibid.]

The poetic vocabulary of the time lends itself to the rich and ingenious treatment of compelling visions: the evocation of the mysterious, the unfathomable, the chiaroscuro is achieved most effectively in lines rich in periphrases and poetic plurals which increase distances and make the *décor* more indefinite and more intriguing:

> . . . Un monstre assez vieux pour lui dire
> Tous les noms des chercheurs de mondes inconnus
>   Qui n'en étaient pas revenus,
> Et que depuis cent ans sous l'abîme avaient vus
>   Les anciens du vaste empire.[VIII,8]

> Le vaste enclos qu'ont les royaumes sombres. . . .[VII,7]

> Les noms et les vertus de ces clartés errantes,
> Par qui sont nos destins et nos mœurs différentes. . . .[XI,4]

> Tous deux, à nager malheureux,
> Allèrent traverser, au séjour ténébreux,
>   Bien d'autres fleuves que les nôtres.[VIII,23]

> Janot Lapin retourne aux souterrains séjours.[VII,15]

> Des tanches qui sortaient du fond de ces demeures.[VII,4]

Sometimes, La Fontaine revels in expressing the ineffable, the transitory, the disconcerting, in a most concise manner which contrasts with that of the *Baroque* poets treating similar themes:

> Il pleut; le soleil luit; et l'écharpe d'Iris. . . .[VI,3]

> Un souffle, une ombre, un rien, tout lui donnait la fièvre.[II,14]

>   . . . Ceux qui cherchent vainement
> Cette fille du sort de royaume en royaume,
> Fidèles courtisans d'un volage fantôme.[VII,11]

La Fontaine, like Ovid,[1] describes the first instants of dawn by means of an ingenious periphrasis:

> A l'heure de l'affût, soit lorsque la lumière
> Précipite ses traits dans l'humide séjour,
> Soit lorsque le soleil rentre dans sa carrière,
> Et que n'étant plus nuit, il n'est pas encore jour. . . .[X,14]

The critics of the time point out the dangers which threaten an author who overestimates his own virtuosity. Bouhours writes:

> 'Comme de la délicatesse au raffinement, il n'y a qu'un pas à faire, le passage est aisé du raffinement au galimatias: l'un tend de lui-même et va droit à l'autre . . . Nous avons des écrivains du premier ordre qui excellent en raffinement. Balzac y est un grand maître, et je ne sais si en prose on peut subtiliser plus qu'il fait. C'est lui qui a dit d'un petit bois assez sombre "Il n'y entre du jour qu'autant qu'il en faut pour n'être pas nuit". N'est-ce pas raffiner que de penser de la sorte?'[2]

Bellegarde's judgement is even more explicit:

> 'Monsieur de La Chapelle, croyait apparemment faire des vers, lorsqu'il disait "Dans le temps qui divise la nuit d'avec le jour, et auquel les faibles rayons de l'aurore commencement à percer les voiles épais des ténèbres". Tout cela est bien poétique; c'est faire bien de la dépense et employer des termes trop magnifiques, pour exprimer le crépuscule.'[3]

But La Fontaine was writing in verse and knew the art of giving refinement the look of supreme naturalness and ease.

Although language, imagery, sounds and subject-matter are closely associated to give his verse poetic intensity, it is, to a certain extent, possible to identify the linguistic and stylistic elements conducive to poetry. Certain words have a poetic quality which is most difficult to assess, the more so as their meaning, from generation to generation and even from individual to individual, is subject to unaccountable variations. Documentary evidence concerning the evocative effect of particular words at any given time is scanty. However, there are, for example, comments made by seventeenth-century critics on the word *vaste*, an

---

[1] Ovid, *Amores*, I, v, *ll*. 5–6, Loeb Classical Library, London, 1958, p. 332. See also *O.D.*, p. 56.
[2] D. Bouhours, *La Manière de bien penser*, pp. 332–3.
[3] J.-B. Morvan de Bellegarde, *Réflexions sur l'élégance*, p. 96.

adjective which La Fontaine uses in some of his most poetic lines. Richelet writes:

> 'Ce mot se dit au figuré et fait une assez belle idée. Cicéron avait l'esprit fort vaste, c'est à dire avait un esprit d'une vaste étendue. Il a de vastes desseins, c'est à dire des desseins qui s'étendent loin.'[1]

Saint-Evremond, in his *Dissertation sur le mot de Vaste* disagrees with this opinion:

> 'Le grand est une perfection dans les esprits; le *vaste* est toujours un vice. L'étendue juste et réglée fait le grand: la grandeur démesurée fait le *vaste* ... Le *vaste* et l'affreux ont bien du rapport: les choses *vastes* ne conviennent point avec celles qui font sur nous une impression agréable. *Vasta solitudo*, n'est pas de ces solitudes qui donnent un repos délicieux, qui charment les peines des amants, qui enchantent les maux des misérables; c'est une solitude sauvage où nous nous étonnons d'être seuls, où nous regrettons la perte de la compagnie, où le souvenir des plaisirs perdus nous afflige, où le sentiment des maux présents nous tourmente.'[2]

The poet's use of *vaste* to describe Hades:

> Le *vaste* enclos qu'ont les royaumes sombres,[VII,7]

and the depths of the sea, 'le *vaste* empire'[VIII,8], conforms to the definition given by Saint-Evremond.[3] But who could say with certainty that La Fontaine restricts the meaning of the word to this acceptation when he refers to the gods' abode as *vastes lambris*[XII,21]? Yet for his contemporaries 'Une *maison vaste* a quelque chose d'affreux à la vue; des *appartements vastes* n'ont jamais donné envie à personne d'y loger';[4] and La Fontaine himself, when celebrating the charm of solitude and wishing to conjure up an unmistakably pleasant vision, chooses another adjective:

> Je ne dormirai point sous de *riches* lambris,[XI,4]

as he does when he evokes the magnificence of wealth:

> Le prince voulut voir ces richesses *immenses*.[X,9]

---

[1] Richelet, *Dictionnaire français*, item *Vaste*.
[2] Saint-Evremond, *Dissertation sur le mot de Vaste à Messieurs de l'Académie Française*, in *Œuvres*, Amsterdam, 1739, vol. IV, pp. 6–7.
[3] Cf. Saint-Evremond, ibid., p. 7. See also *Contes*, vol. II, p. 257 (La Clochette), the lines:
> ... O belles évitez
> Le fonds des bois et leur *vaste* silence,
and Saint-Evremond, ibid., p. 7: '*de vastes forêts* nous effrayent'.
[4] Saint-Evremond, ibid., p. 7.

When, in *Le Vieillard et les trois jeunes hommes*[XI,8], the young men say:

Quittez le long espoir et les *vastes* pensées,

or when the poet, in *Le Loup et le Chasseur*[VIII,27], remarks:

Mais quoi, rien ne remplit
Les *vastes* appétits d'un faiseur de conquêtes,

the word implies ὕβρις but also retains the quality which Richelet sees in it. Thus, one single word of the poetic language evokes several aspects of a complex reality. Another adjective, *profond*, in the lines:

Comment percer des airs la campagne *profonde*?[VIII,16]

Porte un peu tes regards sur ces plaines *profondes*,[VIII,25]

enlarges the vision of the infinity of the firmament and of an extensive stretch of water, already conjured up by two metaphors.

Not only the vocabulary but also syntax may contribute to poetic effects: for example, Vaugelas formulated a very simple rule regulating the use of *aller*, followed by the gerund:

'Cette façon de parler avec le verbe aller, et le gérondif est vieille et n'est plus en usage aujourd'hui, ni en vers, ni en prose, si ce n'est qu'il y ait un mouvement visible auquel le mot d'aller puisse promptement convenir, par exemple, si en marchant une personne chante, on peut dire, elle va chantant. ... De même d'une rivière, on dira fort bien, elle va serpentant, parce qu'en effet elle va, et ainsi des autres.'[1]

La Fontaine derives a fine poetic image from this construction when referring to the fox's tail:

Que faisons-nous, dit-il, de ce poids inutile,
Et qui va balayant tous les sentiers fangeux?[V,5]

Here, the use of the gerund with the *verbum vicarium* enables the poet to shift the emphasis from the action itself to the continuity and slow tempo of this action and thus to suggest the amplitude of the sweep of the fox's tail by a lengthy verbal form. The same device stresses the extension and the persistence of the quest in the lines:

Dieu fait bien ce qu'il fait. Sans en chercher la preuve
En tout cet univers, et *l'aller parcourant*,
Dans les citrouilles je la treuve.[IX,4]

[1] Vaugelas, *Remarques sur la langue française*, pp. 185–6.

Elsewhere, it is true, the construction is used simply for its value as an archaism, as when the sheep replies to the wolf:

> ... Que Votre Majesté
> Ne se mette pas en colère;
> Mais plutôt qu'elle considère
> Que je me *vas désaltérant*. ...[I,10]

The effect of the same construction in:

> Les diadèmes *vont* sur ma tête *pleuvant*,[VII,9]

is more delicate to assess. Malherbe, shocked by Desportes's lines:

> Moissonnant tout joyeux les épis blancs-dorés
> Dont la mère de Cérès *va couronnant* sa tête,

wrote in the margin: 'Cérès se couronne donc en se promenant. C'est une façon bien nouvelle'[1] If La Fontaine's phrasing does not call for the same sarcastic comment, it is because the notion of duration which he has substituted for that of movement, which alone justified the construction in the purists' eyes, is still loosely related to the latter notion. Here, *aller* suggests the continuity and the repetition of the narrator's wild dream. When, in *Les Compagnons d'Ulysse*[XII,1], La Fontaine writes to the Duc de Bourgogne:

> Mon esprit diminue, au lieu qu'à chaque instant
> On aperçoit le vôtre *aller en augmentant*,

the poet, with a disarming smile and a pun,

> Il ne va pas, il court, il semble avoir des ailes,

evades any responsibility and escapes into the heights of poetic fantasy, ignoring Vaugelas who wrote:

> 'On ne dira ... point, ces arbres vont croissant, sa vigueur allait diminuant et autres semblables phrases, comme on disait autrefois.'[2]

3. THE THIRD DIMENSION OF THE LANGUAGE

The poet derives the maximum effect from the affective and evocative value of the language. The poetic aura which glows around certain words,

---

[1] Quoted by Stanislav Lyer, in *La Syntaxe du gérondif et du participe présent dans les langues romanes*, Paris, 1934, pp. 150–2.
[2] Vaugelas, *Remarques sur la langue française*, pp. 185–6.

the echo which prolongs them is most elusive and often depends on fortuitous circumstances, as Giraudoux points out:

> 'Siegfried—Comme les mots qui vous viennent d'un pays nouveau et ouvert sont eux-mêmes ouverts, purs!
> Robineau—Pardon, ce sont là malgré tout des mots français.
> Siegfried (à Geneviève)—Français, certes, mais dans votre bouche, ils ont fait un détour par l'inconnu. Jamais le mot neige n'a touché en France autant de neige qu'au Canada. Vous avez pris à la France un mot qui lui servait à peine quelques jours par an et vous en avez fait la doublure de tout votre langage.'[1]

In other words, at times, the *signifié* no longer exactly corresponds with the *signifiant* and the latter is thereby made to express concurrently a variety of meanings and notions mutually exclusive in everyday speech. As Valéry once remarked:

> 'On sait bien que les conditions de la lecture littéraire sont incompatibles avec une précision excessive du langage.'[2]

In the *Fables*, poetry often resides in the interplay of the various meanings implied in a seemingly simple and direct phrasing. The reader senses poetic ambiguities which the general meaning of the verse does not quite confirm nor exclude. Thus the lines:

> ... un jour
> Qu'il était allé faire à l'Aurore sa cour
> Parmi le thym et la rosée,[VII,15]

conjures up the vision of a classical allegory although, in the words of Rudler, 'c'est à peine si la déesse se distingue du phénomène naturel, dont la fraîcheur riante nous arrive à travers le mot et nous pénètre.' There is, too, an echo of contemporary court life,—l'Aurore devient une sorte de reine; le lapin va à son petit lever'—incongruous and yet acceptable, in the fragrant open-air setting:

> 'Où La Fontaine s'en va-t-il chercher ces idées si lointaines et si contraires pour les rapprocher? Et cela n'est point heurté, et paraît naturel! C'est que cela est court, que l'impression déborde le mot et que l'esprit se perd dans la poésie.'[3]

---

[1] J. Giraudoux, *Siegfried*, I, 6, Paris, 1949, pp. 54–5.
[2] P. Valéry, *Monsieur Teste*, Paris, 1964, p. 8.
[3] G. Rudler, *L'explication française*, pp. 74–5.

Chamfort had already observed an almost similar effect in another fable
when he remarked on

> '... Cet art de savoir, en paraissant vous occuper de bagatelles,
> vous placer d'un mot dans un grand ordre de choses. Quand le loup,
> par exemple, accusant auprès du lion malade, l'indifférence du renard
> sur une santé si précieuse, "daube au coucher du roi son camarade
> absent", suis-je dans l'antre du lion? Suis-je à la cour?'[1]

In the same manner, the poet draws a poetic effect from the interaction of
the concrete and the abstract elements of his vocabulary. The pigeons
become

> ... Une autre nation
> Au col changeant, au coeur tendre et fidèle;[VII,7]

every creature in the world must

> ... Puiser son âme en un trésor commun.[IX,7]

Sometimes, the concrete itself comes very close to the abstract, the two
planes intersect as in the lines:

> ... Sortons de ces riches palais
> Comme l'on sortirait d'un songe,[X,9]

on which Royère comments:

> 'Le berger montre son propre palais, celui où il se trouve présente-
> ment. Il emploie donc le pluriel dans un autre dessein que celui du
> nombre. Or, toutes les fois qu'on le fait, on prête au concret les
> perspectives de l'abstrait. Ce palais disparaît dans sa pluralité comme
> dans un gouffre. Il s'estompe en tant qu'édifice particulier. Il est
> remplacé par son idée et cette idée donne naissance à une image
> complexe: la réalité concrète se transfigure et devient abstraite,
> musicale.'[2]

> ... Les humides bords des royaumes du vent[I,22]

would provide yet another example of the transfiguration operated by the
poetic plural.

Hendiadys, as in:

> Eh! qui guide les cieux et leur course rapide?[IX, *Discours à Mme de la Sablière, l.* 164]

---

[1] Chamfort, *Eloge de La Fontaine*, in *Recueil de l'Académie de Marseille*, pp. 23–4. *Fables*,
VIII, 3.
[2] J. Royère, *Le Musicisme*, p. 63.

Loin du monde et du bruit goûter l'ombre et le frais,[XI,4]

and hypallage, as in:

Nous cultivons en paix d'heureux champs,[XI,7]

Le blé, riche présent de la blonde Cérès,[IX,11]

also constitute ingenious transpositions of concrete and abstract notions,
conducive to poetry.

4. POETIC IMAGERY

Imagery is another element of La Fontaine's poetry. It is infinitely
varied, rich, but never obtrusive. The poet's use of the poetic image co-
incides with the ideal proposed by Rapin:

'Il y a une rhétorique particulière pour la poésie, que les poètes
modernes ne connaissent presque point. Cet art consiste à savoir
bien précisément ce qu'il faut dire figurément et ce qu'il faut dire sans
figure; et à bien connaître où il faut de l'ornement, et où il n'en faut
pas. . . . C'est un effet du génie, que ce discernement, et que cette
rhétorique particulière qui est propre à la poésie.'[1]

Jean Royère stresses the paradoxical nature of La Fontaine's figures of
speech, style and rhetoric, which are both complex and natural; beneath
their apparent variety, he perceives a fundamental attitude of the poet's
mind and, in spite of the variety of the technical names which can be given
to each of these devices, most of them, he thinks, are forms of euphemisms,
a figure particularly rich in virtual poetic developments and discreet in
its external appearance:

'Les vers de La Fontaine, comme ils sont un tissu d'allitérations
et de consonances sont également un système parfait de figures; c'est
l'avers et le revers de ces vers. Toutes ces figures, vues du dedans
sont des euphémismes comme toutes celles de Boileau sont des
métaphores, et toutes celles de Baudelaire des catachrèses . . .
L'euphémisme . . . est en soi un art de penser, moins fort mais plus
efficace que la métaphore . . . Il n'y a pas d'euphémisme sans la
liberté laissée à tous et à soi-même de ne pas toujours l'apercevoir . . .
C'est une manière de faire entendre une chose sans la dire ou de ne

---

[1] Rapin, *Réflexions sur la poétique*, Paris, 1675, pp. 59–60.

N

pas faire entendre une chose en la disant. C'est une sorte d'aparté et un moyen de se duper soi-même pour le plaisir. ... L'esprit qui s'amuse à l'euphémisme se surpasse car il ne connaît pas toute la subtilité de ses feintes ... Il y a beaucoup de mystère et d'obscurité dans le moindre euphémisme. S'il est en lui-même une pensée complète et formulée, il incline les autres vers des pensées qui ne sont encore que probables ... Le langage invente lui-même ses significations par l'euphémisme ... La fable elle-même est un euphémisme ... L'euphémisme de La Fontaine naît du contrôle de l'entendement sur la sensibilité et c'est une sorte de demi-jugement estompé de rêve.'[1]

The fable *Le Lièvre et la Perdrix*[V,17] ends enigmatically on a most evocative euphemism:

> Mais la pauvrette avait compté
> Sans l'autour aux serres cruelles,

which leads the reader to imagine the tragic *dénouement*. Yet the text is compelling; the only possible conclusion has the inevitability of tragedy: this is implied by the position of *cruelles* as the very last word of the fable, whilst the endearing diminutive *la pauvrette* solicits the reader's sympathy in favour of a character so far unworthy of it but whose circumstances are about to change.

Metaphors have often the value of euphemisms in so far as they suggest more than their actual wording tells. In this respect, La Fontaine's metaphors are particularly effective, the more so as the simplicity and naturalness of the expression often conceals the boldness of the *rapprochements* which the reader tends to accept before he recognizes them as such: the poetic idiom of the *Fables* is, on the surface, as direct as everyday speech and yet closer examination reveals a wealth of latent evocations and associations.

> La vase est un épais nuage
> Qu'aux effets du cristal nous venons d'opposer[XII,29]

is not only a picturesque implied comparison, it is also a baroque transposition involving a *transformation à vue*, underwater sights described in terms of open-air landscape.

> ... Le tocsin
> Sonne aussitôt sur lui, l'alarme se promène
> De toutes parts ...,[XI,1]

[1] J. Royère, *Le Musicisme*, pp. 43, 110–11 and 119.

insists on the extension of the hue and cry as well as its haphazard diffusion. The fullness of the evocation contrasts with the conciseness of the sentence and the precision of the wording. When Juno answers the peacock's complaints with the words:

> Est-ce à toi d'envier la voix du rossignol,
> Toi que l'on voit porter à l'entour de ton col
> Un arc-en-ciel nué de cent sortes de soies,[II,17]

the peacock's neck is compared with the rainbow and, by implication, the rainbow with a scarf of graded shades, in a succession of interdependent metaphors to suggest an allusion to *l'écharpe d'Iris* ('à l'entour de ton col...').

Allusions, which Royère calls *raccourcis d'art*[1] often provide fine poetic effects: a few words open rich vistas of texts and legends of our classical heritage. Their prestige reflects on the modern text which is transfigured by the association taking place in the reader's mind. The poetic quality of the modern text must be such as not to be eclipsed by this association and discreet enough to introduce the reference as a natural development and not as a pedantic cliché or a laboured paraphrase. Thus, grief-stricken Hecuba[X,12], the old gardener of the *Georgics*[XII,20], Helen of Troy[IX,7], Amalthea the goat[XII,4], to mention but a few, make, often in a single line, a fleeting but unforgettable appearance. The final lines of *Daphnis et Alcimadure*[XII,24] are particularly evocative and poetic:

> Tout l'Erèbe entendit cette belle homicide
> S'excuser au berger qui ne daigna l'ouïr,
> Non plus qu'Ajax Ulysse, et Didon son perfide.

Proper nouns, classical and lyrical vocabulary, sounds, the elliptical construction, the inversion, everything contributes to the magic power of this incantation which 'lève à demi le voile sur deux des plus beaux passages de deux chefs-d'oeuvre de l'esprit humain: le onzième chant de *l'Iliade* [sic] et le sixième de *l'Enéide*'.[2] The allusion is yet more subtle and purely stylistic when the poet, by the use of a Latinism, a phrase or sometimes a single word, awakens the reader's memories of classical literature. To make such allusions perceptible in translation and in an unexpected context is one of La Fontaine's greatest achievements. Thus, on *Les deux Pigeons*[IX,2], the passionate reproach:

[1] J. Royère, *Le Musicisme*, p. 45.
[2] J. Royère, *Clartés sur la poésie*, p. 46. In fact, the reference is to the *Odyssey* (Book XI) and *not* to the *Iliad*.

> L'absence est le plus grand des maux:
> Non pas pour vous, cruel . . .,

arouses echoes of Dido's *crudelis* and Ovid's *dure*.[1] In *La Lionne et l'Ourse,*[X,12]

> Moi me taire? moi malheureuse!

recalls Eurydice's lament in Vergil:

> Quis et *me*, inquit, *miseram*, et te perdidit, Orpheu?

as well as Ovid's:

> Me miserum! quid agam, si proxima quaeque relinquunt?[2]

In *Le Fermier, le Chien et le Renard*[XI,3], the fox's spite expresses itself in epic style:

> . . . Je jure les puissances
> De l'Olympe et du Styx, il en sera parlé;

it is therefore appropriate that the line:

> Roulant en son cœur ces vengeances,

implicitly compares him with Vergil's wrathful Juno:

> Talia flammato secum dea corde volutans . . .[3]

Whether La Fontaine intended the reference to be to these authors or to any other is irrelevant to our study. What matters is the fact that the poet's choice of certain words has made such *rapprochements* possible. The text invites the reader to go beyond the formulated meaning and to complete the author's writing by adding to it his personal and unpredictable literary experience and sensibility: we cannot but acknowledge in this compelling invitation the efficiency of the poetic and stylistic device.

---

[1] Vergil, *Æneid*, IV, *ll.* 309–11, Loeb Classical Library, London, 1956, p. 416.
> Quin etiam hyberno moliris sidere classem,
> Et mediis properas Aquilonibus ire per altum,
> *Crudelis!*

Ovid, *Tristia*, I, viii, *ll.* 11–14, Loeb Classical Library, London, 1953, p. 40:
> Tantane te, fallax, cepere oblivia nostri,
> Afflictumque fuit tantus adire timor,
> Ut neque respiceres nec solarere jacentem,
> *Dure*, nec exsequias prosequerere meas?

[2] Vergil, *Georgics*, IV, *l.* 494, Loeb Classical Library, London, 1956, p. 230. Ovid, *Tristia*, V, ii, *l.* 39, Loeb Classical Library, p. 216. Cf. also Jean de Schélandre, *Tyr et Sidon*, 2nd Journée, IV, 4:
> Toi méchante et malheureuse moi
in *Ancien Théâtre Français*, Paris, 1856, vol. VIII, p. 194.

[3] Vergil, *Æneid*, I, *l.* 50; IV, *l.* 533; VI, *l.* 185.

5. RELEVANCE AND UNITY

If, on the one hand, La Fontaine relies on the evocative quality of the language to extend the field of poetic vision beyond the limitations of words, on the other, he maintains a fundamental relationship between the poetic variations thus suggested and the theme from which they spring. Thus, beneath the incidental, unpredictable and fragmentary forms taken by reality in the vision, lies unity. The poet, in his flights of fancy, remains conscious of the value of what we shall call for convenience the principle of relevance; he therefore remains *raisonnable*.

First, there is, in the *Fables*, relevance within the more complex images. In the words of Bernard Lamy:

> 'Il faut ... faire que la liaison des images des choses et de leurs noms soit si étroite, que les images et les expressions se présentent de compagnie.'[1]

It is this internal relevance which ensures the coherence of lengthy metaphors such as:

> Nous devons l'apologue à l'ancienne *Grèce*.
> Mais ce *champ* ne se peut tellement *moissonner*
> Que les derniers venus n'y trouvent à *glaner*.
> La feinte est un *pays* plein de terres *désertes*.
> Tous les jours nos auteurs y font des *découvertes*.[III,1]

In the lines:

> Le moindre vent qui d'aventure
> Fait rider la face de l'eau . . .,[I,22]

it is not just mere chance that the verb *rider* and the time-old metaphor 'la face de l'eau' occur in the same line.

The principle of relevance applies also to the whole fable; each *ornement*, the lyrical ones in particular, is related to the mood, the subject-matter or the issue of the apologue. Naigeon remarked of the *Fables* that:

> 'Les ornements y sont répandus avec une sobriété qu'il est plus difficile de rendre, que de saisir; ils naissent immédiatement du fond du sujet, ou y sont liés par des rapports dont La Fontaine semble vouloir faire un secret à ses lecteurs; la marche de son récit n'en est point interrompue, ni l'intérêt affaibli.'[2]

[1] B. Lamy, *L'Art de parler*, p. 182.
[2] J. A. Naigeon, *Éloge de La Fontaine*, p. 56.

Chamfort also made useful observations on the subject. Of the line:

Tout cela, c'est la mer à boire,

in *Les deux Chiens et l'Ane mort*[VIII,25], he wrote:

'M. de Voltaire critique ce vers comme plat et trivial. Il me semble que ce qui rend excusable ici cette expression populaire, c'est qu'elle fait allusion à une fable où il s'agit de boire une rivière.'[1]

It is this kind of relevance to the whole fable or its theme which we observe in La Fontaine's most poetic verse. The subject-matter is transfigured by the reflection and becomes poetic just as it comes to life and becomes a comedy when narrative and dialogue prevail. In *L'Ecolier, le Pédant et le Maître d'un jardin*[IX,5], for example, we are told that an objectionable child steals from a neighbour's garden

> Et fleurs et fruits. Ce voisin, en automne,
> Des plus beaux dons que nous offre Pomone
> Avait la fleur, les autres le rebut.
> Chaque saison apportait son tribut:
> Car au printemps il jouïssait encore
> Des plus beaux dons que nous présente Flore.

The theme of the passage is *les fleurs et les fruits*, *Pomone* and *Flore*, autumn and spring; the vocabulary and imagery contribute to the diffusion of the idea throughout the verse. Thus, to refer to the finest fruit, La Fontaine uses the word *fleur* in its figurative meaning: 'Des plus beaux dons . . . avait la fleur', speaking of *la fleur des fruits*, when he is about to conjure up the vision of the orchard blossoming in spring. From one season to the other, the thematic unity of the passage is preserved through the poetic ambiguity of language. The line:

> Sur les ailes du temps la tristesse s'envole

sums up the whole theme of *La jeune Veuve*[VI,21], the flight of time and inconstancy.[2] In the same fable, the allegory and the metaphor:

> Toute la bande des Amours
> Revient au colombier . . .

are particularly well-chosen since mythology has endowed the *Amours* with wings.

[1] Chamfort, Notes on the Fables, in J. B. Gail, *Les Trois fabulistes, Esope, Phèdre, La Fontaine*, vol. IV, p. 313.
[2] See also *s'envoler, l.* 19.

> ... Le temps, dont les ailes légères
> N'amènent que trop tôt, hélas! chaque saison

is also well suited to the fable *Pour Monseigneur le Duc du Maine*[XI,2] which is an allegory celebrating the precocity of the royal child.[1] In *Du Thésauriseur et du Singe*[XII,3] and *La Chauve-Souris, le Buisson et le Canard*[XII,7], the sea is evoked through periphrases,

> ... Le gouffre enrichi par maint et maint naufrage,

> ... [Le] fond des magasins
> Qui du Tartare sont voisins,

in harmony with the pursuits of the characters, respectively a miser and rich merchants.

> ... Les humides bords des royaumes du vent[I,22]

is no gratuitous periphrasis but a pointed reference to an ominous circumstance which will bring about the *dénouement* of the fable.[2] Gohin writes:

> 'Dans les *Fables*, je ne connais qu'un lieu commun nettement caractérisé; c'est l'exquise définition de l'amour dans *Tircis et Amarante*; encore renferme-t-elle le sujet même de la fable.'[3]

In *Phébus et Borée*[VI,3], the poetic evocation of *l'écharpe d'Iris*, which we have already examined in detail in an earlier chapter, is very appropriate in a fable where the weather and its influence on dress plays an important part. In 1718, Houdart de La Motte already remarked:

> '[Il ne faut pas] se laisser entraîner au plaisir de décrire de façon que la description devienne un écart. Ce qu'il y a de plus heureux, en ce genre, est que la description soit le fait même. Telle est la fable du Roseau et du Chêne aussi bien que celle de Borée et du Soleil.'[4]

This strict relevance gives the fable a poetic unity: poetry invites the reader to enter into the subject by intuition. In the words of Grammont:

---

[1] The Duke had just published *Œuvres diverses d'un auteur de sept ans*, 1677.
[2] The imagery of *Le Savetier et le Financier*[VIII,2], poetic in a lesser degree, is also closely related to the fable. Cf. the metaphor:

> Le sommeil quitta son *logis*,
> Il eut pour *hôtes* les soucis ...

in a fable in which the location of the characters' dwellings plays an important part: *voisin, hôtel, cave*, etc. The periphrasis 'ce qui cause nos peines' contains the gist of the apologue.
[3] F. Gohin, *Les Comédies attribuées à La Fontaine*, Paris, 1935, p. 95, n. 1. *Fables*, VIII, 13.
[4] Houdart de La Motte, *Discours sur la fable*, in *Fables nouvelles*, p. xxxvii.

'Chez lui [La Fontaine] tout est préparé, annoncé soit par un mot, soit par un détail, soit par la forme d'un vers et notre imagination peut à chaque instant envisager d'avance la suite des événements ce qui est l'essence même de la poésie; tout est lié logiquement et l'ensemble forme un tout indissoluble.[1]

This technique is ideally suited to the fable which, by its nature, entails prosaic narrative, pedestrian didactic developments and realistic dialogues. The occasional poetic line casts its light on the whole fable; its effect on the reader's mind lasts considerably longer than the time it takes to read it and, by contamination, the prosaic lines seem less pedestrian. Indeed, by the wit and elegance which distinguish them, these also often participate of the poetic atmosphere. Thus are overcome the limitations of the fable, which is no longer merely a convenient didactic form but becomes the stimulating prelude to an infinite variety of meditations. In this respect, the *Fables* conform to Nicole's definition of books worthy of the name, in his *Traité de la grâce générale*:

'Chaque livre est en quelque sorte double, et imprime dans l'esprit deux sortes d'idées, car il y imprime un amas de pensées formées, exprimées et conçues distinctement, et, outre cela, il y en imprime un autre, composé de vues et de pensées indistinctes, que l'on sent, et que l'on aurait peine à exprimer, et c'est d'ordinaire dans ces vues excitées et non exprimées que consiste la beauté des livres et des écrits.'[2]

[1] M. Grammont, 'L'Art de La Fontaine', *Le Français Moderne*, 1933, p. 114.
[2] Quoted by Manuel de Diéguez, in *L'Ecrivain et son langage*, Paris, 1961, p. 156.

CONCLUSION

A STYLISTIC study of the *Fables*—by its nature bound to review and analyse series of technical devices—cannot but give a fragmentary picture of the poet's art. At no point should the critic forget, when assessing its effect, that each device is to be replaced in its context and considered as a unique case. Moreover, the elements which, gathered together, give us a clear picture of the various qualities of La Fontaine's style—vigour and vividness, familiarity, humour, elegance, poetry—are nearly always interwoven to form the smooth texture of any one fable. All these components overlap and are interdependent: their effects are intentionally blurred or ambiguous; new and subsidiary implications derive from their blending or their juxtaposition. The shifts of tone may, at times, be baffling in their subtlety, and an acknowledgement of their presence in any given instance often amounts to an admission of uncertainty as to the purpose of the writer since any attempt at the 'reconstruction of stylistic values'[1] is perilous and necessarily incomplete. In 1718, Gamaches already remarked on

> 'l'incertitude de nos jugements quand nous voulons nous prononcer sur la manière d'écrire de ceux qui nous ont précédés. Nous savons ce qu'ils ont pensé mais nous ignorons quelles étaient les idées accessoires attachées de leur temps aux expressions dont ils faisaient usage.'[2]

The original text, like a living organism, has, after three centuries, reached a mature state in which early features are still traceable, under the accretions and the alterations caused by age, as tantalizing vestiges of its pristine and elusive youth. In these circumstances, a stylistic analysis can only constitute a preparation to an appreciative reading during which the informed reader derives enjoyment from the intuitive perception of concomitant meanings, values and implications latent under the limpid surface meaning of the writing. In La Fontaine's own words:

> 'Il n'appartient qu'aux ouvrages vraiment solides et d'une souveraine beauté, d'être bien reçus de tous les esprits et de tous les

---

[1] Stephen Ullmann, *Language and Style*, Oxford, 1964, pp. 154–73.
[2] E. S. de Gamaches, *Les Agréments du langage*, p. 262.

siècles, sans avoir d'autre passeport que le seul mérite dont ils sont pleins.'[1]

The rich and intriguing style of the *Fables* constitutes their most durable merit.

If, in the course of this study, we have not mentioned any flaw in our author's style, it is simply because blemishes, not uncommon in La Fontaine's other works, are practically non-existent in the *Fables*. The poet's shrewd use of studied negligence, his tongue-in-the-cheek attitude towards the poetic conventions of his day make any criticism of an occasional *cliché*, *cheville* or repetition rather pedantic.[2] Improprieties and ambiguities are almost always intentional, digressions are pretexts for poetic or humorous developments, and unexpected changes of style are both intended and carefully contrived. However, it is true that to ask of a wasp, even when it is acting as judge,

N'a-t-il point assez léché l'ours?[I,21]

or to write of Dawn:

N'attendez point les *traits* que son *char* fait *éclore*,[XII,28, l. 90]

is unworthy of a poet usually praised for the relevance and the coherence of his metaphors. It is also true that La Fontaine's style, well suited to the lighter passages of the *Discours à Madame de La Sablière*[IX], becomes rather ponderous and inadequate when he theorizes:

Au dire de ces gens, la bête est toute telle:
L'objet la frappe en un endroit;
Ce *lieu* frappé *s'en va* tout droit,
Selon nous, au voisin en porter la nouvelle;
Le sens de proche en proche aussitôt la reçoit.
L'impression se fait, mais comment se fait-elle?

Such lines recall some of the more clumsy ones celebrating the virtue of quinquina.[3] A careful examination of the 'faults' found in the *Fables* by their most critical editors, Sélis, Delille, La Harpe,[4] reveals that these have often been misled in their judgements by their lack of knowledge of seventeenth-century language and syntax, and, in their appreciation of

---

[1] *Contes*, vol. I, p. 4 (Preface to Part I).
[2] See, for example, Alcide Macé's criticism of 'fort civile' and 'fort honnête', in fable I, 9. *La Fontaine et Horace*, Paris, 1944, pp. 58–9.
[3] *Le Quinquina*, O.D., pp. 60–75.
[4] In J. B. Gail, *Observations sur les quatre dernières fables de La Fontaine*.

imagery, by their rigid conformity to the letter rather than to the spirit of the rules of composition.

Other omissions have been deliberate on our part. It might seem profitable to trace the evolution of the poet's art from his first to his last fable, or to stress the differences existing between the two main collections on the one hand, and between these and Book XII on the other.[1] It is however doubtful whether such studies would cast much light on the style of our poet: when La Fontaine began to write fables, his style had already reached a remarkable maturity. If the scope of later fables is, on the whole, wider than that of the earlier ones, their structure more complex, and their tone more lyrical, *Le Chêne et le Roseau* in Book I, *L'Astrologue qui se laisse tomber dans un puits* in Book II, *L'Alouette et ses Petits avec le Maître d'un champ* in Book IV, to take but a few examples, prove that the poet was already, at the time of the first collection, in full command of all the stylistic resources which he was to use, later, in a more lavish manner. The difference between the *recueils* is not one of quality but rather one of inspiration, themes and structures; the style remains, throughout the *Fables*, consistent in its perfection.

This perfection is the result of the exceptional combination of features and qualities found nowhere else in such close association, and which talent, years of practice and experiment, good taste, and maturity of mind enabled La Fontaine to achieve. He conceals his conscientious craftsmanship under the apparent spontaneity of his expression; the gracefulness of this expression and a wealth of implications, which arouses admiration for the poet and the moralist alike, compensate for its restraint. From his remarkable knowledge of language and of all the resources of style, he draws a whole range of effects impressive in their variety, and creates a poetic idiom in which styles reputed incompatible blend harmoniously. His deep appreciation of ancient and contemporary literatures is revealed in his numerous free adaptations, references, allusions, and his erudition, paradoxically, often assumes the form of humour; his human warmth counterbalances his sharp wit, and his familiarity towards the reader, his attitude of detachment to his work. The multiple aspects of La Fontaine's style constitute a faithful representation of multiple aspects of a complex reality, expressed, with elegant economy of means, in terms rich in evocative power.

One cannot but marvel that all the features characteristic of the aesthetic ideal of the time are found, in their purest form, in one single

---

[1] See Margarete Cordemann, *Der Umschwung der Kunst zwischen der ersten und zweiten Fablesammlung La Fontaines*, Munich, 1917.

work which is the only great non-dramatic poetry of the age.[1] It is fitting that Valéry's definition of French classicism describes perfectly the style of the *Fables*.

'Il est admirable, il fut réservé à la France, que, sous l'empire de l'intelligence volontaire, un art qui fut le comble de la grâce fût créé; et qu'une aisance supérieure dans le style, une intimité continue des formes avec les pensées, une pudeur délicieuse aient été les fruits étonnants d'une contrainte extraordinaire.'[2]

[1] O. de Mourgues, *La Fontaine, Fables*, p. 7.
[2] Paul Valéry, *Remerciement à l'Académie Française*, in *Œuvres*, Pléiade, Paris, 1957, vol. I, p. 741.

BIBLIOGRAPHY

The editions given below are those which have been consulted, and are not necessarily the first editions.

Editions of La Fontaine Referred to

RÉGNIER, Henri (ed.). *Œuvres de Jean de la Fontaine*, Grands Ecrivains de la France, Paris, 1883–92, 11 vols.

CLARAC, Pierre (ed.). *Fables choisies mises en vers par M. de La Fontaine*, Association pour la diffusion de la pensée française, Paris, 1946.

COUTON, Georges (ed.). *Fables choisies mises en vers*, Garnier, Paris, 1962.

GESLIN, Lucien (ed.). *Fables*, de Gigord, Paris, 1950.

GUILLEMIN, Henri (ed.). *Fables*, Editions du Milieu du Monde, Geneva, 1945.

GOHIN, Ferdinand (ed.). *Fables choisies mises en vers*, Textes Français, Paris, 1934, 2 vols.

RADOUANT, René (ed.). *Fables*, Hachette, Paris, 1929.

SAULNIER, Verdun-Louis (ed.). *Fables*, Bibliothèque de Cluny, Paris, 1950, 2 vols.

CLARAC, Pierre (ed.). *Contes et nouvelles en vers*, Textes Français, Paris, 1934, 2 vols.

PILON, Edmond, GROOS, René, SCHIFFRIN, Jacques (ed.). *Fables, contes et nouvelles*, Pléiade, Paris, 1932.

CLARAC, Pierre (ed.). *Œuvres diverses*, Pléiade, Paris, 1942.

BUSSON, Henri & GOHIN, Ferdinand (ed.). *Discours à Madame de La Sablière*, Geneva & Lille, 1950.

Seventeenth-Century Lexicographers, Grammarians and Theorists of Language and Style

ALEMAND, Louis Auguste. *Nouvelles observations ou guerre civile des Français sur la langue*, Paris, 1688.

ARNAULD, Antoine & LANCELOT, Claude. *Grammaire générale et raisonnée contenant les fondements de l'art de parler expliqués d'une manière claire et naturelle*, Paris, 1660.

BARBIER D'AUCOURT. *Sentiments de Cléante sur les Entretiens d'Ariste et d'Eugéne*, Paris, 1671.

BARY, René. *La Rhétorique française où l'on trouve de nouveaux exemples sur les passions et sur les figures, où l'on traite à fond de la matière des genres oratoires et où le sentiment des puristes est rapporté sur les usages de notre langue*, Paris, 1653.

BELLEGARDE, Jean-Baptiste Morvan de. *Réflexions sur l'élégance et la politesse du style*, Amsterdam, 1706.

BELLINGEN, Fleury de. *Etymologie des proverbes français*, The Hague, 1656.

BOISREGARD, Nicolas Andry de. *Réflexions sur l'usage présent de la langue française ou remarques nouvelles et critiques touchant la politesse du langage*, Paris, 1689.

—— *Suite des Réflexions sur l'usage présent de la langue française*, Paris, 1693.

BOREL, Pierre. *Trésor de recherches et antiquités gauloises et françaises*, Paris, 1655.

BOUHOURS, Dominique. *La Manière de bien penser dans les ouvrages d'esprit*, Paris, 1687.

—— *Les Entretiens d'Ariste et d'Eugène*, ed. Radouant, Paris, 1920; (1st ed. 1671).

—— *Remarques nouvelles sur la langue française*, Paris, 1675.

BRETTEVILLE. *L'Eloquence de la chaire et du barreau selon les principes les plus solides de la rhétorique sacrée et profane*, Paris, 1689.

BUFFET, Marguerite. *Nouvelles observations sur la langue française*, Paris, 1668.

CALLIÈRES, François de. *Des bons mots et des bons contes, de leur usage, de la raillerie et des railleurs de notre temps*, Paris, 1692.

—— *Du bon et du mauvais usage dans les manières de s'exprimer. Des façons de parler bourgeoises et en quoi elles sont différentes de celles de la cour*, Paris, 1693.

CHAPELAIN, Jean. *Opuscules critiques*, ed. A. C. Hunter, Paris, 1936.

CHIFLET, Laurent. *Nouvelle et parfaite grammaire française ou l'on trouve en bel ordre tout ce qui est de plus nécessaire et de plus curieux pour la pureté, l'orthographe et la prononciation de cette langue*, Paris, 1722 (1st ed. Anvers, 1659).

COTGRAVE, Randle. *A Dictionarie of the French and English Tongues Compiled by Randle Cotgrave Whereonto Is Also Annexed a Most Copious Dictionarie of the English Set Before the French by R S L* (Robert Sherwood Londoner), London, 1632.

DANGEAU, Louis de. *Opuscules sur la grammaire*, ed. Manne Ekman, Uppsala, 1927.

DESMARETS DE SAINT-SORLIN, Jean. *La Comparaison de la langue et de la poésie française avec la grecque et la latine et des poètes grecs, latins et français*, Paris, 1670.

Dictionnaire de l'Académie Française, Paris, 1694, 2 vols.

DU MARSAIS, C. Chesneau. *Des Tropes ou des différents sens dans lesquels on peut prendre un même mot dans une même langue*, Paris, 1766 (1st ed. 1730).

DU PLAISIR. *Sentiments sur les Lettres et l'Histoire avec des scrupules sur le style*, Paris, 1683.

DU VAIR, Guillaume. *Œuvres*, Paris, 1625.

FRAIN DU TREMBLAY, Jean. *Traité des langues où l'on donne des principes et des règles pour juger du mérite et de l'excellence de chaque langue et en particulier de la langue française*, Paris, 1703.

—— *Discours sur l'origine de la poésie, sur son usage, et sur le bon goût*, Paris, 1713.

FRÉMOND D'ABLANCOURT, Nicolas. *Nouveau dictionnaire de rimes*, Paris, 1648.

FURETIÈRE, Antoine. *Dictionnaire universel contenant généralement les mots français tant vieux que modernes et les termes de toutes les sciences et des arts* . . ., The Hague & Rotterdam, 1690, 3 vols.

GAMACHES, Etienne S. de. *Les Agréments du langage réduits à leurs principes*, Paris, 1718.

GIBERT, Balthazar. *Jugement des Savants sur les auteurs qui ont traité de la rhétorique*, Paris, 1712–19, 3 vols.

GIRAC, Paul Thomas de. *Réponse à la défense des œuvres de M. de Voiture faite par M. Costar*, Paris, 1655.

GUÉRET, Gabriel. *L'Orateur*, Paris, 1672.

IRSON, Claude. *Nouvelle méthode pour apprendre facilement les principes et la pureté de la langue française*, Paris, 1656.

JOUVENCY, Joseph. *L'Elève de rhétorique, Candidatus rhetoricae*, ed. & trans. H. Ferté, Paris, 1892.

—— *De la Manière d'apprendre et d'enseigner, De ratione discendi et docendi*, ed. & trans. H. Ferté, Paris, 1892.

LA CROIX, A. Phérotée de. *L'Art de la poésie française et latine avec une idée de la musique sous une nouvelle méthode*, Lyon, 1694.

LA MOTHE LE VAYER. *Considérations sur l'éloquence française de ce temps*, Paris, 1638.

LAMY, Bernard. *L'Art de parler avec un discours dans lequel on donne une idée de l'art de persuader*, Paris, 1676.

LA NOUE, Odet de. *Le Dictionnaire des rimes françaises* . . . *auquel deux traités sont ajoutés, l'un des conjugaisons* . . . *plus un amas d'épithètes recueilli des œuvres de G. de Salluste Seigneur Du Bartas*, Cologne, 1624.

LA NOUE, Pierre de. *Synonyma et æquivoca gallica phrasibus sententiisque proverbialibus illustrata in usum linguae gallicae studiosorum digesta et latina eorum interpretatione donata*, Lyon, 1618.

LA PORTE, Maurice de. *Les Epithètes françaises, livre non seulement utile à ceux qui font profession de la poésie, mais fort propre aussi pour illustrer toute autre composition française*, Paris, 1571.

LA TOUCHE, N. de. *L'Art de bien parler français*, Amsterdam, 1696, 2 vols.

LE DUC, Jean. *Proverbes en rimes ou rimes en proverbes tirés en substance tant de la lecture des bons livres que de la façon ordinaire de parler et accommodés en distiques ou manières de sentences qui peuvent passer pour maximes dans la vie* . . ., Paris, 1665.

LEMOYNE, Pierre. *De l'art des devises. Avec divers recueils de devises du même auteur*, Paris, 1666.

L'ESTANG, Gaspard de Tende de. *Règles de la traduction ou moyens pour apprendre à traduire le Latin en Français, tirées de quelques unes des meilleures traductions du temps*, Paris, 1660.

MÉNESTRIER, Claude François. *L'Art des Emblèmes*, Lyon, 1662.[1]

—— *L'Art des Emblèmes où s'enseigne la morale par les figures de la fable, de l'histoire et de la nature*, Paris, 1684.

[1] The Bibliothèque Nationale copy (*Rés.Z2522–3*) is bound together with *Livret de Emblèmes de Maître André Alciate mis en rime française et présenté à Monseigneur L'Amiral de France*, Paris, 1536, which belonged to François Louis Jamet (1713–78): Marginalia in Jamet's hand quote La Fontaine opposite emblems which recall some of his fables.

MONTFAUCON DE VILLARS, Nicolas Pierre Henri de. *De la délicatesse*, Paris, 1671.

MONTMÉRAN, Antoine de. *Synonymes et épithètes françaises*, Paris, 1645.

NICOLE, Pierre. *Traité de la beauté des ouvrages d'esprit et particulièrement de l'épigramme, traduit du Latin par L S G L A C*, (from *Delectus epigrammatum*, Paris, 1659), in Pierre Costar, *Recueil des plus beaux endroits de Martial*, Toulouse, 1689, vol. II.

NICOT, Jean. *Trésor de la langue française tant ancienne que moderne*, Paris, 1960, fac-simile of the 1621 ed.

OUDIN, Antoine. *Curiosités françaises pour supplément aux dictionnaires ou recueil de plusieurs belles propriétés avec une infinité de proverbes et quolibets pour l'explication de toutes sortes de livres*, Paris, 1656 (1st ed. 1640), in La Curne de Sainte-Palaye, *Dictionnaire historique de l'ancien langage français*, Paris, 1882, vol. X.

—— *Recherches italiennes et françaises. Dictionnaire contenant outre les mots ordinaires une quantité de proverbes et de phrases pour l'intelligence de l'une et l'autre langue*, Paris, 1643.

PALSGRAVE, John. *L'Eclaircissement de la langue française composé par maître Jehan Palsgrave, Anglais*, ed. F. Génin, Paris, 1852 (1st ed. London, 1530).

Parterre de la rhétorique française émaillé de toutes les plus belles fleurs d'éloquence qui se rencontrent dans les œuvres des orateurs tant anciens que modernes, ensemble le verger de la poésie, ouvrage très utile à ceux qui veulent exceller en l'un et l'autre art, Lyon, 1659.

RAPIN, René. *Réflexions sur la poétique de ce temps et sur les ouvrages des poètes anciens et modernes*, Paris, 1675.

—— *Réflexions sur l'éloquence. la poétique, l'histoire et la philosophie, avec le jugement qu'on doit faire des auteurs qui se sont signalés dans ces 4 parties des Belles Lettres*, vol. II of *Œuvres diverses du R.P.R. Rapin concernant les Belles Lettres*, 2 vols., Amsterdam, 1686.

—— *R. Rapini S.J. Hortorum libri IV*, Paris, 1723.

RENAUD, André. *Manière de parler la langue française selon les différents styles*, Lyon, 1697.

La Rhétorique de l'honnête homme ou la manière de bien écrire des lettres, de faire toutes sortes de discours . . . celle d'acquérir l'usage de la langue française et d'imiter les poètes . . . où l'on a ajouté à la fin le catalogue des livres dont un honnête homme doit former sa bibliothèque, Amsterdam, 1699.

RICHELET, Pierre. *Dictionnaire de rimes françaises*, Paris, 1692.

—— *Dictionnaire français contenant plusieurs nouvelles remarques sur la langue française . . .*, Geneva, 1680.

—— *La Versification française ou l'art de bien faire et de bien tourner les vers*, Paris, 1677.

—— *Les plus belles lettres des meilleurs auteurs français avec des notes*, Lyon, 1689.

RICHESSOURCE, Jean de la Sourdière de. *Les Plaisirs et les avantages de la lecture du cabinet ou les délicatesses et l'élégance de la prose française par les lumières de la critique rectifiante, raisonnée . . .*, Paris, 1680.

SAINT-RÉAL. *Traité de la critique*, Utrecht, 1693.

VAUGELAS, Claude Favre de. *Remarques sur la langue française*, Paris, 1934, fac-simile of the 1647 ed.
VAUMORIÈRE, Pierre D'Ortigue de. *Harangues sur toutes sortes de sujets avec l'art de les composer*, Paris, 1693.

OTHER WORKS CONSULTED

ADAM, Antoine. *Histoire de la Littérature française au XVIIème siècle*, Paris, 1962, 5 vols.
—— See BOILEAU, *Les Premières Satires*. . . .
ALBALAT, Antoine. *Le Travail du style enseigné par les corrections manuscrites des grands écrivains*, Paris, 1923.
ARNOULD, Louis. *La Terre de France chez La Fontaine; bêtes et gens*, Tours, 1924.
—— *Racan, histoire anecdotique, et critique de sa vie et de ses œuvres*, Paris, 1896.
ARTHOS, John. *The Language of Natural Description in Eighteenth-Century Poetry*, Ann Arbor, Michigan, USA, 1949.
ASCOLI, Georges. *La Critique littéraire au XVIIème siècle*, Cours de Sorbonne, Paris, 1934, 4 vols.
AUERBACH, Richard. Der Stil La Fontaines in seinen Briefen, Unpublished thesis, Mainz, 1953.
BAÏF, Jean Antoine de. *Les Mimes, enseignements et proverbes*, ed. Blanchemain Paris, 1880.
BAILLET, Adrien. *Jugement des Savants sur les prinicipaux ouvrages des auteurs*, Paris, 1685–86, 9 vols.
BAILLY, Auguste. *La Fontaine*, Paris, 1937.
—— *L'Ecole classique française. Les doctrines et les hommes*, Paris, 1941.
BALZAC, Jean Louis Guez de. *Œuvres*, ed. L. Moreau, Paris, 1854, 2 vols.
BAR, Francis. *Le Genre burlesque en France au XVIIème siècle, étude de style*, Paris, 1960.
—— 'Style burlesque et langue populaire', *Cahiers de l'Association Internationale des Etudes Françaises*, No. 9, June 1957, pp. 221–37
BAR-SAMFIRESCO. *Ménage polémiste, philologue et poète*, Paris, 1902.
—— 'Essai sur V. Conrart grammairien', in *Mélanges de philologie offerts à M. F. Brunot*, Paris, 1904, pp. 303–10.
BARCHILON, J. 'Wit and Humor in La Fontaine's Psyché', *French Review*, XXXVI, 1962, pp. 23–31.
BASSOMPIERRE, François de. *Mémoires du Maréchal de Bassompierre*, ed. Petitot, Collection des Mémoires relatifs à l'histoire de France, vols. XIX-XXI, Paris, 1822–23.
BAUDIN, Emile. *La Philosophie morale des Fables de La Fontaine*, Neuchâtel, 1950.
BÉDIER, Joseph & HAZARD, Paul. *Littérature française*, Paris, 1948, 2 vols.
BELLESSORT, André. 'Réflexions sur La Fontaine', *Revue des Deux Mondes*, XVIII, 1913, pp. 873–909.
—— *Sur les grands chemins de la poésie classique*, Paris, 1914.
BENSERADE, Isaac de. *Les Œuvres de Monsieur de Benserade*, Paris, 1697, 2 vols.

BLOCH, Oscar & WARTBURG, W. Von. *Dictionnaire étymologique de la langue française*, Paris, 1950.

BOILEAU-DESPREAUX, Nicolas. *Les Premières Satires de Boileau, I–X, édition critique et commentaire*, ed. A. Adam, Paris, Lille, 1941.

—— *Les Satires de Boileau commentées par lui-même, reproduction du commentaire inédit de Pierre Le Verrier avec les corrections autographes de Despréaux*, ed. Lachèvre, Le Vésinet, 1906.

—— *Lettres à Brossette*, ed. Boudhors, Paris, 1942.

—— *Œuvres complètes*, ed. A. C. Gidel, Paris, 1870–73, 4 vols.

—— *Œuvres de Mr. Boileau-Despréaux avec des éclaircissements historiques donnés par lui-même*, Geneva, 1716, 4° ed., 2 vols; 12° ed., 4 vols.

BOILLOT, Félix. *Les Impressions sensorielles chez La Fontaine*, Paris, 1926.

—— *Psychologie de la construction dans la phrase française moderne*, Paris, 1930.

BOISROBERT, Francois le Métel de. *Epîtres en vers*, ed. M. Cauchie, Paris, 1921, 2 vols.

BOIVIN, Jean, dit de Villeneuve. *Apologie d'Homère et bouclier d'Achille*, Paris, 1715.

BORGERHOFF, E. B. O. *The Freedom of French Classicism*, Princeton, New Jersey, USA, 1950.

BOURGET, Paul. *Études et Portraits; I. Portraits d'écrivains et notes d'esthétique*, Paris, 1905.

BOURGOIN, Auguste. *Les Maîtres de la critique au XVIIème siècle*, Paris, 1889.

BOUVIER, Ernest. 'Des Perfectionnements que reçut la langue française au XVIIème siècle', *Annales des Universités de Belgique*, 1851–52, pp. 169–508.

BRAY, René. *Les Fables de La Fontaine*, Paris, 1929.

BRERETON, Geoffrey. *An Introduction to the French Poets; Villon to the Present Day*, London, 1956.

BRODY, Jules. *Boileau and Longinus*, Geneva, 1958.

—— 'Platonisme et Classicisme', *Saggi e Ricerche di Letteratura Francese*, Milan, 1961, vol. II, pp. 7–30.

BRUNETIÈRE, Ferdinand. 'Vaugelas et la théorie de l'usage', in *Etudes critiques sur l'histoire de la littérature française, 7ème série*, Paris, 1922, pp. 27–54.

BRUNOT, Ferdinand. *Histoire de la langue française des origines à 1900*, Paris, 1905–53, 13 vols.

CALVET, Jean. *Histoire de la littérature française*, vol. IV, Paris, 1934.

CAUDAL, Ange. Lettres de La Fontaine à sa femme. Relation d'un voyage en Limousin. Texte avec introduction et notes. Unpublished thesis, Paris, 1956.

CAVENS, A. 'La Fontaine et Rabelais', *Revue du XVIème siècle*, 1922, pp. 175–9. Also, *La Renaissance d'Occident*, XXVI, 1928, pp. 177–216.

CAYROU, Gaston. *Le Français classique. Lexique de la langue du XVIIème siècle*, Paris, 1948.

CERNY, Vaclav. 'Le "je ne sais quoi", de Trissotin', *Revue des Sciences Humaines*, No. 103, July–Sept. 1961, pp. 367–78.

CHAIGNET, A. E. *La Rhétorique et son histoire*, Paris, 1888.

CHAMFORT, Sebastien Roch Nicolas, dit. *Eloge de La Fontaine*, see *Recueil de l'Académie de Marseille*.

—— Notes sur les Fables, see J. B. GAIL, *Les Trois Fabulistes.* . . .

CHASLES, Robert. *Les Illustres françaises,* ed. Deloffre, Paris, 1959, 2 vols. (1st ed. 1713).

CLARAC, Pierre. *La Fontaine, l'homme et l'œuvre,* Paris, 1947.

—— *La Fontaine par lui-même,* Paris, 1961.

—— 'Six pages inédites de La Fontaine', *Revue d'Histoire Littéraire de la France,* LI, 1951, pp. 61–8.

—— 'Variations de La Fontaine dans les six derniers livres des Fables', *L'Information Littéraire,* January–February 1951, pp. 1–9.

CLÉMENT, Pierre. *Les Cinq années littéraires ou nouvelles littéraires etc., des années 1748, 1749, 1750, 1751 et 1752.* The Hague, 1754, 4 vols.

CONS, Louis. 'La préface des Fables de La Fontaine, une correction', *Modern Language Notes,* XXXVII, 1932, pp. 246–8.

CORDEMANN, Margarete. *Der Umschwung der Kunst zwischen der ersten und zweiten Fabelsammlung La Fontaines,* Munich, 1917.

CORNEILLE, Pierre. *Œuvres,* ed. Marty-Laveaux, Grands Ecrivains de la France, Paris, 1862–68, 12 vols.

COSTAR, Pierre. *Recueil des plus beaux endroits de Martial,* Toulouse, 1689, 2 vols.

COUTON, Georges. *La Poétique de La Fontaine,* Paris, 1957.

D'ASSOUCY, Charles Couppeau. *Aventures burlesques,* ed. Colombey, Paris, 1858.

DAUDET, Alphonse. *Lettres de mon moulin,* Charpentier, Paris, 1934.

DAUZAT, Albert. *Dictionnaire étymologique de la langue française,* Paris, 1947.

DESPORTES, Philippe. *Les Amours d'Hippolyte,* ed. V. E. Graham, Paris, 1960.

DELASSAULT, Geneviève. 'Le Maistre de Sacy et La Fontaine traducteurs de Phèdre', *Revue des Sciences Humaines,* 1952, pp. 281–94.

DIÉGUEZ, Manuel de. *L'Ecrivain et son langage,* Paris, 1961.

DONCIEUX, Georges. *Le Père Bouhours,* Paris, 1886.

DOUCET. 'La Fontaine orateur', *Les Etudes Classiques,* XXIII, 1955, pp. 427–39.

DU BARTAS, Guillaume de Salluste. *Works,* ed. Holmes, Lyons & Linker, Chapel Hill, N. Carolina, USA, 1935–40, 3 vols.

EDELMAN, Nathan. *Attitudes of Seventeenth-century France Towards the Middle-Ages,* New York, 1946.

ELUARD, Paul. *Première anthologie vivante de la poésie du passé,* Paris, 1951, 2 vols.

EMPSOM, William. *Seven Types of Ambiguity,* Penguin Books, London, 1961.

Encyclopédie de la Pléiade, Histoire des littératures, Paris, 1958, vol. III.

ETTMAYER, Karl. 'Die Rolle der Verba vicaria im poetischen Stil La Fontaines', in *Hauptfragen der Romanistik, Festschrift für P. A. Becker,* Heidelberg, 1922, pp. 3–36.

FAGUET, Emile. *Dix-septième siècle, études littéraires,* Paris, n.d., Boivin.

—— *Histoire de la Poésie française de la Renaissance au Romantisme,* Paris, 1930, vol. IV, *La Fontaine.*

FÉNELON. *Lettre sur les occupations de l'Académie Française,* ed. Cahen, Paris, 1908.

FISCHER, M. & HACQUARD, G. *A la Découverte de la grammaire française*, Paris, 1959.

FISCHER, Walter P. *The Literary Relations between La Fontaine and L'Astrée of Honoré d'Urfé*, Philadelphia, Pennsylvania, USA, 1913.

FRANCE, Anatole. *Le Génie latin*, Paris, 1919.

FURETIÈRE, Antoine. *Fables morales et nouvelles*, Paris, 1671.

—— *Recueil des Factums d'Antoine Furetière contre quelques uns de cette Académie* ed. Asselineau, Paris, 1859.

GAIL, Jean-Baptiste. *Les Trois fabulistes, Esope, Phèdre, La Fontaine*, Paris, 1796, 4 vols. Vols. 3–4, *Fables de La Fontaine avec les notes de Chamfort*.

—— *Observations sur les quatre dernières fables de La Fontaine restées jusqu'ici sans commentaire, par Sélis, Delille et La Harpe, recueillies par J.-B. Gail*, Paris, 1821.

GAILLARD, Gabriel Henri. *Éloge de La Fontaine*, 1744, see P. L. SOLVET.

GARAPON, Robert. *La Fantaisie verbale et le comique dans le théatre français du Moyen-âge à la fin du XVIIème siècle*, Paris, 1957.

GIRAUDOUX, Jean. *Juliette au pays des hommes*, Paris, 1924.

—— *Siegfried*, Paris, 1949.

GODEFROY, Frédéric. *Dictionnaire de l'ancienne langue française et de tous ses dialectes*, Paris, 1881–1902, 10 vols.

—— *Lexique de l'Ancien Français*, Paris & Leipzig, 1901.

GOHIN, Ferdinand. *La Fontaine, études et recherches*, Paris, 1937.

—— *L'Art de La Fontaine dans ses Fables*, Paris, 1929.

—— *Les Comédies attribuées à La Fontaine*, Paris, 1935.

GRAMMONT, Maurice. *Psychologie linguistique: style et poésie*, Paris, 1950.

—— 'L'Art de La Fontaine', *Le Français Moderne*, 1933, pp. 97–115.

GRENTE, Georges. *Dictionnaire des Lettres françaises. Le XVIIème siècle*, Paris, 1954.

GUDRA J. *Die Sprache La Fontaines in seinen Fabeln, zweiundzwanzigster Jahres-Bericht der kaiserlkön. ober-Realschule im III. Bezirk (Landstrasse) in Wien, für das Schuljahr 1872–73*, Vienna, 1873; 25 pp.

GUILLAUMIE, Gaston. *Jean-Louis Guez de Balzac et la prose française, contribution à l'étude de la langue et du style pendant la première moitié du XVIIème siècle*, Paris, 1927.

GUISAN, G. 'L'Evolution de l'art de La Fontaine d'après les variantes de l'Adonis', *Revue d'Histoire Littéraire de la France*, XLII, 1935, pp. 161–80 & 321–43.

GUITON, Margaret. *La Fontaine, Poet and Counterpoet*, Rutgers University Press, New Jersey, USA, 1961.

GUTMANN, R. A. *Introduction à la lecture des poètes français*, Paris, 1946.

HAASE, A. *Syntaxe française du XVIIème siècle*, trans. Obert, Paris, 1925.

HARASZTI, Jules. *En Glanant chez La Fontaine*, Paris, 1922.

HARCOURT, Bernard d'. *Maurice de Guérin et le poème en prose*, Paris, 1932.

HELLO, Ernest. *L'Homme*, Paris, 1941.

HEPP, Noemi. 'Esquisse du vocabulaire de la critique littéraire de la querelle du Cid à la querelle d'Homère', *Romanische Forschungen*, LXIX, 1957, pp. 332–408.

HERVIER, Marcel. *Les Écrivains français jugés par leurs contemporains, I, XVIème et XVIIème siècles*, Paris, 1911.

HOPE, Quentin M. *Saint-Evremond, the Honnête Homme as Critic*, Bloomington, Indiana, USA, 1962.

HORACE. *Satires, Epistles and Ars poetica*, Loeb Classical Library, London, 1961.

HUET, Pierre Daniel. *Huetiana ou pensées diverses de M. Huet, évêque d'Avranches*, ed. d'Olivet, Paris, 822 [sic]; (1722).

HUGUET, Edmond. *Le Langage figuré au XVIème siècle*, Paris, 1933.

—— *Petit glossaire des classiques français du XVIIème siècle*, Paris, 1922.

JACQUIOT, Josèphe. 'Devises pour les médailles et jetons de Louis XIV composées par Jean Racine', in *Actes du Premier Congrès International Racinien*, (Uzès, September 7th–10th 1961), Uzès, 1962, pp. 77–94.

Journal Étranger, Paris, 1754–62, 45 vols.

KOHN, Renée. *Le Goût de la Fontaine*, Paris, 1962.

KÖTZ, Otto. 'Der Sprachgebrauch La Fontaines in seinen Fabeln', *Die Neueren Sprachen*, XVII, 1909, pp. 257–78; 321–40; 402–20.

LA BRUYÈRE, Jean de. *Œuvres*, ed. Servois, Grands Écrivains de la France, Paris, 1922, 5 vols.

LADBOROUGH, R. W. 'Translation from the Ancients in Seventeenth-Century France', *Journal of the Warburg Institute*, II, 1938, pp. 85–104.

LAFENESTRE, Georges. *La Fontaine*, Paris, 1895.

LAGANE, R. & DUBOIS, J. *Dictionnaire de la langue française classique*, Paris, 1960.

LA HARPE, Jean François de. *Éloge de La Fontaine*, see *Recueil de l'Académie de Marseille*.

LA MOTTE, Antoine Houdart de. *Fables nouvelles*, Paris, 1719.

LANSON, Gustave. 'Études sur les rapports de la littérature française et de la littérature espagnole au XVIIème siècle', *Revue d'Histoire Littéraire de la France*, III, 1896, pp. 45–70; 321–31.

—— *L'Art de la prose*, Paris, 1908.

LANTOINE, Henri. *Histoire de l'enseignement secondaire en France au XVIIème et au début du XVIIIème siècle*, Paris, 1874.

LAUSBERG, Heinrich. *Handbuch der literarischen Rhetorik*, Munich, 1960, 2 vols.

—— *Elemente der literarischen Rhetorik*, Munich, 1949.

LECLERC, Jean. *Bibliothèque universelle et historique*, Amsterdam, 1686–1702, 25 vols.

LE HIR, Yves. *Rhétorique et stylistique, de la Pléiade au Parnasse*, Paris, 1960.

LERBER, Walter de. *L'influence de Clément Marot aux XVIIème et XVIIIème siècles*, Lausanne, 1920.

LE VERRIER, Pierre. *Commentaire des Satires de Boileau*, see BOILEAU, *Les Satires de Boileau commentées par lui-même*.

LIPS, Marguerite. *Le Style indirect libre*, Paris, 1926.

LITTRÉ, Émile. *Dictionnaire de la langue française*, Paris, 1877, 4 vols.

LIVET, C. L. *Lexique de la langue de Molière comparée à celle des écrivains de son temps, avec des commentaires de philologie historique et grammaticale*, Paris, 1895–97, 3 vols.

LOMBARD, Alf. 'L'Infinitif de narration dans les langues romanes', *Skrifter utgivna av kungl. humanistika vetenskapssamfundet i Uppsala*, XXX, 1936-37.

LORIN, Théodore. *Vocabulaire pour les œuvres de La Fontaine, ou explication et définition des mots, locutions, formes grammaticales etc. employés par La Fontaine et qui ne sont plus utilisés*, Paris, 1852.

LUGLI, Vittorio. *Il Prodigio di La Fontaine*, Milan, 1939.

LYER, Stanislav. *La Syntaxe du gérondif et du participe présent dans les langues romanes*, Paris, 1934.

MACÉ, Alcide. *La Fontaine et Horace*, Paris, 1944.

MALHERBE. *Œuvres*, ed. Lalane, Grands Écrivains de la France, Paris, 1862, 4 vols.

MAROT, Clément. *Œuvres complètes*, ed. Abel Grenier, Paris, n.d., Garnier, 2 vols.

MAROUZEAU, J. 'Comment aborder l'étude du style', *Le Français Moderne*, XI, 1943, pp. 1-6.

—— *Lexique de la terminologie linguistique*, Paris, 1951.

MARTY-LAVEAUX. *Essai sur la langue de La Fontaine*, Paris, 1853.

MAUCROIX, François de. *Œuvres diverses*, ed. Louis Paris, Paris, 1854, 2 vols.

—— *Œuvres postumes de M. de Maucroix*, ed. d'Olivet, Paris, 1710.

MÉRÉ, Antoine Gombaud de. *Lettres de Monsieur le chevalier de Méré*, Paris, 1682, 2 vol.

—— *Œuvres complètes*, ed. Ch. H. Boudhors, Paris, 1930, 3 vols.

MICHAUT, Gustave. *La Fontaine*, Paris, 1913-14, 2 vols.

MOLIERE. *Œuvres*, ed. E. Despois, Grands Écrivains de la France, Paris, 1921-22, 13 vols.

MONCHESNAY, Jacques de Losme de. *Bolæana ou entretiens de M. de Losme de Monchesnay avec Boileau*, Amsterdam, 1742.

MONK, Samuel Holt. 'A Grace beyond the Reach of Art', *Journal of the History of Ideas*, V, 1944, pp. 131-50.

MONTESQUIEU. *Œuvres complètes*, ed. Masson, Paris, 1950-55, 3 vols.

MONTFAUCON DE VILLARS, Nicolas Pierre Henri de. *La Critique de Bérénice*, Paris, 1671, 2 vols.

MONTFLEURY, Zacharie Jacob, dit. *Théâtre*, Paris, 1705, 2 vols.

MOREAU, Pierre. *Thèmes et variations dans le Premier Recueil des Fables de La Fontaine*, Cours de Sorbonne, Paris, 1960.

MOURGUES, Odette de. *La Fontaine, Fables*, London, 1960.

—— *O Muse, fuyante proie . . .*, *Essai sur la poésie de La Fontaine*, Paris, 1962.

MOUSSET, Joseph. *Der Stil La Fontaines in seinen Contes*, Münster, 1936.

NAIGEON, Jacques-André. *Éloge de La Fontaine*, Bouillon, 1775.

NAVES, Raymond. *Le Goût de Voltaire*, Paris, n.d. Garnier.

OELSNER, Hermann. 'Änderungen von La Fontaines Hand an seinen Amours de Psyché et de Cupidon', *Archiv für das Studium der neuren Sprachen und Litteraturen*, XCIX, 1897, pp. 389-94.

OVID. *Heroides and Amores*, Loeb Classical Library, London, 1958.

—— *Tristia and Ex Ponto*, Loeb Classical Library, London, 1953.

PARKIN, R. Price. *Poetic Workmanship of Alexander Pope*, Univ. of Minnesota, USA, 1955.

PASCAL. *Pensées*, ed. Bruncshvicg, Paris, 1946.
PELLISSON & D'OLIVET. *Histoire de l'Académie Française*, ed. Ch. Livet, Paris, 1858, 2 vols.
PERRAULT, Charles. *Des Hommes illustres qui ont paru en France pendant le XVIIème siècle*, Paris, 1696–1701, 2 vols.
—— *Recueil de divers ouvrages en prose et en vers*, Paris, 1676.
PIGANIOL DE LA FORCE, Jean Aimard. *Nouvelle description des châteaux et parcs de Versailles et de Marly*, Paris, 1724, 2 vols (1st ed. 1701).
PITOU, Spire. 'Rabelais, La Fontaine, Richelet and la touselle,' *Modern Language Notes*, LXV, 1950, pp. 399–403.
POTTHOFF, W. *La Fontaines Stil, mit besonderer Berücksichtigung der syntaktischen Archaismen*, Marburg, 1894.
QUINTILIAN. *Institutio Oratoria*, Loeb Classical Library, London, 1920–22, 4 vols.
QUIRK, Randolph. *The Use of English*, London, 1962.
RABELAIS. *Œuvres*, ed. Louis Moland, Paris, n.d. Garnier.
RACAN, Honorat de Bueil de. *Œuvres*, ed. Louis Arnould, Paris, 1937, 2 vols.
RACINE, Jean. *Œuvres*, ed. Paul Mesnard, Grands Ecrivains de la France, Paris, 1867–73, 8 vols.
RAHIR, Edouard. 'L'Edition originale d'une fable de La Fontaine', *Revue des Livres Anciens*, 1917, vol. II, pp. 159–62.
RAT, Maurice. *Grammairiens et amateurs de beau langage*, Paris, 1963.
Recueil de l'Académie des Belles Lettres, Sciences et Arts de Marseille, pour l'année 1774, Marseilles, 1774.
RÉMOND DE SAINT-MARD, Toussaint. *Œuvres*, The Hague, 1734, 3 vols.
REMY DE GOURMONT. 'La vie des animaux et la morale dans les Fables de La Fontaine', *Mercure de France*, LVII, 1905, pp. 510–23; LVIII, 1905, pp. 24–39.
—— *Promenades littéraires*, Paris, 1904–13, 5 vols.
ROBERT, R. 'Des Commentaires de première main sur les chefs-d'œuvre les plus discutés de Molière', *Revue des Sciences Humaines*, No. 81, January–March 1956, pp. 19–55.
ROCHE, Louis. *La Vie de Jean de La Fontaine*, Paris, 1913.
ROQUES, Mario. 'Jean de La Fontaine; un octogénaire plantait', *Revue d'Histoire Littéraire de la France*, XLVII, 1947, pp. 257–62; See also XLVIII, 1948, pp. 191–2.
ROSEN, Charles W. Style and Morality in La Fontaine, Princeton, New Jersey, USA, 1951. Unpublished thesis.
ROSSET, T. *Entretiens, doutes, critique et remarques du P. Bouhours sur la langue française, 1671–92*, Paris, 1908.
ROUSSEL, Louis. *La Fable troisième du Livre onze commentée par Louis Roussel*, Paris, 1951.
ROYÈRE, Jean. *Clartés sur la poésie*, Paris, 1925.
—— *Le Musicisme, Boileau, La Fontaine, Baudelaire*, Paris, 1929.
—— 'Le Symbolisme verbal chez La Fontaine', *Renaissance Politique, Littéraire Artistique*, July 9th, 1921.
RUDLER, Gustave. *L'Explication française, principes et applications*, Paris, 1948.

SAINT-AMANT, Marc Antoine Girard de. *Œuvres poétiques*, ed. Léon Véranne, Paris, 1930.
SAINTE-BEUVE, Charles Augustin. *Œuvres*, ed. Maxime Leroy, Pléiade, Paris, 1949–50, vols. I and II.
SAINT-EVREMOND, Charles de. *Œuvres*, ed. Des Maizeaux, Amsterdam, 1739. 7 vols.
SAINTE-PALAYE, La Curne de. *Dictionnaire historique de l'ancienne langue française depuis son origine jusqu'au siècle de Louis XIV*, Paris, 1875–82, 10 vols.
SARASIN, Jean Francois. *Œuvres*, ed. Festugière, Paris, 1926, 2 vols.
—— *Œuvres de M. Sarasin*, Paris, 1656.
SCARRON, Paul. *Poésies diverses*, ed. Maurice Cauchie, Paris, 1948–62, 3 vols.
SCHÉLANDRE, Jean de. *Tyr et Sidon*, ed. Viollet Le Duc, in vol. VIII of *Ancien Théâtre français depuis les Mystères jusqu'à Corneille*, Paris, 1854–57, 10 vols.
SCHENK, A. *Table comparée des observations de Callières sur la langue de la fin du XVIIème siècle*, Kiel, 1908.
SEARLES, Colbert. 'La Fontaine's Imitation', *Philological Quarterly*, I, 1922, pp. 56–70.
SENECA. *Moral Essays*, Loeb Classical Library, London, 1931–35, 3 vols.
SERVAN, O. 'A propos de La Fontaine et de Rabelais', *Revue du XVIème siècle*, XIV, 1927, pp. 170–6.
SÉVIGNÉ, Mme de. *Lettres*, ed. Gérard Gailly, Pléiade, Paris, 1953–57, 3 vols.
SIEGERT, Clemens. *Die Sprache La Fontaines mit besonderer Berücksichtigung der Archaismen*, Meissen, n.d. (1885).
SIMON, Pierre-Henri. 'Le "je ne sais quoi" devant la raison classique', *Cahiers de l'Association Internationale des Etudes Françaises*, No. 11, May 1959, pp. 104–17.
SOLVET, P. Louis. *Etude sur La Fontaine ou notes et excursions littéraires sur ses Fables par PLS ... T*, précédées de son éloge par Gaillard, Paris, 1812.
SÓTÉR, Istvän. *La Doctrine stylistique des rhétoriques du XVIIème siècle*, Budapest, 1937.
SPITZER, Leo. *Critica stilistica e storia del linguaggio*, Bari, 1954.
—— 'Die Kunst des Übergangs bei La Fontaine', *Publications of the Modern Language Association of America*, LIII, 1938, pp. 393–433.
—— 'Zum französischen historischen Infinitiv', *Zeitschrift für romanische Philologie*, L, 1930, pp. 533–47.
STENDHAL. *Journal*, Le Divan, Paris, 1937, 5 vols.
—— *La Chartreuse de Parme*, ed. Martineau, Paris, 1946.
—— *Pensées*, Le Divan, Paris, 1931, 2 vols.
TAINE, Hippolyte. *Essai sur les Fables de La Fontaine*, Paris, 1853.
—— *La Fontaine et ses Fables*, Paris, 1860.
TALLEMANT DES RÉAUX, Gédéon. *Historiettes*, ed. Georges Mongrédien, Paris, 1932–34, 8 vols.
TRISTAN L'HERMITE, François. *Les Amours et autres poésies choisies*, ed. P. Camo, Paris, 1925.
ULLMANN, Stephen. *Language and Style*, Oxford, 1964.
—— *Précis de sémantique française*, Bern, 1952.

VALÉRY, Paul. *Monsieur Teste*, Paris, 1946.
—— *Œuvres*, ed. Jean Hytier, Pléiade, Paris, 1957–60, 2 vols.
—— *Tel Quel I*, Paris, 1941.
—— *Variété I*, Paris, 1921.
—— *Variété II*, Paris, 1926.
VERGIL. *Eclogues, Georgics, Æneid, The Minor Poems*, Loeb Classical Library, London, 1956–60, 2 vols.
VERSCHOOR, Jan Adriaan. *Etude de grammaire historique et de style sur le style direct et les styles indirects en Français*, Groningen, 1959.
VIAL, Francisque & DENISE, Louis. *Idées et doctrines littéraires du XVIIème siècle*, Paris, 1920.
VIANEY, J. 'Les Grands poètes de la nature en France. I, Ronsard. La Fontaine.' *Revue des Cours et Conférences*, XXVII, 1925–26, pp. 3–19.
VIROLLE, R. 'Explication de texte: l'amitié selon La Fontaine', *L'Ecole*, XLVII, 1956, pp. 252–5.
VOITURE, Vincent. *Œuvres de Voiture, lettres et poésies*, ed. Ubicini, Paris, 1855, 2 vols.
VOLTAIRE. *Œuvres complètes*, ed. A. A. Renouard, 1819–25, 66 vols.
VOSSLER, Karl. *La Fontaine und sein Fabelwerk*, Heidelberg, 1919.
WADSWORTH, P. A. 'La Fontaine as Critic and Student of Malherbe', *Symposium*, III, 1949, pp. 130–9.
—— *Young La Fontaine, a Study of his Artistic Growth in his Early Poetry and First Fables*, Evanston, Illinois, USA, 1952.
WALTZ, René. 'Phèdre et La Fontaine', *L'Information Littéraire*, VI, 1954, pp. 91–2.
WESPY, Leon. 'Die historische Entwickelung der Inversion des Subjekts in Französischen und der Gebrauch derselben bei La Fontaine', *Zeitschrift für französische Sprache und Literatur*, VI, 1884, pp. 150–209.
WIEMANN, Heinrich. *Impressionismus im Sprachgebrauch La Fontaines*, Munster, 1934.
WINEGARTEN, Renée. *French Lyric Poetry in the Age of Malherbe*, Manchester, 1954.
WINKLER, E. *La Doctrine grammaticale française d'après Maupas et Oudin*, Halle, 1912.

INDEX TO THE FABLES

INDEX OF TECHNICAL TERMS

204

INDEX OF PROPER NAMES

Stendhal, 87 n. 1, 118, 118 n. 1, 127, 128 n. 1, 167 n. 4

Taine, xi, xi n. 7
Tallemant des Réaux, 28 n. 7, 44 n. 4, 45 n. 4, 61 n. 3
Terence, 34, 95 n. 4
Théophile de Viau, 30 n. 2, 49
Toscanella, 9 n. 3
Trebutien, 63 n. 1
Tristan L'Hermite, 30 n. 2, 99, 99 n. 2

Ullmann, 163, 163 n. 5, 183, 183 n. 1
Urfé, 51 n. 3, 167 n. 1

Valéry, xi, xi n. 3, xii n. 1, xvi, xvi n. 1, 128, 173, 173 n. 2, 186, 186 n. 2
Vaugelas, 27, 27 n. 3, 29 n. 3, 52 n. 3, 68, 68 n. 4, 104 n. 1, 137 n. 2, 144, 145, 145 n. 1, 171, 171 n. 1, 172, 172 n. 2

Vaumorière, 145, 145 n. 2
Vergil, 160, 178, 178 n. 1, n. 2, n. 3
Verschoor, 89 n. 2
Vial, 1, 1 n. 4
Villiers, 137
Virolle, 66, 66 n. 2, 132, 132 n. 2
Voiture, 17, 18, 20, 21, 25, 29 n. 3, 34, 46, 46 n. 1, 56 n. 2, 57, 79, 94, 104, 122, 122 n. 2
Voltaire, 94 n. 3
Vossler, xi, xi n. 6

Wadsworth, xi, xi n. 8, 1, 1 n. 3, 11, 11 n. 4
Waltz, 2, 2 n. 5
Wartburg, 43 n. 4, 45 n. 3
Wespy, xiii, xiii n. 1
Wiemann, xiii, xiii n. 4, 74 n. 1
Winegarten, 26, 26 n. 6
Winkler, 70 n. 3